Understanding the Culture of Markets

How does culture shape economic life? Is culture like a ball and chain that actors must lug around as they pursue their material interests? Or, is culture like a toolkit from which entrepreneurs can draw resources to aid them in their efforts? Or, is being immersed in a culture like wearing a pair of blinders? Or, is culture like wearing a pair of glasses with tinted lenses? *Understanding the Culture of Markets* explores how culture shapes economic activity and describes how social scientists (especially economists) should incorporate considerations of culture into their analysis.

Although most social scientists recognize that culture shapes economic behavior and outcomes, the majority of economists are not very interested in culture. *Understanding the Culture of Markets* begins with a discussion of the reasons why economists are reluctant to incorporate culture into economic analysis. It then goes on to describe how culture shapes economic life, and critiques those few efforts by economists to discuss the relationship between culture and markets. Finally, building on the work of Max Weber, it outlines and defends an approach to understanding the culture of markets.

In order to understand real world markets, economists must pay attention to how culture shapes economic activity. If culture does indeed color economic life, economists cannot really avoid culture. Instead, the choice that they face is not whether or not to incorporate culture into their analysis but whether to employ culture implicitly or explicitly. Ignoring culture may be possible but avoiding culture is impossible. *Understanding the Culture of Markets* will appeal to economists interested in how culture shapes economic life, in addition to economic anthropologists and economic sociologists. It should be useful in graduate and undergraduate courses in all of those fields.

Virgil Henry Storr is a Senior Research Fellow and the Director of Graduate Student Programs at the Mercatus Center, George Mason University, USA. He is also a Research Associate Professor in the Department of Economics at George Mason University.

'Storr issues a challenge to the entire discipline of economics in this deep and innovative study. It should be required reading in every undergraduate class on markets and economic theory. A brave and spirited work that carves out new intellectual territory for economics, this book opens a crucially important conversation between economists and other social scientists, asking fundamental questions about what determines behavior in markets. Storr is definitely pushing the boundaries of economics, opening up the most fundamental issues in the theory of markets. This work will be welcomed by social scientists in many disciplines, and it should be read by any serious student of markets.'

Richard Wilk, Provost's Professor of Anthropology,
Indiana University, USA

'Storr's beautifully written book puts forward a theory of the 'animating spirit' in an economy, in the style of Max Weber's ethic—without the Protestantism. He replies to Samuelsonian economists who want to reduce everything to Capital and to Austrian economists who are not willing to take the next step into culture that their theories demand. In short, he and a handful of others, may their tribe increase, are initiating a 'humanomics,' that is, an economics with people instead of sociopaths at its center.'

Deirdre McCloskey, Distinguished Professor of Economics, History,
English, and Communication, University of Illinois at Chicago, USA

'Economists have all too often either ignored culture completely, or failed to do justice to it by assimilating it to some other phenomenon—such as capital—that provides a poor model for understanding its true nature and significance. Virgil Storr is different. He has thought hard about how to conceptualize culture, about the relationship between culture and economic activity, and about how an appreciation of culture should affect the way that economists carry out applied work. This careful, insightful, and persuasive book is the outcome of his reflections. Economists who want a more sophisticated way of thinking not only about culture but also, given culture's impact on economic activity, about markets, will benefit greatly from reading it. Social scientists from other disciplines who have previously despaired of finding a culturally literate economist will also find much to ponder and value in this fine work of scholarship.'

Paul Lewis, Reader in Economics and Public Policy,
King's College London, UK

'In one of the most controversial works in social science, Max Weber argued that without taking 'the spirit of capitalism' into account, you cannot understand the modern economy. More than a century later, Virgil Storr argues that without taking 'the spirits that animate markets' into account, you cannot understand the modern economy. Was Weber right or wrong; is Storr right or wrong? Different readers will no doubt give different answers. But all will agree that Storr raises questions that are absolutely essential to get a better grip on the modern economy.'

Richard Swedberg, Professor of Sociology, Cornell University, USA

'In *Understanding the Culture of Markets* Virgil Storr makes a major contribution to the under-explored intersection between cultural and economic processes. The customary perspective the economics discipline brings to cultural analysis is either to collapse nuanced cultural processes into a rational choice model of human decision making or to cast culture in the role of economic spoiler—as a set of constraints that stands in the way of productive life. In Storr's hands, culture receives the nuanced treatment it deserves as he explores the ways in which culture shapes and undergirds all of productive life. In short, Storr delivers on his promise to offer an economics of meaning.'

Emily Chamlee-Wright, Professor of Economics and Provost,
Washington College, USA

'The reason some countries prosper while others languish in abject poverty is ultimately a function of the institutions of governance that are operating within each country. Peaceful and prosperous countries have institutions that curb public and private predation; poor, sick and violent countries have institutions that leave public and private predation unchecked. This observation is in many ways as old as economics as a discipline, and certainly was a central message of Adam Smith's description about the difference between barbarism and opulence. But the puzzle of how peoples are able to move from one set of institutions to another is not as obvious. Smith's recipe of 'peace, easy taxes, and a tolerable administration of justice' must be supplemented by a deeper examination of the cultural preconditions that allow such an institutional configuration to take root in any society. Those cultural preconditions become evident to us through the stories societies tell about themselves, and the tacit presuppositions that underlie social intercourse in specific social contexts. Political economy, in other words, must ultimately move from the pure theory of price and the institutional analysis of development to an understanding of the culture of markets if an adequate explanation of the wealth and poverty of nations is to emerge. Enter Virgil Storr's concise, readable, learned, and penetrating discussion of the beliefs, norms, mores, attitudes, and 'spirits' that make human societies tick. *Understanding the Culture of Markets* is required reading for any student of society and the doings of human action regardless of disciplinary background and ideological disposition. Storr provides his reader with not only a primer on cultural economy, but also an examination of the methodological and analytical adjustments required by economics if the discipline is to realize its full potential as a science of human action.'

Peter J. Boettke, University Professor of Economics and Philosophy,
George Mason University, USA

Routledge Foundations of the Market Economy
Edited by Mario J. Rizzo, *New York University* and
Lawrence H. White, *University of Missouri at St Louis*

A central theme in this series is the importance of understanding and assessing the market economy from a perspective broader than the static economics of perfect competition and Pareto optimality. Such a perspective sees markets as causal processes generated by the preferences, expectations and beliefs of Economic agents. The creative acts of entrepreneurship that uncover new information about preferences, prices and technology are central to these processes with respect to their ability to promote the discovery and use of knowledge in society.

The market economy consists of a set of institutions that facilitate voluntary cooperation and exchange among individuals. These institutions include the legal and ethical framework as well as more narrowly "economic" patterns of social interaction. Thus the law, legal institutions and cultural and ethical norms, as well as ordinary business practices and monetary phenomena, fall within the analytical domain of the economist.

Previous books in this series include:

Understanding the Culture of Markets

Virgil Henry Storr

Routledge
Taylor & Francis Group

LONDON AND NEW YORK

First published 2013
by Routledge
2 Park Square, Milton Park, Abingdon, Oxon OX14 4RN

Simultaneously published in the USA and Canada
by Routledge
711 Third Avenue, New York, NY 10017

Routledge is an imprint of the Taylor & Francis Group, an informa business

British Library Cataloguing in Publication Data
A catalogue record for this book is available from the British Library

Library of Congress Cataloging in Publication Data
Storr, Virgil Henry
  Understanding the culture of markets/Virgil Storr.
  p. cm.—(Routledge foundations of the market economy; 31)
  Includes bibliographical references and index.
  1. Economics—Sociological aspects. I. Title.
  HM548.S76 2012
  330—dc23
  2012011066

ISBN: 978-0-415-77746-9 (hbk)
ISBN: 978-0-203-09549-2 (ebk)

Typeset in Times New Roman
by Florence Production Ltd, Stoodleigh, Devon, UK

Printed and bound by CPI Group (UK) Ltd, Croydon, CR0 4YY

For Don Lavoie

Contents

Preface

For a young scholar, one of the greatest thrills you can experience is having an established scholar that you admire take an interest in your work. You can, thus, imagine how thrilled I was when I received a letter from Professor Israel Kirzner commenting on a paper that I presented at a colloquium at New York University.[1] Kirzner was already an emeritus professor at the time and was no longer a regular attendee at the workshop. But he received the papers in the mail and took the time to write me his reactions to my piece. In this book, I will attempt to convince economists as well as anthropologists and sociologists that they ought to pay attention to the culture of markets. In that paper, I advanced a parallel argument to the one presented here. If economists wanted to develop a more complex theory of the market, I suggested, they should focus on the meaningful social relationships that can and do form in markets. "The market," I argued, is "a social space where people form friendships, meet their husbands and wives, and connect with their parents, children, and siblings" (Storr 2008: 148). The market is a social space where meaningful conversations occur: "conversations that express more than bid–ask; conversations that are not just bartering and negotiations; conversations between socially bonded market participants concerned with more than simply making a deal" (ibid.: 137).

The first few paragraphs of Kirzner's response were extremely generous. He, for instance, described the paper as "stimulating," "highly interesting," "a *most* useful contribution," and "evidencing wide scholarship and careful analysis." But he followed those kind remarks with a gentle but firm chiding. I was, of course, correct that the market was a social phenomenon in its own right. But I was quite wrong that economists qua economists should pay any attention to the market as a social phenomenon in its own right. In pushing for a richer conception of the market, I was, he explained, repeating the errors of "the enemies of economic theory who—beginning with early nineteenth century critics of economics, continuing with the German and British 'historical schools,' and continuing further in the twentieth century with the American Institutionalists (and especially with Thorstein Veblen)—have uniformly criticized economic theory for failing to take into account the extra-economic relationships which might (in the critic's opinion) call for drastic modification of the conclusions of economic theory." The "chains of *purely economic causation*" that occur within markets, Kirzner argued, "can be identified and understood only by deliberately *abstracting* from the extra-economic relationships occurring in markets." At the end of the day, my work was simply not economics. "I am puzzled," he concluded, "by your unwillingness to recognize that your work is an exploration of a field (or, better, of an aspect of markets) which lies *outside* the scope of economic theory itself—and from which economic theorists themselves deliberately and *altogether properly (!)* abstracted."

I, of course, respectfully disagree. But, admittedly, Kirzner's contention that my paper was urging economists qua economists to step outside the bounds of economics is a view that would be shared by almost any economist who reads it. This current project faces a similar danger. Most economists, I must confess, believe that they *"altogether properly (!)"* abstract from culture.[2] This book, however, is an attempt to convince them that they are wrong. And, to lend support to those who are already convinced that they are wrong. Indeed, I believe that our analysis of markets in the real world is impoverished if we fail to account for culture.

It is true that a small but growing number of economists are arriving at the position that we can no longer afford to abstract from culture. Unfortunately, many of them misunderstand culture by treating it as a form of capital. Culture, however, is not reducible to an item in our production functions but must be thought of as being partially responsible for what makes it into our production functions. It guides our evaluation of the tools that we have at our disposal and helps us to pick out the appropriate ones. Following noted anthropologist Clifford Geertz, I view culture throughout the book as "webs of significance" and "patterns of meaning." As such, we ought to think of culture as shaping how we see our environment and our opportunities, guiding our (economic) behavior, and, ultimately, coloring economic outcomes.

I believe that there is a way to take full account of how culture conceived of as "patterns of meaning" shapes markets without giving up on rational choice or our belief in a universal rationality, and without ignoring the critical role played by institutions in structuring human interactions, and without our having to abandon empirical analysis. In short, there is a way, a way that I attempt to outline here, to study the culture of markets while remaining within the scope of economics.

Of course, this book could not have been written without a lot of help. In fact, I owe tremendous thanks to a number of people who aided in the development of this book. At the top of that list is my mentor and dear friend, the late Don Lavoie. Don taught me a number of lessons that I will always carry with me: that you should always be open to the arguments and ideas of even your staunchest critics; that it isn't enough to be a good economist (narrowly construed) but that you have to read widely in philosophy and anthropology and sociology if you want to call yourself a scholar; that being a teacher means that you have to give generously not only of your ideas but of your time; that you should never take shortcuts—ideas are too important for that; that you ought to reserve your most pointed and focused critiques for your own work. Don wrote convincingly about how culture impacted entrepreneurship and consistently encouraged me to think deeply about how culture affected our (economic) choices. Don is why I first read Weber, and Geertz, and several of the scholars that factor prominently in this book. I have spent my career since he passed away trying to deserve the attention that he so generously gave me and fearing that I am falling short.

I also owe a tremendous debt to two of Don's students: Emily Chamlee-Wright and Peter Boettke. They are by far my favorite teachers and my most trusted advisors. Their guidance has been critical as I have attempted to work out these ideas as well as navigate my career. Additionally, their patience with me, even when I was critical of their own efforts to mine the same territory, has been more important to my own development than they will ever know. Both are also tremendous friends who offer useful critiques when appropriate, tease when deserved, and encourage when required. I could not wish for better siblings.

I also owe a heartfelt thanks to my frequent co-author Arielle John. She has played a critical role in the development of this manuscript. She provided summaries of a handful of the articles that I engage. Additionally, her eagerness to discuss the arguments that I attempt to advance in this book as well as her critical comments on several drafts of each of the chapters has been invaluable.

Special thanks are also owed to my closest colleagues at George Mason University, Peter Leeson and Chris Coyne. From when I met them in graduate school, they have been ever-present reminders that I could and should be working harder, writing much more consistently, reading more carefully, and having more fun doing economics.

Thanks are owed to Rob Garnett who has played a key role in the development of this book through to its publication. Special thanks are also owed to my good friend Paul Lewis as well as to John Meadowcroft and Mark Pennington who hosted me for a weeklong visit at King's College London and organized as well as participated in a conference on an earlier draft of this manuscript. Their comments have been critical as I have developed these ideas. I also wish to thank Alex Padilla for organizing a panel session around this manuscript at the 2012 Association for Private Enterprise Education Annual Meeting.

Additionally, I would like to thank Israel Kirzner, Deidre McCloskey, Stephen Gudemann, Richard Swedberg, Mark Granovettor, Lawrence White, Steve Horwitz, Roger Koppl, Everlyn Hawthorne, James Witte, Susan Trencher, Paul Dragos Aligica, Frederic Sautet, Sanford Ikeda, Dominique Lazanski, André Azevedo Alves, Paul Gunn, Nicola Virgill-Rolle, John Rolle, Laura Grube, Solomon Stein, and T. Clark Durant for very helpful discussions and comments on earlier drafts of the arguments presented here. The usual caveat applies. I also want to thank Lane Conaway, Peter Lipsey, and Taylor Barkley for their invaluable administrative and research support. Special thanks are similarly owed to Jack Howells of Florence Production for managing the production of this manuscript.

I would like to thank Springer for allowing me to reuse portions of my articles, "Weber's Spirit of Capitalism and the Bahamas' Junkanoo Ethic" (*Review of Austrian Economics*), "Schütz on Meaning and Culture" (*Review of Austrian Economics*) and "The Social Construction of the Market" (*Society*). Similarly, I would like to thank Edward Elgar Publishing for allowing me to reuse portions of "The Facts of the Social Sciences are What People Believe and Think." And, I would like to thank the *Journal of Caribbean Literatures* for allowing me to use portions of "B' Rabby as a True-True Bahamian: Rabbyism as Bahamian Ethos and Worldview in the Bahamas' Folk Tradition and the Works of Strachan and Glinton-Meicholas."

This book could not have been written without the financial support of the Mercatus Center at George Mason University. Nor could it have been written without the consistent efforts of Brian Hooks to maintain a vibrant intellectual environment at Mercatus.

Finally, I would like to thank my wife Nona for being exactly what I needed at every moment during the development of this project. I have asked her to be my coach, my counselor, my cheerleader, and my copy-editor and she has performed every role amazingly. I have also asked her to help me work out and clarify a number of the key claims that I make in this book. Her love and patience have been critical to this effort.

1 Introduction

Culture shapes economic behavior and outcomes. Although most economists believe that culture does not matter, if I am right that culture colors economic life, economists cannot really avoid culture. They can attempt to ignore it. But it will implicitly sneak into their studies. They can attempt to articulate the assumptions that they are making about the role of culture when they abstract from it or they can explicitly integrate cultural considerations into their theories and empirical research. This, however, raises the question of how best to incorporate culture into economic analysis. What, for instance, is the relationship between culture and markets? How does culture impact economic life? Is culture like a ball and chain that actors must lug around as they pursue their material interests? Perhaps, lighter and less burdensome in some contexts, while in others the dead hands of past generations severely hampering economic life. Or, is culture like a toolkit from which entrepreneurs can draw resources to aid them in their efforts? Everyone's toolbox stocked with different cultural assets that they can employ as they go about their business. Or, is being immersed in a culture like wearing a pair of blinders? Some prospects kept out of the entrepreneur's field of vision, and others more easily brought into view. Or, is culture like wearing a pair of glasses with tinted lenses? Some opportunities easier to find and focus on than others while looking through the lenses, and everything appearing to have a particular tint.

Grappling with these questions has become more common within economics in recent years. Indeed, several recent articles and books within economics have explored how culture impacts economic life.[1] In his seminal paper, Greif (1994) explores the relationship between cultural beliefs and the structure of economic institutions.[2] As he explains, cultural beliefs shape institutions and, because cultural beliefs persist, they come to determine the character of the social and economic institutions that are adopted as well as the path of institutional development. According to Greif (ibid.: 914), his "findings suggest the theoretical and historical importance of culture in determining societal organizations, in leading to path dependence of institutional frameworks, and in forestalling successful intersociety adoption of institutions." Studying the Maghribi traders of the eleventh century and the Genoese traders of the twelfth century, Greif (ibid.) found that the economic institutions that these groups adopted differed because their cultures differed.[3] The Maghribis had collectivist beliefs while the Genoese had more individualist beliefs.[4] The Maghribis, having more collectivist beliefs, invested in information sharing and (albeit rarely) employed collective punishment (ibid.: 923). Moreover, when the Maghribis expanded their trading to new centers they relied on other Maghribis to serve as agents (ibid.: 930). "Among the Maghribis," Greif (ibid.: 936) explains, "collective cultural beliefs led to a collectivist society with an economic self-enforcing collective punishment, horizontal agency relations, segregation, and an in-group social communication network." The Genoese, having more individualist beliefs, did not invest in information sharing nor did they employ collective punishment (ibid.: 923). Additionally, they relied on both Genoese and non-Genoese agents when they expanded their trade (ibid.: 931). "Among the Genoese," Greif (ibid. 936) explains, "individualist cultural beliefs led to an individualist society with a vertical and integrated social structure, a relatively low level of communication, and no economic self-enforcing collective punishment." These differences in cultural beliefs, thus, explain why the individualist Genoese developed formal legal and political arrangements in order to facilitate collective actions while the collectivist Maghribis were able to rely on informal institutions.[5]

Guiso et al. (2006), similarly, explore whether or not culture affects economic outcomes. They argue that culture affects beliefs and values and that those beliefs and values, in turn, affect economic performance. They claim, for instance, that culture determines a group's religious values and that religious values in turn shape the group's saving decisions and also its taste for redistribution. Catholic countries, they note, tend to have higher national savings rates and lower tax rates than Protestant countries. These findings lead the authors to conclude that cultural differences in beliefs can produce important differences in economic performance. Additionally, Guiso et al. (2009) find that cultural factors such as religion, a history of conflicts, and genetic similarities can affect individuals' willingness to trust citizens of other countries and so their willingness to trade with foreigners.

Tabellini (2008, 2010) has also argued that culture is the "missing link" that explains economic backwardness in certain contexts. Norms of morality, he suggests, emerge from institutions of the previous eras. As he explains, cultures that practice "generalized morality" (i.e. where everyone in society is treated according to norms of good conduct) perform better than cultures practicing "limited morality" (i.e. where norms of good conduct only apply to the limited group of people that the individual feels close to). This is because transaction costs tend to be lower where a "generalized morality" exists. According to Tabellini (2008: 8), for instance, "law enforcement is easier" in cultures that practice generalized morality

> because citizens are more likely to be law abiding; bureaucrats are more likely to refrain from corruption; and voters expect and demand higher standards of behavior from political representatives, and are more inclined to vote based on general social welfare rather than personal benefit criteria.

Cultures that are individualistic and engender mutual trust, these studies tend to conclude, facilitate economic exchange. The cultural legacy of communism, collectivism, colonialism and corruption, on the other hand, stands in the way of development in the transitioning and developing worlds. Economists in this area have tended to highlight the extent to which cultures can stand in the way of economic progress. In this regard, Harrison's *Who Prospers? How Cultural Values Shape Economic and Political Success* (1992) is a classic example. "Some cultures are progress-prone," Harrison offers bluntly, "while others are not." The world, in his view, is divided into cultures that "nurture human creative capacity and progress" and "those that don't." More recently, in *Understanding the Process of Economic Change*, North (2005) has argued that the way people perceive the world influences their belief systems, that their beliefs in turn influence the institutions they select to constrain the choices they make, and that the choices they make lead to the outcomes that we observe in the world. Like Guiso et al. and Greif, North underscores the importance of religious beliefs and collectivist/ individualist beliefs in leading to the adoption of institutions that can either facilitate economic development or hamper it.

Arguably, these efforts to explore the relationship between culture and markets within economics tend to employ fairly narrow notions of culture.[6] Outside of economics, especially within economic sociology and economic anthropology, richer conceptions of culture tend to be employed. Following Max Weber, for instance, economic anthropologist Clifford Geertz (1973: 5) has defined culture as webs of significance in which human beings are suspended and which they themselves have spun.[7] Culture, Geertz (ibid.: 89) explains, "denotes an historically transmitted pattern of meanings embodied in symbols, a system of inherited conceptions expressed in symbolic forms by means of which men communicate, perpetuate, and develop their knowledge about and attitudes toward life." This definition deserves unpacking. Human beings are born into, raised and come to be enmeshed in a complex collection (i.e. a "pattern of meanings embodied in symbols") of shared beliefs about how the world works (i.e. "knowledge about" life) and ethical values (i.e. "attitudes toward life") that have evolved over time (i.e. are "inherited" and "historically transmitted"). A cultural system, Geertz (ibid.: 90) further explains, consists of a people's worldview and ethos that both confront and mutually confirm one another. "A group's ethos," Geertz (ibid.) writes,

> is rendered intellectually reasonable by being shown to represent a way of life ideally adapted to the actual state of affairs the world view describes, while the world view is rendered emotionally convincing by being presented as an image of an actual state of affairs peculiarly well-arranged to accommodate such a way of life.

For Geertz, then, a cultural system, like all systems, is a complex integrated whole that is not defined by any one or even any subset of its constituent parts.[8]

Following Geertz, I define culture as a historically transmitted pattern of meanings that is shared by a group of people and learned by new members as they become a part of the group.[9] Additionally, I argue that understanding the pattern of meanings that shape an individual's identification and assessment of desirable ends and appropriate means is critical to understanding his/her (economic) behavior. As Geertz (1973: 14) explains, "understanding a people's culture exposes their normalness without reducing their particularity. . . . It renders them accessible: setting them in the frame of their own banalities, it dissolves their opacity." Reality is processed through the lens of culture. As such, different cultural lenses can and do give rise to different conceptions of the good, different economic choices and so different economic outcomes.

Rather than treating culture as a pattern of meanings, however, the temptation for most economists examining the role of culture is to identify one or a few easily measurable factors and to have those serve as proxies for entire cultures (see, for instance, Guiso et al. 2006; Tabellini 2008; Fernandez and Fogli 2009; Williamson and Mathers 2011). Unfortunately, this approach (i.e. employing a few easily measurable factors as proxies for entire cultures) risks treating cultures as homogenous and static systems.[10] Cultures, however, are not homogenous. Even in so-called "progress-resistant" cultures, there are attitudes and beliefs that work to promote progress. A definite spirit of enterprise can be found in the most unlikely places. Slaves throughout the Caribbean, for instance, grew produce for market on their quasi-private plots during their free time and traded their surplus produce in an effort to improve their living standards (Tomich 1991; Storr 2004). While there may be prevailing attitudes in a particular culture that hamper progress, there is no such thing as a culture that cannot develop. To be sure, it is possible for some of the attitudes, views and values within a particular culture to be a barrier to entrepreneurship and so economic development. But no culture is entirely progress-resistant and all cultures are heterogeneous and have competing beliefs, some of which will promote enterprise and others that will discourage it. Of course, certain values are more compatible with markets than others but we should not be so pessimistic as to assume that there are large pockets in the world where we cannot locate market-friendly values.

Similarly, although cultural change is necessarily path dependent, cultures are not static. So-called "progress-resistant" cultures can grow more "progress-prone" over time. Chinese institutions and attitudes, for instance, are inarguably more individualistic and supportive of profit seeking in the 2010s than they were in the 1970s (see Allison and Lin 1999; Chow 2010). The same is true for India where the attitudes that supported central planning in the 1950s and 1960s gave ground to attitudes that supported technological innovation in the 2000s (see Rodrik and Subramanian 2005). A culture can change over time to reflect shifting beliefs, new information, and even contact with other cultures. And, though cultural systems survive and are transmitted throughout successive generations, changes do take place, a people's ethos and worldview do evolve.

Rather than homogenous and static, cultures are both heterogeneous and dynamic. As Lavoie and Chamlee-Wright (2000: 13) point out,

> culture is not an immutable given with which a society must learn to live. Nor is it homogenous within nations, or even within families. It is a complex of diverse tensions, ever evolving, always open to new manifestations and permutations.

How, then, should economists study the culture of markets? As I will argue, economists should look to Max Weber for insight into how to study the culture of markets.[11]

Perhaps economists should adopt a Weberian approach to studying the culture of markets

Max Weber is among the most important figures in modern social science and his writings have crossed into a number disciplines including economics, sociology, political science, anthropology and jurisprudence. Within economics, Weber is arguably best known (and either roundly criticized or enthusiastically embraced) for *The Protestant Ethic and the Spirit of Capitalism* (1905), *General Economic History* (1927), and perhaps his writings on the methodology of the social sciences. Although economists still engage his economic histories and methodological writings, his other contributions to economics (e.g. to marginal utility theory or institutional economics) have gone largely unnoticed, and his influence on the discipline is rather minimal.[12] Outside of economics, however, Weber is quite influential. As Kalberg (2005: 1) writes, "of the three major founders of modern sociology, Max Weber spans the widest horizon." "Among sociologists," as Käsler (1988: ix) also describes, "Weber is recognized as one of the principal 'founding fathers' of the discipline." And, "Weber has become regarded throughout the world as an undisputed 'classic' of sociology. Every lexicon or 'history' of this discipline mentions his name as central and emphasizes his authoritative influence on its development" (ibid.: 211). Similarly, as Coser (2005: xxv) remarks, "Weber's impact on modern social science is similar to that of Lord Keynes on modern economics. Like the work of Keynes, the work of Weber is a landmark. There is a pre-Weberian and a post-Weberian sociology." His two-volume *Economy and Society* (1978), for instance, is viewed as a foundational text within modern sociology. Similarly, his works on the religions of India and China as well as on Ancient Judaism are considered seminal works. The methodological discussions and substantive claims he advanced in those volumes have helped to shape a number of sub-disciplines within sociology, especially economic sociology, the sociology of religion, the sociology of law, urban sociology, industrial sociology, and political sociology.

Importantly, for our purposes here, Weber's *Sozialökonimik* or "social economics" also offers a fruitful approach to studying the culture of markets. According to Weber (1949: 65), social economics is concerned with a wide range of subjects; "the domain of such subjects extends naturally . . . through the totality of cultural life." "The basic element in those phenomena which we call . . . 'social economic'," Weber (ibid.: 64) explains,

> is constituted by the fact that our physical existence and the satisfaction of our most ideal needs are everywhere confronted with the quantitative limits and the qualitative inadequacy of the necessary external means, so that their satisfaction requires planful provision and work, struggle with nature and the association of human beings.

Social economics, thus, recognizes scarcity as the fundamental social scientific problem that it must confront. Its chief task is to explain the consequences of the scarcity of means; specifically, that the satisfaction of our wants requires that we plan, that we work, and that we cooperate with others.

For Weber, social economic phenomena fall into three different categories: (a) "pure" economic phenomena, (b) economically relevant phenomena, and (c) economically conditioned phenomena.[13] Economic phenomena, Weber (1949: 64) explains, are "events and constellations of norms, institutions, etc., the economic aspect of which constitutes their primary cultural significance for us." Economic events such as exchange and competition, economic norms such as offering employees a lunch break, economic institutions such as money and credit, economic relationships such as those between buyer and seller, and economic organizations such as banks and multinational corporations would all fall into this category because it is their economic aspect that interests social economists.[14]

The second category, economically relevant phenomena, is comprised of

> phenomena, for instance, religious ones, which do not interest us, or at least do not primarily interest us with respect to their economic significance but which, however, under certain circumstances do acquire significance in this regard because they have consequences which are of interest from the economic point of view.
>
> (ibid.)

This would include "all the activities and situations constituting an historically given culture [that] affect the formation of the material wants, the modes of satisfaction, the integration of interest groups and the types of power which they exercise" (ibid.: 66). Gender, racial, ethnic and class relations and biases, religious and political beliefs and institutions, and aesthetic considerations would, thus, fall into this category because they affect actors' preferences and decisions, the nature of economic life and the direction of economic development.

The third category, economically conditioned phenomena, consists of

> phenomena which are *not* "economic" in our sense and the economic effects of which are of no, or at best slight, interest to us . . . but which in individual instances are in their turn more or less strongly influenced in certain aspects by economic factors.
>
> (Weber, 1949:64)

The form and function of families and friendships, the fiscal aspects of the state, and attitudes towards neighboring populations and even immigrants, to the extent that they are influenced by economic phenomena, would fall into this category.[15]

Obviously, the boundary lines between these categories are not indelible. Moreover, since the non-economic phenomena that affect economic phenomena can in turn be affected by economic phenomena, it would be possible, even if the boundary lines were rigid, for the same phenomena to be both economically relevant and economically conditioned. For instance, social friendships both influence economic activity as is often pointed out in the literature on social capital (Coleman 1988; Portes 1998, 2000) and can grow out of economic relationships as is argued in the literature on the market as a social space (Storr 2008, 2009, 2010; Storr and John 2011; Meadowcroft and Pennington 2008). Similarly, attitudes about slavery or restrictions on immigration both affect and are affected by economic phenomena. Likewise, culture, within Weber's social economic framework, is both economically relevant and conditioned.

Weber, however, not only offers epistemological justification for the study of culture within economics but also offers methodological direction for economists hoping to examine how culture impacts economic life and vice versa. As hinted at above, he was committed to *verstehen* (i.e. interpretive understanding as a key method of the social sciences) and endorsed the use of thicker descriptions and more concrete ideal types in both theoretical and historical work than economists studying the culture of markets typically employ.

Weber's *sozialökonimik* is at root an interpretive social science that aims at understanding the meanings that individuals attach to their actions and the social world that they inhabit as well as the cultural significance of economic, economically conditioned and economically relevant phenomena. As Weber (1978: 4) writes,

> "meaning" may be of two kinds. The term may refer first to the actual existing meaning in the given concrete case of a particular actor, or to the average or approximate meaning attributable to a given plurality of actors; or secondly to the theoretically conceived *pure type* of subjective meaning attributed to the hypothetical actor or actors in a given type of action.

Arguably, the only way to get at the meanings that individuals attach to their circumstances, their relationships and their interactions is to look to the social stock of knowledge (i.e. the set of shared beliefs and values) from which their meanings are drawn.[16] Examining the social stock of knowledge, in turn, requires that we rely on ethnography and other qualitative approaches.[17]

The *verstehen* method that Weber advocated self-consciously employs ideal types.[18] Ideal types are constructs derived from historical reality but they are not simply historical generalizations. As Weber (1949: 90) writes,

> an ideal type is formed by the one-sided accentuation of one or more points of view and by the synthesis of a great many diffuse, discrete, more or less present and occasionally absent concrete individual phenomena, which are arranged according to those one-sidedly emphasized viewpoints into a unified analytical construct. . . . In its conceptual purity, this mental construct . . . cannot be found empirically anywhere in reality.[19]

Although some social scientific approaches do not explicitly employ or refer to their constructs as ideal types, all social science relies on ideal types of varying degrees of abstractness.[20] The more abstract an ideal type, the broader its applicability but the less useful it is in gaining insight into real world phenomena. For most social scientists, then, the goal is to construct ideal types that are not so abstract or idealized that they cease to be useful for doing applied social science but are not so concrete that they cease to be universal propositions. Every social science, for instance, is based on a particular anthropology. The traditional economic model of man as a rational, purposive actor is a fairly abstract ideal type. Similarly, the entrepreneur as an agent of change who is alert to profit opportunities is a more concrete ideal type than the economic man though it remains fairly abstract. The American entrepreneur as a maverick with a range of particular characteristics (i.e. a certain willingness to take heroic risks) is quite concrete though it remains potentially a useful theoretical construct (e.g. in making sense of the growth of the United States' economy). It is, likewise, possible to construct ideal types that describe social arenas and social processes.[21] Market, mall, indoor shopping mall and the Mall of America are all ideal types that range in levels of abstractness. Similarly, a business cycle, a business cycle precipitated by a housing bubble, and a business cycle precipitated by a housing bubble that was caused by a credit expansion are increasingly concrete ideal types. That these ideal types might not exist anywhere (at least in "pure" form) is actually an advantage of self-consciously adopting this approach. That they can be compared to real world phenomena and the differences between them and real world phenomena can be highlighted constitutes their chief benefit. [22]

In his explorations of the culture of markets, Weber (1951, 1958, 2002) employs the ideal type of the economic spirit to great effect. This ideal type represents the set of culturally derived attitudes and orientations that can and does animate a given economic market by shaping the way market participants conceive of their opportunities as well as the strategies that they adopt as they pursue their goals. As Weber (2002) explains, the differences that we observe in real world markets are partly due to those markets being governed by different bundles of institutions and partly due to those markets being home to different economic spirits. In studying the culture of specific markets, then, the goal would be to construct concrete ideal types based on his economic spirit typification that are developed from the particular histories and speak to the specific circumstances of those markets and their participants. Arguably, employing this strategy allows economists to do more than simply identify cross-cultural differences in economic practices and outcomes. Indeed, I believe that adopting a Weberian approach can lead to the development of a richer (theoretical and empirical) appreciation of the culture of markets and so of what actually occurs in markets than currently exists within the economics literature.[23] This book, thus, argues that economists should not only focus on the culture of markets but that, in doing so, they should adopt a Weberian approach.

And so, this book is organized as follows

This book outlines and defends an approach to understanding the culture of markets that builds on the work of Max Weber but also relies on the efforts of economists from several schools of thought as well as anthropologists, sociologists and historians.[24] Chapter 2, "Economists should study culture," thus, argues that economics ought to be a science of meaning and, as such, economists ought to pay attention to culture as they seek to understand both the meanings that actors attach to their decisions as well as the social significance of those decisions. Unfortunately, most economists are not all that interested in culture. There are, arguably, several reasons behind their reluctance to introduce considerations of culture into their theoretical and empirical analysis. First, they believe that culture is too nebulous a concept to usefully include in economic analysis. Second, they believe that, even if culture does play an important role in shaping economic behavior, in their role as economists they are not in the business of offering cultural explanations for economic phenomena. Culture, if it matters at all, operates at the level of preferences and so outside the domain of economics. Third, they believe that differences in economic behavior have less to do with differences in culture and more to do with differences in incentives. Although there is some validity to these concerns, none are dispositive, especially if the case can be made (as I attempt to do) that ignoring culture impoverishes both economic theory and empirical economics.

Next, Chapter 3, "But economists often misunderstand the relationship between culture and markets," critiques the relatively few efforts to explore the culture of markets within economics.[25] These efforts, I argue, tend to treat culture as capital (i.e. as a resource that can be employed in economic dealings). There are, however, problems with the culture as capital metaphor. Treating culture as capital, for instance, misunderstands capital and its essential features as well as culture and its significance. Additionally, it exaggerates the homogeneity of cultures, the degree to which actors are slaves to their cultures, and the degree to which cultural change is path dependent. Moreover, it treats culture or rather the lack of the "right" cultural traits or tools as a potential barrier to economic development.

Chapter 4, "Economists ought to be looking at the spirits that animate markets," makes explicit the approach that I recommend for exploring the culture of markets and suggests why the benefits of adopting this approach are likely to outweigh the costs. And Chapter 5, "This does *not* mean that economists have to abandon economics," argues that in adopting this approach economists do not have to reject rational choice or downplay the role of institutions. But, I argue, empirical efforts to explore the spirits that animate markets ought to be qualitative. Although the central conclusions of Weber's *The Protestant Ethic and the Spirit of Capitalism* have been roundly and rightly criticized, I maintain that the method that he pursued in attempting to illuminate the culture of modern capitalist markets ought to be embraced as a strategy for examining the culture of markets across contexts. Following Weber, I believe that the first step in this effort is to recognize that—and how—markets are animated by particular spirits. The next step, as economists move toward applied analysis, would be to outline the specific historical roots of the various and often competing spirits that animate some particular market, to outline their characteristics and to explore how they affect that market.

Finally, in the Epilogue, I offer concluding remarks. In summary, although their reluctance is understandable, economists ought to study the culture of markets. Unfortunately, when they do consider culture, they often misunderstand the relationship between culture and markets. Examining the spirits that animate markets, however, promises to be a fruitful approach to understanding how culture impacts economic behavior.

2 Economists should study culture

The truism is apt: context matters. Consider, for instance, how we understand the meaning of a sentence. Of course, the meaning of the individual words in the sentence matter a great deal. The meaning of the sentences that immediately preceeded and followed it as well as the broader conversation of which it is a part also matter, as does the speaker and her tone, her dialogical partners, her relationships to her dialogical partners, and the location where she is speaking. Is she being serious or sarcastic? Is she issuing a command or making a plea or voicing a complaint? When Henry II of England, for instance, asked aloud if someone would "rid him" of "this meddlesome priest"—his close friend and Archbishop of Canterbury Thomas Becket—we understand both that he likely meant it as a lament and also why his subjects assumed it was a royal edict and carried out Becket's assassination.

It is simply not enough to know the words in a sentence if we wish to understand its meaning. We have to know something about its context. As Gadamer (1994: 44) explains,

> when we want to understand sentences that have been handed down to us, we engage in historical reflections, from which it is determined just where and how these sentences are said, what their actual motivational background is and therewith what their actual meaning is. When we want to represent a sentence as such to ourselves we must, therefore, represent its historical horizon.

The same is true for understanding the actions of others. Recall Ryle's (2009) now famous insight that we cannot figure out the meaning of an action without some knowledge of the context and the actor's motivations. A twitch is an involuntary, reflexive opening and closing of an eye that has no intended recipient and no special meaning. A wink, on the other hand, looks identical to a twitch, but, unlike a twitch, a wink is done intentionally as a communicative act and is meant as a signal or to convey some sly meaning; it has an intended recipient and is meant to convey a particular message. The external physical changes to an individual's body that occur when he/she winks or blinks do not tell us anything about the meaning of those movements. Did the wind just blow an irritant into Ruthie's left eye? Or, are Ruthie and Tara best friends who are about to play a practical joke on another? Or, is Ruthie's gesture not aimed at Tara at all, but at the cute boy that is staring at her from across the room? How, Ryle asks, can we distinguish between a wink (a conspiratorial gesture between compatriots) and an eye twitch (an involuntary response to an irritant) without knowing anything else about its context? Of course, we cannot. As Geertz (1973: 6) explains, "the two movements are, as movements, identical; from an I-am-a-camera, 'phenomenalistic' observation of them alone, one could not tell which was twitch and which was wink, or indeed whether both or either was twitch or wink." We simply cannot tell the difference between a meaningful action and a reflex without knowing something more about the incident than that someone's left eye closed and opened rapidly. We would need to know a lot more about the scene in order to conclude that it was a twitch or not. "Yet the difference, however unphotographable, between a twitch and a wink," as Geertz (ibid.) reminds us, "is vast; as anyone unfortunate enough to have had the first taken for the second knows." We cannot distinguish Ruthie's wink from a simple twitch and cannot determine what her wink, if it is a wink, is meant to signal unless we know a great deal about her situation and the circumstances surrounding the act. As Schütz (1967: 27) explains, "questions of subjective meaning . . . cannot be answered by merely watching someone's behavior." Instead, "we first observe the bodily behavior and then place it within a larger context of meaning" (ibid.).[1]

Although economists have always been comfortable examining context in the form of constraints (i.e. the limited resources or rules prohibiting certain activities), they have been less eager to look to context in the form of culture and cultural systems. Economic anthropologists and economic sociologists, however, have not been so reticent to study the impact of culture on economic behavior.

Economic anthropologists have focused on how culture affects preferences as well as economic practices and performance. For economic anthropologists, culture is something that shapes economic behavior. As Henrich (2002: 255) summarizes, for "most economic anthropologists . . . 'culture' may provide individuals with certain preferences, perspectives, or context-specific heuristic rules." Similarly, Bird-David (1990: 190) has argued that cultures organize their economic activities and relationships on the basis of "primary metaphors" that "not only offer [a] means of 'seeing' the world but also govern everyday functioning [of individuals] down to the most mundane details."[2] And, as Wilk and Cliggett (2007: 143) explain, for economic anthropologists who focus on culture, "understanding economic behavior depends on mapping the symbolic and social order that underlies it, gives people the values they pursue, and constrains the strategies they follow."[3]

Most efforts by economic anthropologists to study the relationship between culture and economic phenomena highlight the folk models that individuals employ as they engage in economic activity. Bird-David (1990), for instance, has contrasted the Nayaka, a South Indian hunter-gatherer people, with neighboring communities in order to show how patterns of economic distribution and property relations vary widely depending on the "primary metaphors" or "metaphorical models" of the people in question.[4] Because the Nayaka consider the forest as a parent and each other as siblings, she explains, the Nayaka economy is one based on familial giving. As Bird-David (ibid.: 191) writes,

> Nayaka give to each other, request from each other, expect to get what they ask for, and feel obliged to give what they are asked for. They do not give resources to each other in a calculated, foresighted fashion, with a view to receiving something in return, nor do they make claims for debts.

Furthermore, since the forest as parent provides "unconditionally" to its children, the Nayaka believe that land cannot be owned by anyone.

Browne (2004: 10) has, similarly, explained how the creole culture that emerged in Martinique as a result of over 400 years of uninterrupted French control pushes Martiniquais "to make undeclared money in ways that earn them social status as well as income." Martiniquais, she asserts, prefer to work for themselves. Martiniquais, Browne (ibid.: 11) explains, also aspire to be thought of as *débrouillards* (i.e. as willing to pursue economic success in ways that "may extend beyond what is legal") though not beyond what is moral and as not only gifted, intelligent and resourceful but also "economically cunning and successful in unorthodox ways." According to Browne, both aspirations (i.e. personal autonomy and to be perceived as cunning) make sense given Martinique's creole culture and can be traced to their experiences during slavery and colonialism.

Economic sociologists have also attempted to demonstrate how culture shapes economic life. As Swedberg (2003: 218) suggests, economic sociologists have recognized that "for a full understanding of economic phenomena, it is not only necessary to pay attention to their political and legal dimension, but also to the role that is played by culture." Similarly, as Zukin and DiMaggio (1990: 17) explain, for economic sociologists,

> culture sets limits to economic rationality: it proscribes or limits market exchange in sacred objects and relations (e.g., human beings, body organs, physical intimacy) or between ritually classified groups. . . . Culture provides scripts for applying different strategies to different classes of exchange. Finally, norms and constitutive understandings regulate market exchange, causing persons to behave with institutionalized and culturally specific definitions of integrity even when they could get away with cheating.

In addition to being embedded in systems of social relations as well as in a political/legal institutional matrix, for economic sociologists, economic behavior is, thus, also culturally embedded (DiMaggio 1997). Moreover, as Levin (2008: 114) describes, the "new sociology of markets incorporates culture into analyses of economic action by treating culture as something that constitutes markets or else affects their operation." For sociologists, then, culture is either something that affects how markets are developed or it is something that affects how markets work.[5]

Most efforts by economic sociologists to study the economic impact of culture treat it as constitutive of markets or as constraining markets. Nee (1998), for instance, stresses the role of informal constraints—norms and networks—in shaping social interactions within organizations. He has argued that where informal constraints match the formal rules, the costs of monitoring and enforcement are low and organizational performance is high. Similarly, Zelizer (1978) has explored how culturally prescribed prohibitions against establishing monetary equivalents for certain objects and relationships can limit exchange and how cultural shifts can legitimize enterprises that had previously been proscribed.[6] The life insurance industry in the United States, Zelizer (ibid.: 597) explains, was not successful when it first emerged because there was, at the time, a "cultural aversion" to treating death as a commercial or monetary event. As Zelizer (ibid.: 598) writes,

> particularly, although not exclusively, during the first half of the nineteenth century, life insurance was felt to be sacrilegious because its ultimate function was to compensate the loss of a father or husband with a check to his widow or orphans.

By the second half of the nineteenth century, however, life insurance came to be seen as a secular ritual parallel to the religious ritual of the funeral that helped the bereaved to overcome the sadness of losing a loved one. Having life insurance also came to characterize what it meant to "die a good death" and a way to promote (economic) immortality. "As an efficient mechanism to ensure the economic provision of dependents," Zelizer (ibid.: 603) states, "life insurance gradually came to be counted among the duties of a good and responsible father." And, "theological concern with personal immortality was replaced in the nineteenth century by a growing concern with posterity and the social forms of immortality." The change in cultural attitudes toward life insurance allowed the industry to thrive. Culture, then, determines what and what does not count as a legitimate commodity. All successful commodities have to be culturally or at least sub-culturally sanctioned.

These accounts by economic anthropologists and sociologists of how culture affects economic behavior and outcomes can certainly be reconciled with economic accounts. Still, there are several reasons why economists should not be altogether pleased with a division of labor where economists focus exclusively on institutions and incentives and leave the study of the relationship between culture and economics to others. First, focusing exclusively on institutions and incentives and excluding culture is not actually a possibility. Of course, culture, which acts as a lens through which economic actors make sense of the world and their options in it, has not been and need not be at the fore of any economic analysis. But, if culture really is a source of meanings, if it really does play a key role in shaping choices and preferences, then culture necessarily enters into every economic analysis.

Second, there is something dissatisfying, at least from the perspective of an economist, with the efforts of economic anthropologists and economic sociologists to examine the relationship between culture and markets. Economic anthropologists sometimes make arguments that, for an economist, are simply too relativistic.

Consider, for instance, Gudeman's (1986) claim that non-Westerners filter their economic decisions through "local economic models" that bear little resemblance to the economic models deployed by Westerners. Modern Western economic behavior, for him, is simply different than economic behavior in non-Western, primitive, or exotic cultures. An economist, however, would insist that, even if preferences and the makeup of utility functions differ across contexts, economic actors across all contexts are in some respects quite similar (e.g. they prefer more of what they value to less, etc.). Additionally, rather than agreeing with Bird-David (1992a: 30) that the hunter-gatherers that she is describing "care about going on forays just as they do about the value of their products," an economist would likely insist that, if it is true that these hunter-gatherers occasionally walk through the forest with no hope of collecting something of value, we should consider the forays themselves as a good that they desire. Similarly, economic sociologists sometimes make arguments that, for an economist, focus too heavily on how culture shapes economic activity at the exclusion of how culture is shaped by economic activity. For instance, while Zelizer (1978) is certainly correct that the "cultural aversion" to treating death as a commercial event had to be overcome before the life insurance industry could thrive, she arguably understates the role that the life insurance industry played in bringing about the requisite cultural shift.

Third, and perhaps most importantly, absent a focus on how culture affects economic activity, economists can only offer (woefully) incomplete explanations of cross-cultural variations in economic behavior. Admittedly, some economists are beginning to recognize that they should not leave the study of the culture of markets to the economic anthropologists and the economic sociologists.[7] But, with a few exceptions, economists have little interest in studying how culture affects economic behavior. This chapter explores why economists should study culture.

With a few exceptions, economists have little interest in studying the effects of culture

If you pressed an economist to explain why he/she was not all that interested in culture, he/she would likely offer one or more of the following reasons: (a) culture may be important but it is a hazy concept, it is difficult to define and isolate; (b) culture may be important but anthropologists and sociologists (i.e. non-economists) should focus on it; and (c) culture is not that important, it is not cultural shifts and their effect on preferences but price differences and price changes that explain economic behavior (*de gustibus non est disputandum*).[8] Each of these reasons, I believe, is understandable and widely held by economists but, ultimately, as I shall argue toward the end of the chapter, invalid. Let us, however, take each in turn.

(a) Because economists believe that culture is a hazy concept

One justification that an economist might offer for ignoring cultural considerations in economic analysis is that culture is simply too vague a concept. Culture is difficult to define and almost impossible to separate from other factors that condition human behavior. As such, measuring culture presents a challenge for economists. In this view, economists simply cannot meaningfully talk about culture, whether they would want to or not. As Casson and Godley (2000: 2) write, "culture is a potentially nebulous concept. Many economists deny culture any place in their theories on the grounds that the concept is so imprecise." Similarly, as Fukuyama (2001: 3132) explains, economists are reluctant to study culture because "cultural factors are, methodologically, very difficult to measure and to disentangle from other kinds of variables."[9] Likewise, as Guiso et al. (2006: 23) explain,

> until recently, economists have been reluctant to rely on culture as a possible determinant of economic phenomena. Much of this reluctance stems from the very notion of culture: it is so broad and the channels through which it can enter economic discourse so ubiquitous (and vague) that it is difficult to design testable, refutable hypotheses.

Indeed, that culture is arguably a part of every potential factor that affects economic behavior means that it is problematic to treat it as a separate causal factor.

The recent increase in the number of economists who are exploring the role of culture suggests that they have found strategies for isolating and measuring cultural factors (ibid.). Even those economists who have attempted to examine how culture affects the economic aspects of behavior, however, have pointed to the challenges of incorporating culture into economic analysis. According to Tabellini (2008: 259), for instance, culture is an "ambiguous" term that has at least two different meanings within economics. As Tabellini (ibid.) explains,

> the most common meaning of culture [within economics] is that it refers to the social conventions and individual beliefs that sustain Nash equilibria as focal points in repeated social interactions or when there are multiple equilibria. . . . An alternative interpretation is that culture refers to more primitive objects, such as individual values and preferences.

Although "the two interpretations are not mutually exclusive" and "beliefs and values could interact in systematic fashions," Tabellini (ibid.) argues that the two are distinct. Notice, as Tabellini (ibid: 260) points out, that beliefs and values change at different rates; beliefs being less persistent than values. Ultimately, Tabellini (ibid.) settles on the prevalence of certain individual values and codes of good conduct, specifically codes of conduct that suggest either limited or generalized morality as being the aspect of culture that is relevant for explaining differences in economic performance. And he concludes that the diffusion of generalized morality is positively associated with economic development.

Importantly, the measures of the diffusion of generalized morality that Tabellini (ibid.: 262) employs are, by his own admission, "imperfect indicators." In his study, he constructed two variables from the *World Values Survey*, one measuring generalized trust toward others and the second measuring tolerance and respect for others (ibid.: 261). As Tabellini (ibid.: 262) confesses, not only are they measured with error, but their interpretation is also somewhat ambiguous. . . . besides measuring individual values, these variables might also capture social conventions or beliefs about others. Even interpreting them as values, their specific meaning in terms of the distinction between generalized vs. limited morality is only one of the possible interpretations.

Tabellini has, thus, focused on the diffusion of generalized morality as the important aspect of culture that explains economic outcomes and has attempted to construct measures that indicate the levels of generalized morality in various countries but concedes that he cannot be confident that his measures really do capture levels of generalized morality nor can he be confident that they are not capturing some other aspect of culture that may, thus, be more or as important for economic development. Moreover, as Tabellini (2010: 711) confesses, "culture" in his work "is still largely a black box." His goal is to establish *that* aspects of culture can shape economic outcomes, not to explain *how* culture does shape economic outcomes. Because Tabellini finds culture difficult to isolate and measure, he also finds that establishing the relationship between culture and economic outcomes is a challenge and explaining the relationship between culture and economic outcomes is even more difficult.

Of course, this difficulty of isolating and measuring culture as well as explaining how culture affects economic outcomes is not peculiar to Tabellini's specific approach.[10] If true, the supposedly nebulous nature of culture would present a challenge for any economist who attempted to advance a cultural explanation of economic phenomena and might explain some economists' reluctance to emphasize the role of culture. Indeed, the incorporation of culture into economics, they must feel, presents challenges at both the theoretical and empirical levels. Even if they wished to incorporate culture into their analysis, because they believe that culture is so difficult to define, isolate and quantify, it would make sense for them to doubt that they can successfully do so. That incorporating culture into economics presents certain (perceived) theoretical and empirical challenges might explain why economists are reluctant to focus on culture but is ultimately separable from the question of whether or not economists should pay attention to culture.

(b) Because economists believe that cultural considerations are outside the domain of economics

A second justification that an economist might offer for ignoring culture is that cultural considerations remain outside the domain of economics even if examining the role of culture may be important to understanding economic phenomena. Unlike anthropology, sociology and the other social sciences, which ought to be and are deeply concerned about the role of culture, economics, in this view, is only interested in a particular aspect of human behavior (i.e. rational decision-making subject to preferences). Tastes and their origins, thus, ought to be considered data to the economist. The role of the economist qua economist in explaining differences in behavior ends when differences in tastes come into question. Culture, in this view, both can and should be kept out of economic analysis.

Robbins' (1932: 16) assertion that economics is "the science which studies human behavior as a relationship between ends and scarce means which have alternative uses" is consistent with and could very well be the source of this view.[11] Rather than seeing economics as being principally concerned with particular activities such as exchange, consumption and production or with particular phenomena such as the accumulation of material wealth or with behavior that occurs within a particular domain such as market behavior, Robbins (ibid.) sees economics as being chiefly concerned with a particular aspect of all activities (i.e. "the disposal of scarce means.") As Robbins (ibid.) explains, the economist

> is interested in the way different degrees of scarcity of different goods give rise to different ratios of valuation between them, and he is interested in the way in which changes in conditions of scarcity, whether coming from changes in ends or changes in means—from the demand side or the supply side—affect these ratios.

Since all human behavior involves the use of scarce goods and services that could have been employed elsewhere, all human behavior can be said to have an economic aspect and so aspects of every human action falls within the domain of economics. As Robbins (ibid.: 17) writes, "it follows from this, therefore, that in so far as it presents this aspect, any kind of human behavior falls within the scope of economic generalizations. . . . There are no limitations on economic science save this."

It follows from this definition of economics as being concerned with a particular aspect of all human behavior that economists qua economists should not be concerned with the origins, nature or ethical status of the various ends that individuals pursue. As Robbins (ibid.: 24) writes, "economics is entirely neutral between ends; . . . in so far as the achievement of any end is dependent on scarce means, it is germane to the preoccupations of the economist. Economics is not concerned with ends as such." It would, thus, not matter to an economist whether the goal is to accumulate treasures on earth or in heaven, it would not matter to an economist whether the goal is profane or sacred, the economist would only be concerned with how the scarcity of means limits the attainment of desired ends. And, since time is necessarily scarce, all goals that require an investment of time are of interest to economists. Time, for instance, cannot simultaneously be spent in active efforts to accumulate wealth and in quiet meditation, so there is a necessary trade-off between material and spiritual riches. In this case, the economist would be concerned with how the scarcity of time results in this trade-off not with the ends being traded off. For an economist, then, ends are to be the starting point of an inquiry into how the satisfaction of various competing ends is affected by the scarcity of means.

It also follows from this definition of economics as being concerned with the disposal of scarce means that economists qua economists should not be concerned with the various ways that particular means can be used or the context in which the disposal of scarce means occurs. The "technical arts of production" and "the social environment" are, for Robbins, outside the scope of economics. As Robbins (ibid.: 33) explains, these "are simply to be grouped among the given factors influencing the relative scarcity of different economic goods." Consider the writing of books. The tools used to produce books (e.g. the editorial services, the word processing technology, the printing presses) can be used for various other purposes. Moreover, the social status of books has changed over time as literacy levels, the availability of other sources of entertainment and information, the availability of other mechanisms for transmitting the written word, and the esteem given to publishers and authors have changed. The technical aspects of the production of books and the social setting in which book production occurs, however, would not be relevant to economists. Instead, economists are to be concerned with how the existence of particular techniques for producing books, which can also be used to produce other goods, and with how the social factors affecting the production of books, influence the adaptations that book manufacturers make to any changes in the valuation of books by consumers.

For an economist, then, that particular means are capable of satisfying various ends and that the disposal of means occurs within particular social environments would be the *starting point* of an economic inquiry.

Economics, according to Robbins, should primarily be concerned with the linking of available scarce means to the satisfaction of particular ends. As Robbins (ibid.: 36) asserts, "it is one of the characteristics of the world as we find it that our ends are various and that most of the scarce means at our disposal are capable of alternative application." In this view, the reason and process through which particular ends come to be desired and the reason and process through which particular means come to be viewed as appropriate for the satisfaction of particular wants are, thus, beyond the scope of economics. The domain of economics, Robbins (ibid.: 38) argues,

> is essentially a series of relationships—relationships between ends conceived as the possible objectives of conduct, on the one hand, and the technical and social environment on the other. Ends as such do not form part of this subject-matter nor does the technical and social environment. It is the relationships between these things and not the things in themselves which are important for the economist.

The cultural aspect of human behavior and the economic aspect of human behavior are, thus, conceptually separate and practically separable. Jackson (2009) has pointed to Robbins' narrowing of the field of economics as being responsible for the removal of cultural considerations from economics. As Jackson (ibid.: 89) writes,

> By the mid-twentieth century, the Robbins definition of economics as the scientific study of scarcity and resource allocation had narrowed the scope as

a discipline. . . . The severing of economics from culture was now institutionalized . . . culture is not an active issue, since considering it would take them outside the domain of economics.[12]

Similarly, Beugelsdijk and Maseland (2011) have described the disappearance of culture from economics as being linked to this conception of economics as a subject principally concerned with the economic aspects of human behavior. As Beugelsdijk and Maseland (ibid.: 47) explain, "the distinction between cultural factors and economic phenomena was a first step in the removal of context from economics. The second step was the redefinition of non-orthodox economists as not really economists." Veblen, Beugelsdijk and Maseland (ibid.) argue, was described as doing something other than economic theory because he challenged the removal of culture, psychology and institutions from economics. Beugelsdijk and Maseland (ibid.), similarly, explain that Weber came to be viewed as a sociologist because he was interested in behavior that could not be fully explained using marginal utility.

In this view, culture is conceived of as "a pattern of meanings" that conditions the desirability of particular ends and perceptions of the appropriateness of particular means to the satisfaction of those ends would only be of indirect relevance to economists. The effect that particular cultural characteristics (i.e. specific tastes and preferences) had on the disposal of scarce means, however, would be relevant. Arguably, Parsons' (1935: 666) complaint that, "in the theoretical sense, there has been . . . too much sociology (as well as biology, psychology, etc.) in economics and too much economics in sociology" is consistent with the notion advanced by Robbins that the various social sciences ought to concern themselves with different aspects of human behavior. Like Parsons, Robbins would undoubtedly agree that economists should be interested in the disposal of scarce means and leave the concern over the other aspects of human behavior (i.e. the cultural, psychological and sociological aspects) to the other disciplines.

A potential modification of this view is that while cultural considerations have no place in economic theory (e.g. in Kirzner's theory of entrepreneurship), because of the important role that culture plays in shaping human behavior, discussing culture might be permissible and even necessary in the applied branches of economics such as economic history.[13] As Kirzner (1994: 329) has suggested, the observation that culture influences the economic aspects of human behavior should matter in the application of economic theory but not in the formulation of economic theory. As Kirzner (ibid.) argues, "it does not follow that, for the purposes *within economic theory* for which the entrepreneurial role has been introduced, it is necessary to go beyond the bare propensity of being alert." It is not necessary to consider culture *within economic theory*. However, "in *applying* economic theory," Kirzner (ibid.) explains, "one immediately looks for the cultural, historical, and social detail . . . through which the economic processes make themselves manifest." According to Kirzner, to the extent that understanding some particular real world phenomena requires that we pay attention to culture then the economic theory employed to describe it would necessarily be incomplete. But, "to suggest that the 'incompleteness' of such pure theory is in any way an inadequacy," Kirzner (ibid.) explains, "would be an unfortunate misunderstanding of what theory is all about." Admittedly, recent efforts to discuss the relationship between culture and economic behavior have primarily been within applied economics.[14] They have not (with a few exceptions) attempted to advance economic theory. In fact, rather than incorporating culture into economic theory, economists are beginning to theorize about the economic aspects of culture (see, for instance, Bisin and Verdier 2000, 2001, 2011).

(c) Because they believe it is all about prices and price changes[15]

A third justification for eschewing cultural considerations in economic analysis is that much of what is frequently explained or explained away by reference to culture can be explained using economic theory. There are, goes this argument, non-economic aspects of human behavior but the economic aspects of human behavior and so the scope for economics are much larger than is frequently supposed.[16] In this view, tastes need not be treated as data by economists or as explainable only by referencing non-economic factors. Instead, tastes can be examined using economic theory. According to Stigler and Becker (1977), saying that people behave differently because they have different tastes is too simplistic and is ultimately unsatisfactory. Recourse to cultural considerations, they contend, offers little analytically. "No significant behavior," Stigler and Becker (ibid.: 87) argue,

> has been illuminated by assumptions of differences in tastes. Instead, they, along with assumptions of unstable tastes, have been a convenient crutch to lean on when the analysis has bogged down. They give the appearance of considered judgment, yet really have only been ad hoc arguments that disguise analytical failures.

Rather than assuming that differences in tastes are pronounced or that tastes are unstable, Stigler and Becker (ibid.: 89) assert that tastes are remarkably stable over time and do not differ importantly among individuals. Consequently, "all changes in behavior," Stigler and Becker (ibid.: 89) argue, "are explained by changes in prices and incomes, precisely the variables that organize and give power to economic analysis." Consider, for instance, the apparent change in tastes for certain addictive goods that occurs as we spend increasing amounts of time consuming them. Over time, we appear to acquire a greater taste for certain kinds of music, foods and friends as well as for drinking certain beverages and smoking certain substances. Stigler and Becker (ibid.: 78) argue, however, that this apparent change in tastes is really a change in the (non-monetary) price of consuming these goods. As we consume these goods, they assert, we build "consumption capital" that actually lowers the costs of consuming them in the future. Thus, it actually becomes cheaper to consume those addictive goods than their alternatives. With types of music it is that over time one additional minute spent listening to the type of music that an individual has built up consumption capital in becomes increasingly more enjoyable relative to one minute spent listening to other types of music, *ceteris paribus*. The type of music that the individual has consumption capital in, thus, becomes relatively cheaper. Doing useful economics, according to Stigler and Becker (ibid.: 89), requires that "one searches, often long and frustratingly, for the subtle forms that prices and incomes take in explaining differences among men and periods."

Stigler and Becker (ibid.: 81) directly challenge the analytical efficacy of referencing custom and tradition in order to explain why and under what conditions behavior will sometimes remain stable in the face of changing conditions. According to Stigler and Becker (ibid.: 82), people continue to behave traditionally in the face of changing circumstances when behaving in step with tradition is cheaper than breaking with tradition. Customs and traditions, they explain, "result from investments of time and other resources in the accumulation of knowledge about the environment, and of skill with which to cope with it." Customs and traditions, for them, act as a form of capital.[17] Since decision-making involves our searching for relevant information about the environment as well as analyzing and making use of that information, customs and traditions, they argue, can lower the cost of decision-making. "The costs of searching for information and of applying the information to a new situation," Stigler and Becker (ibid.) write, "are such that habit is often a more efficient way to deal with moderate or temporary changes in the environment than would be a full, apparently utility-maximizing decision." When a temporary change in the environment occurs, it often does not make sense to abandon traditions or to invest in the acquisition of different types of knowledge about the environment or different recipes for negotiating it. When a permanent change in the environment occurs, those who are relatively young—those individuals who have a greater incentive to disinvest from capital attuned to the old environment and to develop capital relevant to the new environment than to retain and act consistently with customs and traditions—will tend to do adopt new modes of behavior. In this view, people maintain certain modes of behavior over generations not because they are under the sway of particular customs and traditions but because it is often prohibitively expensive to learn to do things differently. Economic theory can, they argue, explain behavior that is consistent with habits as well as deviations from habitual behavior.

If Stigler and Becker (ibid.) are correct, it would, thus, not be necessary to reference culture or other non-economic factors in order to explain unstable behavior where environments are stable or to explain stable behavior in the face of changing environments. Price and income shifts rather than cultural shifts or cultural constancy would explain human behavior. Arguably, this view explains Stigler's (1984) advocacy of economic imperialism (i.e. the belief that economics can explain ostensibly non-economic phenomena even though the reverse is not true). Moreover, Hirshleifer's (1985) claim that there is "only one social science" is also consistent with this view. "It is ultimately impossible," Hirshleifer (ibid.: 53) writes,

> to carve off a distinct territory for economics, bordering upon but separated from other social disciplines. Economics interpenetrates them all, and is

reciprocally penetrated by them. . . . What gives economics its imperialist invasive power is that our analytical categories—scarcity, cost, preferences, opportunities, etc.—are truly universal in applicability. . . . Economics really does constitute the universal grammar of social science.

Economics is, thus, (almost) all that we need to use in order to understand human behavior, if by economics we mean the study of rational decision-making in a world where ends are plenty and resources are necessarily scarce.

In this view, it is simply unclear what culture would add to the economist's analytical apparatus. Consider, for instance, Acemoglu and Robinson's (2010) discussion of why African societies are so poor. Rejecting cultural explanations of African development that point to cultural disincentives to entrepreneurship because "we have little systematic evidence of such ideas," and there is much evidence that there is dynamic entrepreneurship in Africa, Acemoglu and Robinson (ibid.) advance an institutional argument. "The current poverty of African societies," Acemoglu and Robinson (ibid.: 45) argue, "is explained by the nature of their institutions, not their geography or cultures." Absent secure property rights, markets cannot thrive and economic growth will not occur. Policies that undermine private property, control prices and restrict profits, stifle market exchange and retard wealth creation. Where the institution of private property is tenuous, they argue, underdevelopment necessarily follows. According to Acemoglu and Robinson (ibid.: 22),

> the main reasons that African nations are poor today is that their citizens have very bad interlocking economic and political incentives. Property rights are insecure and very inefficiently organized, markets do not function well, states are weak and political systems do not provide public goods.

Institutions and not culture, they conclude, play the key role.

If economists are going to reference culture, it would thus follow from this view, they should not treat it as an independent factor that impacts economic behavior. Instead, culture can and should be understood using the tools of economics. Bisin and Verdier (2001), for instance, argue that cultural attitudes are endogenously determined.[18] For them, "preferences of children are acquired through an adaptation and imitation process which depends on their parents' socialization actions, and on the cultural and social environment in which children live" (ibid.: 299). In their analysis, parents are rational, paternalistic agents who wish to produce children who share their preferences (because they believe it is in their children's own interest). Parents, thus, determine which cultural traits to transmit to their children and how much to invest in socialization. Because the socialization of children within the family and children's cultural adaptation from society are substitutes, families who belong to cultural minorities will socialize their children more intensely than families who are a part of the majority since members of majority groups can rely on the transmission of cultural traits by the society at large. As a result, Bisin and Verdier (ibid.: 300) explain, "there exists a heterogeneous distribution of preferences in the population, which is globally stable."

This way of justifying the exclusion of culture as an independent factor from economic analysis (i.e. economics explains culture but culture does not explain economic behavior) is notably different from the view that the other social sciences (e.g. anthropology, political science, sociology, etc.) have unique and important contributions to make to our understanding of human behavior that are simply outside the purview of economics. In this view, economics or rather rational choice theorizing is the only valid approach to understanding social phenomena.

But economics is a science of meaning, and so economists should look at the role of culture

Friedman (1953) has argued that economics ought to be a predictive science.[19] As Friedman (ibid.: 4) writes,

> its task is to provide a system of generalizations that can be used to make correct predictions about the consequences of any change in circumstances. Its performance is to be judged by the precision, scope, and conformity with experience of the predictions it yields. In short, positive economics is, or can be, an "objective" science, in precisely the same sense as any of the physical sciences.

The goal, then, is not to understand economic behavior but to predict economic behavior. The concern is how individuals will respond to this or that stimulus not why they respond as they do to some particular stimulus. As such, the realism of assumptions is beside the point. As Friedman (ibid.: 14) writes, "truly important and significant hypotheses will be found to have 'assumptions' that are wildly inaccurate descriptive representations of reality, and, in general, the more significant the theory, the more unrealistic the assumptions (in this sense)."

If economics is a predictive science, then whether or not to include culture in an analysis would simply be an empirical question. It will depend on its predictive power. If economics, however, is an interpretive science, then the case for including culture becomes quite strong. There are, in fact, good reasons to believe that economics is and ought to be an interpretive science.

Arguably, the essential data of all of the social sciences including economics are subjective in character. The facts of social sciences are the meanings that individuals attach to their actions and their environments. As Knight (1990: 226) argues, "we can learn about human phenomena, in the significant sense of knowledge, chiefly by studying, and practicing, communication with other minds." Similarly, as Mises (1949: 26) argues, "we cannot approach our subject if we disregard the meaning which acting man attaches to [his] situation." And, "the task of the [social sciences] is the comprehension of the meaning and relevance of human action" (ibid.: 51). Likewise, as Hayek (1979: 53) argues, "unless we can understand what . . . people mean by their actions any attempt to explain them . . . is bound to fail." Also, the facts of the social sciences are merely opinions, views held by the people whose actions we study. They differ from the facts of the physical sciences in being beliefs or opinions held by particular people, beliefs which as such are our data, irrespective of whether they are true or false.

(Hayek 1942: 279)

And, "in the social sciences the things are what people think they are" (Hayek 1943: 3). In order to explain social phenomena, the social sciences must be concerned with what people think and believe, their assessments and valuations, the importance they place on particular relationships vis-à-vis others, and the way they see the world and their place within it.

The opinions and beliefs that guide the actions of the individuals under study simply cannot be ignored, even if those beliefs are wrong, or irrational, or based on superstition rather than reason. The interactions between two individuals, for instance, are explainable only in terms of what they believe about the nature of their relationship (Hayek 1948: 60). If Latoya believes that Keisha is her blood relative, whether Latoya is in fact mistaken or not is irrelevant to any explanation of Latoya's behavior toward Keisha. Similarly, if Latoya and Keisha were in fact blood relatives but neither of them knew it, a valid explanation of Latoya's behavior toward Keisha or Keisha's toward Latoya could not be based on their genetic connection to one another. The same is true, of course, for efforts to explain religious rituals. It is not the social scientists' "objective" assessments of the efficacy of prayer but individuals' "subjective" perceptions of the power of prayer that explains why some people pray and others do not. Reference to what people think and believe is necessary in order to explain why people accept certain metal discs as money and not others, why they eat certain animals and plants and not others, why they ingest certain chemical concoctions when they are sick and not others. Like all the other social sciences, then, economics is a science that must be preoccupied with meanings.

What, though, does it mean to be a science of meaning? Schütz's (1967) efforts are quite helpful in this regard. To say that a person's experience has meaning, that it is a meaningful lived experience, Schütz (ibid.: 41) informs, is to say that acting man has reflected upon it and isolated it "from the abundance of experiences coexisting with it, preceding it, and following it" and, in so doing, has constituted it as meaningful.[20] As Schütz (ibid.: 71) explains, "the reflective glance signals out an elapsed lived experience and constitutes it as meaningful." And, in constituting an item as meaningful, the item is "selected out" and "rendered discrete by a reflexive act" (ibid.: 19). Meaning then, in a generic sense, is a certain way of regarding an item or experience. "*Meaning,*" as Schütz (ibid.: 42) points out, "*is a certain way of directing one's gaze at an item of one's own experience.*"

It becomes clear at this point that "meaningfulness," contrary to Weber's view, is not a useful criterion for distinguishing between mere behavior and action (what Weber called "meaningful behavior").[21] In fact, Weber's hope to separate out meaningful behavior (as rational, purposive action) from purely emotional behavior and traditional/habitual behavior completely breaks down when we think of meaning as a way of seeing an item.[22] "It is useless to say that what distinguishes action from behavior," Schütz (ibid.: 19) writes, "is that the former is subjectively meaningful and the latter meaningless. On the contrary, each is meaningful in its own way." All of my experiences can be selected out and distinguished from other experiences and so constituted as meaningful, be they "purposive" in Weber's sense or merely "automatic" reactions to stimuli. In fact, even my involuntary responses to stimuli (e.g. coughing, sneezing, choking, etc.) can be isolated and made meaningful. As Schütz (ibid.) states, "when I look closely, I find that none of my experiences is entirely devoid of meaning."[23]

What, then, is the difference between action and mere behavior? Can we draw any meaningful distinctions between them? In which way are actions meaningful? According to Schütz (ibid.: 61), *"action is the execution of a projected act,"* and *"the meaning of any action is its corresponding projected act."* A person acting rationally first chooses a goal or an end. He/she then imagines a completed act and that projection becomes the thing that he/she tries to bring about through action. Consider, for example, Michaela wanting to get out of bed to go into the living room. "What is visible to the mind," Schütz (ibid.: 60) explains, "is the completed act, not the ongoing process that constitutes it." She does not count her steps before beginning to head to the living room nor does she, at least at this initial stage, think of the obstacles she will encounter along the way (i.e. she does not see the doors she will have to open, the furniture she will have to walk around, etc.). Instead, what she projects (at first) is "herself in the living room." Next, she identifies the means that are necessary to achieve the desired ends and, perhaps, projects those as intermediate goals. This process, Schütz (ibid.: 61) explains, is a recognition of "a certain causal regularity" between the means available to her and her particular goal. To continue with our example, Michaela is able to conceive of a plan that gets her from her bed to the living room because she is aware (through experience in this case) that lifting herself from her bed, walking toward the bedroom door, opening said door and walking through it will get her from the bed to the living room. An action (and the sub-actions that contribute to bringing about a particular act), as Schütz (ibid.: 63) concludes, "are meaningless apart from the project that defines it."

Although the "projected act" can be fairly thought of as "the meaning of an action," reference to the projected act only gives us the "in-order-to motive" of the action.[24] As Schütz (ibid.: 89) explains,

> if, therefore, I give as the motive of my action that it is in-order-to-such-and-such, what I really mean is the following: The action itself is only a means within the meaning-context of the project, within which the completed act is pictured as something to be brought to fulfillment by my action. Therefore, when asked about my motive, I always answer in terms of "in-order-to" if the completed act is still in the future.

But the term "motive" can mean more than "the orientation of the action to a future event" (ibid.: 87). It can also mean "its relation to a past lived experience" (ibid.). Stating that a murderer committed murder for money is an "in-order-to" statement. Stating that a murderer committed murder because he grew up under difficult circumstances is an altogether different kind of statement. Although we are inclined, Schütz (ibid.: 91) explains, to call this second statement an "explanation of the deed," it is ultimately only a statement that "certain past experiences of the murderer have created a disposition on the part of the murderer to achieve his goals by violence rather than by honest labor." The so-called "explanation of the deed" speaks to the "genuine because-motive" of the action.

Determining the "genuine because-motive" of an action, as Schütz (ibid.: 95) points out, is a backward looking effort.[25] As Schütz (ibid.: 93) explains, "the formulation of a genuine why-question is generally possible only after the motivated experience has occurred and when one looks back on it as something whole and complete in itself." Moreover, the motivating experience must certainly be past at the time that a genuine because-statement is made. A future event cannot be the genuine because-motive of a past event. As Schütz (ibid.) notes, "the meaning-context of the true because-motive is thus always an explanation after the event." Suppose, for instance, we say that the murderer killed his victim because his victim was going to kill him at some later date. Notice that the in-order-to motive behind the murderer's killing was to prevent his own demise in the future. And, that the because-motive is not really his impending doom but his past perception of the possibility of his future death. It is his prior realization of the threat to his life and not his future death that motivated him to kill.

Identifying how meaning is constituted, however, does not tell us anything about its content nor does it tell us anything about how, if at all, we can gain access to the in-order-to motives let alone the genuine because-motives of others. There is, according to Schütz, no method available to us which we can follow in hopes of gaining access to the actual intended meanings of others, the in-order-to and genuine because-motives of an actor as the actor understands them. As Schütz (ibid.: 218) explains, "it is one thing to interpret one's own experience and quite another to interpret the experiences of someone else." We have "direct" access to our own experiences. We only have access to the external signs, products and indications of each other's lived experiences. In order to interpret the experiences of someone else, we have to begin with these signs and trace them back to their (possible) subjective meanings.[26] This process of tracing signs back to subjective meanings of the actor is not without its challenges. There is not a one to one mapping between signs and meanings. Instead, "the subjective meaning that the interpreter *does* grasp is at best an approximation to the . . . [individual's] intended meaning, but never that meaning itself, for one's knowledge of another person's perspective is always necessarily limited" (ibid.: 129). Although our knowledge of another person's perspective is limited, interpretation is nonetheless possible because everyone's actions belong to an "intersubjective world common to us all" (ibid.: 218).

The task of a science of meaning that aims at exploring the actions of others must attempt to explicate the interpretive schemes that actors employ to understand their own acts and the stock of knowledge from which they draw the subjective meanings of their actions.

Schütz has stressed the importance of the "social stock of knowledge" in providing individuals with "interpretive schemes," "relevance systems," "skills," "useful knowledge" and "recipes."[27] As Schütz and Luckmann (1973: 100) explain, "each situation [that individuals encounter and experience in the everyday life-world] is defined and mastered with the help of the stock of knowledge." An individual's "subjective stock of knowledge" contains everything that he has "learned" over the course of his life; how to walk, talk, read, ride a bicycle, drive a car, relate to his friends and colleagues, program a computer, reason like an economist; what his capabilities are and his limitations; what is appropriate and inappropriate in a variety of the circumstances; what is typically relevant and what is usually irrelevant in various situations; which phenomena he should view as common and which uncommon; his own life history; the stories he was told as a child; what he gained through interacting with his fellows; the customs and folklore of his community. When an event occurs or he is confronted with a (novel or not so novel) state of affairs, he draws on his subjective stock of knowledge as he defines his circumstances and decides his path.

Although some of an individual's subjective stock of knowledge was developed as a result of his own experiences in the life-world, much of it was derived from the social stock of knowledge. As Schütz and Luckmann (1973: 254) explain, "when the individual enters into a situation, he brings with him a biographically modeled, and to a large extent socially derived, stock of knowledge." And, "the subjective stock of knowledge consists only in part of 'independent' results of experience and explication. It is predominantly derived from elements of the social stock of knowledge" (ibid.: 262).

All social knowledge, Schütz and Luckmann (ibid.: 262) point out, is the result of the "subjective acquisition of knowledge" that occurs through experience in the life-world. The social stock of knowledge, however, contains both "more" than the sum of each individual's subjective stock and "less" than each individual's subjective stock. "More" in the sense that no person in any community is in possession of all of that community's social stock of knowledge; there is a social distribution of knowledge (ibid.: 264). "Less" in the sense that the individual's subjective stock of knowledge contains elements that were acquired during novel or unique experiences and so do not make their way into the social stock of knowledge (ibid.).

Arguably, it is possible to think of the social stock of knowledge as culture.[28] Recall, culture is fairly thought of as a collection of meanings that we received from our predecessors. Again, as Geertz (1973: 89) writes, "it denotes an historically transmitted pattern of meanings . . . a system of inherited conceptions . . . by means of which men communicate, perpetuate, and develop their knowledge about and attitudes toward life." Like Schütz's "social stock of knowledge," cultural systems have both moral and cognitive aspects that shape our decisions regarding good and bad ways of thinking about and behaving in the world.

As a science of meaning, then, economics must highlight the role of the social stock of knowledge (i.e. it must be concerned with culture if economists are to understand the in-order-to and genuine because-motives of actors). This is true at a theoretical level where the economist should (when appropriate) point out how culture can affect economic behavior. This is also true at an empirical level where the economist should (when appropriate) point out how specific cultures have affected the economic behavior of certain individuals and groups and led to certain economic outcomes. Rather than ignoring, or explaining away, or leaving the study of the relationship between culture and economic behavior to others, economists should pay attention to how culture would affect the actors in their models and how culture does affect the actors that they study. Economics is and should be recognized as a cultural science.

And the market order is a cultural phenomenon

The market is typically conceptualized as an area where buyers and sellers exchange goods and services. It could refer to a particular geographic location or marketplace where a variety of goods and services are exchanged (e.g. the local shopping plaza). Or, it can be conceived of as the sphere where buyers and sellers trade a particular good (e.g. the market for tennis shoes).

Conceived of in one or both of these ways, the market ought to be of interest to economists. It should be a central category within economics. After all, price theory and its constituents (i.e. consumer and producer theory) are efforts to tease out the implications of rational choice in a market setting. They are ultimately efforts to elucidate market behavior. Consumers and producers are market figures. Competition and exchange are activities that take place within and lead to the emergence of markets. Much of economic theory is, therefore, concerned with market phenomena.

Ironically, the market has not been a central concern for economists. This peculiarity has not gone unnoticed by economists. For instance, as North (1977: 710) observes, "it is a peculiar fact that the literature on economics . . . contains so little discussion of the central institution that underlies neo-classical economics —the market." Similarly, as Coase (1988: 7) remarks, "although economists claim to study the working of the market, . . . in the modern textbook, the analysis deals with the determination of market prices, but discussion of the market itself has entirely disappeared." And, as Stigler (1967: 291) observes, "economic theory is concerned with markets much more than with factories or kitchens. It is, therefore, a source of embarrassment that so little attention has been paid to the theory of markets." Non-economists have also noticed this peculiarity. As Lie (1997: 342), for instance, has argued,

the market is [allegedly] a central category of economics. . . . It is then curious that the market receives virtually no extended discussion in most works of economic theory or history. . . . The market, it turns out, is the hollow core at the heart of economics.

Similarly, as Swedberg (1994: 257) observes, "astonishingly little work has been done" on the market within economic thought.

The market, thus, occupies a strange position within economics (Storr 2008). It is in a sense ever-present. It is the site where much of the activity that interests economists takes place. But it is more often than not in the background of the analysis.[29] As I have argued elsewhere,

> in economics, we often portray markets as sterile spaces lacking either souls or sounds. We talk about transactions and prices and profits but seldom mention people (except when we refer to the faceless profit maximizing suppliers and hedonistic utility maximizing demanders).
>
> (ibid.: 141)

Bringing the market to the forefront of economic analysis would require recognizing it as a social structure in its own right where both competition and exchange occur that is supported by a variety of norms and more formal institutions which enable it to function. In the real world, "markets . . . are vibrant, colorful social spaces" (ibid.).

It is probably uncontroversial to suggest that real world markets are cultural phenomena. The differences between the New York Stock Exchange, the Mall of America in Minnesota, the Makola Market in Ghana and Amazon.com are obvious to anyone familiar with them. Of course, in many respects, the actors in these markets are very similar to each other. Buyers in all of these markets are hoping to pay as little as possible. Sellers in all of these markets are hoping to earn a profit. All participants are trying to advance their subjectively perceived interests as best they are able to given their constraints. But there are also key differences. Haggling, for instance, does not generally occur in the American mall or when buying from an e-commerce website (except for resellers and auction sites) but is acceptable and expected in an African bazaar and is even essential to the functioning of a stock exchange. Similarly, the nature of the relationships between trading partners in different markets can vary considerably. If electronic commerce offers the possibility for largely anonymous exchange, trading partners in stock exchanges and bazaars tend to have more intimate relationships. Additionally, what would constitute a fair deal can differ across markets.

Consider, for instance, Geertz's (1963) discussion of the differences between the culture of markets in Modjokuto and Tabanan, two towns in Indonesia. As Geertz (ibid.: 122) describes, "Modjokuto's entrepreneurs emerge directly from a bazaar economy in which individualistic, every-man-for-himself activity is carried almost to an extreme in contrast to the lineage-like organization of the relatively solidary and corporate ruling family from which Tabanan's new men come." While the Modjokuto peddlers are ego-focused, Tabanan traders are group-focused. Tabanan markets are high trust environments. Because deception is rampant in Modjokuto's bazaar economy, however, Modjukutans develop shrewd bargaining skills in order to overcome the low level of trust that overlays economic activity. Not surprisingly, the more successful merchants in Modjokuto are the pious Muslims, who embrace more systematic, stable, and efficient business behaviors and are able to set themselves apart from the more opportunistic peddlers in the bazaar.

Modjokuto and Tabanan's different entrepreneurial cultures have shaped the types of transactions that occur as well as the nature and size of the enterprises that exist in each town. "Almost all Modjokuto's modern enterprises," Geertz (ibid.) explains, "are individual or immediate concerns, and capital must be raised either through personal savings or (increasingly) through government loans . . . In Modjokuto even partnerships . . . are almost non-existent." In Tabanan, however, partnerships and large cooperatives are fairly typical and modern enterprises are able to raise capital from villagers to support large-scale collective efforts. Unlike the Modjokutans, Geertz (ibid.) explains, "the cultural tradition from which [Tabananers] draw provides ready-made forms for collective activity." One Tabananer cultural tradition that has proven especially useful in this regard is the *seka* group. According to Geertz (ibid.: 84), village life in Tabanan is best described as a series of overlapping *seka* groups which are organized to serve some specific political, social or economic function. Tabananers can belong to as many as a dozen of these groups. The existence of these *seka* groups, Geertz (ibid.) offers, explains why economic activities in Tabanan tend to be strongly collective.

It is quite clear how employing culture might improve economists' understanding of (actual, existing, real world) markets. Economists' understanding of the (conceptual) market, however, would also improve by treating it as a cultural phenomenon. The concepts that economists employ to explain market interactions are all culturally constructed. Culture (partly) determines who can buy and sell, when a deal between them is properly consummated, which items buyers and sellers can trade, and what counts as an acceptable unit of exchange. Moreover, culture (partly) determines why entrepreneurs notice some opportunities and not others as well as why they chose to pursue certain paths to exploit the opportunities that they notice and not others. Since culture plays a significant role in determining who can legitimately engage in market transactions, what constitutes an acceptable exchange, which items and services can be traded and what counts as money, it would seem to make sense for economists to concern themselves with how culture affects economic behavior.

Besides, the choice is really between employing culture implicitly or employing it explicitly

Ignoring culture may be possible but avoiding culture is impossible. While it is not inaccurate to assert, as many economist do, that relative price shifts, or differences in the size of expected profits, or differences in the institutional framework can explain *all* of the meaningful differences in economic behavior and outcomes, it is not accurate to assert that prices, profits and property can explain *any* of the meaningful differences in economic behavior and outcomes without (at least implicitly) employing culture.[30]

The choice before economists is not between employing culture or not employing culture. Instead, it is a choice between implicitly or explicitly employing culture. Changes in relative prices do explain why individuals might begin to use a particular good more sparingly that they once used wastefully (Hayek 1948). Differences in the size of expected profits do explain why entrepreneurs pursue some opportunities and not others (Kirzner 1973). Differences in the rules governing property do explain why individuals in some contexts engage in productive entrepreneurship and individuals in other contexts engage in destructive entrepreneurship (Baumol 1990). But what meaning should be attached to price changes, when a difference between revenues and expenses in fact signifies a large enough profit to make pursuing an opportunity attractive, and what constitutes an appropriate disposition of property, are all (partly) determined by culture.

The meanings attributed to price changes are culturally constructed. Recall that the price system, as Hayek (1948: 87) explains, can be thought of

> as a kind of machinery for registering change, or a system of telecom-munications which enables individual producers to watch merely the movement of a few pointers, as an engineer might watch the hands of a few dials, in order to adjust their activities to changes of which they may never know more than is reflected in the price movement.

The "marvel" of the market, as Hayek (ibid.) asserts, is that with very little information thousands of people respond appropriately to a change in the relative scarcity of a product without anyone issuing a directive. But, notice, price changes have to be interpreted. The meaning of a price shift is not unambiguous. A price increase could reflect a permanent or temporary change is the scarcity of a good. An individual's response will undoubtedly differ depending on whether or not she decides that the shift is temporary.[31] Of course, she could invest in obtaining additional information about the underlying cost of the price shift and will certainly do so as long as the expected returns from investing in additional information is greater than the cost of acquiring additional information. Correctly weighing expected benefits against expected costs of searching for additional information, however, requires that she not only correctly assesses the value of the information sought and the cost of searching but that she accurately assigns a probability to her finding the desired information. Our assessments of value and our assignments of probabilities come from our stocks of knowledge, parts of which are derived from the social stock of knowledge. Assuming that the meaning of the price change is unambiguous, or that she will neither be overly pessimistic nor optimistic in assessing the costs and benefits of acquiring additional information or estimating the likelihood that her search will be successful, then, is to assume that she possesses an appropriate cultural frame.[32]

The meanings attributed to profit opportunities are similarly culturally constructed. Recall that "the entrepreneurial element in the economic behavior of market participants," as Kirzner (1973: 15–16) writes, "consists . . . in their alertness to previously unnoticed changes in circumstances which may make it possible to get far more in exchange for whatever they have to offer than was hitherto possible." Entrepreneurship, Kirzner (ibid.) explains, consists in recognizing opportunities to buy low and sell high. But, again, the entrepreneur does not uncover unambiguous opportunities. Entrepreneurship requires interpretation. Assuming that profit opportunities are like dollar bills lying on the beach waiting to be picked up, as Kirzner (ibid.) has, might make the act of interpretation a trivial one but does not eliminate the need for interpretation. A piece of paper lying on the ground could be a dollar bill that can be exchanged for valuable items or it could be a worthless piece of paper. Whether an entrepreneur will bend down to pick up the piece of paper or not will depend on whether she believes that the paper represents a dollar bill or a worthless scrap. It will also depend on whether or not she believes that she can successfully pick up the paper without exerting more effort than the piece of paper is worth. And, it will depend on whether or not she believes that the piece of paper is hers for the taking. It may, in fact, belong to someone that she does not yet notice. Again, her assessments will be influenced by her stock of knowledge, part of which is derived from her social stock of knowledge. And, again, assuming her assessments will be correct is to assume that she possesses an appropriate cultural frame.[33]

That culture has to be (implicitly or explicitly) employed when pointing to differences in the rules of the game (i.e. the institutional matrix) as an explanation for differences in economic outcomes is perhaps easier and is certainly less controversial than arguing that prices and profit opportunities are culturally constructed. Recall that, as Baumol (1990: 898) writes,

> the exercise of entrepreneurship can sometimes be unproductive or even destructive . . . whether it takes one of these directions or one that is more benign depends heavily on the structure of payoffs in the economy—the rules of the game.

The rules of the game, however, both emerge from a society's cultural system and are interpreted through a cultural lens. As North (2005: 49) explains, "the institutional structure reflects the accumulated beliefs of the society over time. And change in the institutional framework is usually an incremental process reflecting the constraints that the past imposes on the present and the future." Also, as North (ibid.) continues, "there is an intimate relationship between belief systems and the institutional framework." Cultural systems comprised of belief and value systems are thus the source of society's pay-off structure. To say that the rules of the game in one society encourage productive entrepreneurship and that the institutional matrix in another encourages unproductive or even destructive entrepreneurship is to make a statement about those societies' cultures.

Economists, simply, cannot avoid making assumptions about the relationship between culture and economic behavior. If the aim of economics is prediction, then, not specifying and not defending the cultural assumptions embedded in a particular economic analysis might not matter all that much. As Greif (1994) and others have shown, however, there is reason to believe that including cultural factors into our models could improve their predictive power. If the aim is to explain and understand economic behavior, then, leaving our assumptions about culture implicit (and so unspecified and undefended) necessarily impoverishes our analysis.

Conclusion

The classical economists were aware of the important role that culture plays in shaping economic behavior and discussed the role of culture, particularly in the form of belief systems, customs and habits, in their analysis. For instance, Mill (1848: II. IV. 3) observes in a chapter on competition and custom that

> it is only in the great centres of business that retail transactions have been chiefly, or even much, determined, by competition. Elsewhere it rather acts, when it acts at all, as an occasional disturbing influence; the habitual regulator is custom, modified from time to time by notions existing in the minds of purchasers and sellers, of some kind of equity or justice.

Similarly, as Say (1803: I. XXI. I) observes when discussing the nature of money, "custom . . . and not the mandate of authority, designates the specific product that shall pass exclusively as money, whether crown pieces or any other commodity whatever." Likewise, Smith (1776: I. I. II) observes that "the difference between the most dissimilar characters, between a philosopher and a common street porter, for example, seems to arise not so much from nature, as from habit, custom, and education," and Smith (ibid.: I. I. IX) also discusses how custom can make certain kinds of employment fashionable and other kinds unattractive.

Early in the twentieth century, however, most economists stopped talking about culture. As economics became more formal, culture began to seem too vague a concept to incorporate into economic analysis. As the other social sciences developed, culture was seen as the province of these other disciplines; economists could leave the analysis of culture's role to the anthropologists and the sociologists. As economics began to be seen as the grammar of the social sciences, it seemed as if cultural differences should be explained using the tools of economics rather than treated as an independent factor. Although these three reasons for the removal of culture from economics push in the same direction, they are not all consistent with one another. Stressing that there is an economic aspect of all human action (as Robbins does), for instance, does not imply that the economic aspect of all human behavior is the only important aspect of human behavior (as Stigler and Becker do). Similarly, claiming that culture is too nebulous a concept to be incorporated into economics undermines the claim that culture can be explained using economic analysis.

But if economics is to be viewed as a science of meaning then it must pay attention to culture. There are, of course, better and worse ways to incorporate culture into economics. In Chapters 4 and 5, I recommend an approach to studying the culture of markets and suggest why the benefits of adopting this approach are likely to outweigh the costs. Culture need not be seen as a nebulous concept nor need it be seen as the domain of other disciplines. Economists can still be imperialists if they wish but that implies that they should engage in export (i.e. utilize rational choice theorizing to explore subjects outside the traditional domain of economics) as well as import (i.e. they should benefit from the methods and substantive efforts of social scientists from other disciplines). The next chapter critiques some of the recent efforts to incorporate culture into economic analysis. These efforts, I argue, tend to treat culture as a form of capital. As I suggest, however, there is something unsatisfactory about this analogy.

3 But economists often misunderstand the relationship between culture and markets

Few economists are interested in importing insights, concepts or findings from the other social sciences. This lament, of course, is a familiar one. As Lewin (1996: 1295) complains, "it appears that throughout this century, economists have been reluctant to acknowledge the interdependence between economics and its sister disciplines, particularly sociology and psychology." And, "economists tend to downplay the relevance (to economics) of the other human sciences. In particular, we tend to ignore outside criticism" (ibid.). Examining the citation patterns of social scientists, Rigney and Barnes (1980) as well as Pieters and Baumgarther (2002) find that economists rarely cite anthropology, political science, psychology or sociology. As Pieters and Baumgarther (ibid.: 504) summarize, "economics builds only slightly on knowledge from its sister disciplines."

Interestingly, though few economists are interested in importing from the other social science disciplines, many economists have felt quite comfortable exploring subjects that have traditionally been seen as outside the scope of economics. Indeed, economists are generally very comfortable attempting to export their concepts and theories to other subject areas and disciplines. Rather than adopting or adapting the concepts and formulations of its sister disciplines, however, economists tend to utilize the language of economics when they do study phenomena traditionally viewed as being outside of their purview.

Often, these export ventures are quite fruitful. Consider their efforts to study politics and crime using rational choice.[1] Public choice's application of rational choice theory to the study of political behavior, for instance, is a significant contribution to the field of political science. Its insistence that all individuals, even bureaucrats and politicians, rationally seek to maximize their self-interest has improved (among other things) our understanding of why bureaucracies grow, why interest groups are effective and why voters are typically uninformed (rationally ignorant) and often maintain unfounded beliefs (rationally irrational).[2] Similarly, the economics of crime and punishment has contributed to the field of criminology. Its treatment of criminals as rational individuals who weigh the expected costs and benefits of engaging in crime has improved (among other things) our understanding of why markets in illicit substances and behavior persist, how the likelihood of engaging in criminal activity is affected by the likelihood of being apprehended as well as the severity of expected punishments, and how members of criminal organizations are able to overcome the threat of predation by their leaders without relying on the formal court system to enforce agreements.[3]

Arguably, "capital" as a concept has been an even more popular export than rational choice theory. As Baron and Hannan (1994: 1123) observed with regards to sociology, "a minor sociological industry has arisen to construct sociological parallels to human capital." As a result, "a plethora of capitals" now exists. Religious and spiritual capital, for instance, has been used within religious studies and the sociology of religion to describe the mastery of particular religious practices and the emotional ties to a particular religion that individuals develop as a result of their participation in religious services and training (Iannaconne 1990; Stark and Finke 2000). The more religious capital an individual possesses, the more likely they are to attend religious services and the less likely they are to change religions. Additionally, political capital has been used within political science to describe the political power that politicians and others possess as a result of their political dealings and connections as well as the trust placed in them by their supporters (Remmer 1993). Individuals expend their political capital in order to advance their political agendas.

Social capital has likewise been a much-used concept within sociology and several other disciplines. Although social capital has come to be a fairly broad concept, as Woolcock (1998: 155) argues, a consensus has emerged in the sociological literature regarding the meaning of social capital. Social capital (i) is used by individuals or groups in order to advance their ends; (ii) is comprised of either generalized norms or durable relationships and the resources associated with group membership; and (iii) increases rather than decreases with use. An already large and still burgeoning literature exists within sociology which describes how individuals and groups utilize social capital to help them perform a number of functions from getting a job to recovering from a disaster.[4] Moreover, measures of social capital have been found to be positively correlated with various measures of individual and societal well-being.[5]

Admittedly, not all of their (export) ventures, however heralded by economists, have been successful. In some spheres, the language of economics in general and the language of capital specifically can seem out of place and soulless. For example, though it is possible to think of children and sexual compatibility with one's spouse as marriage-specific capital (Becker 1973) and to conclude that the greater the investment in marriage-specific capital the less likely a couple is to get a divorce (Becker et al. 1977), most (non-economists) would insist that there is more to childrearing, sexual relationships and the other interactions within marriage than capital investment.[6] Although there may be predictive value to this kind of analysis, it is unclear if it adds to our understanding of the phenomenon being studied.[7]

The study of the relationship between culture and markets is another area where economists risk employing an ill-suited economic concept. Often, economists treat culture as a resource. Treating culture as a form of capital, however, can result in economists misunderstanding the culture of markets. This chapter critiques this approach to exploring how culture affects economic behavior.

Most economists write about culture as if it is a form of capital

Most economists studying the relationship between culture and markets (implicitly and explicitly) treat culture as a kind of resource. Individuals and communities either possess a set of cultural tools that can be used for economic development or they have a toolkit comprised of cultural tools that cannot be used for economic development. Most of these studies point to one or more cultural resources as being positively correlated with economic progress. The analysis typically proceeds by first identifying the set of tools that are believed to be consistent with positive economic outcomes and then linking the existence or absence of that toolkit within a particular group to that group's economic performance.

There have been several studies, for instance, that have explored how levels of generalized trust and civic cooperation in a society are related to economic performance. The basic logic is that trust reduces transaction costs and so promotes economic growth (Arrow 1972).[8] Consider Knack and Keefer's (1997) study of whether "culture variables" such as trust and civic cooperation have an economic pay-off. Like most of the studies that explore the economic impact of trust, Knack and Keefer (ibid.) measure a society's level of trust using *World Values Survey* responses to the question, "Generally speaking, would you say that most people can be trusted, or that you can't be too careful in dealing with people?"[9] They use the percentage of respondents in a country who replied that most people can be trusted as that country's trust indicator. Similarly, they assess norms around civic cooperation using survey responses to questions asking people, among other things, if they cheated on their taxes, avoided paying bus fares, or fraudulently claimed government benefits. Not surprisingly, Knack and Keefer (ibid.: 1252) find that trust and norms of civic cooperation "are associated with stronger economic performance" and "are stronger in countries with formal institutions that effectively protect property and contract rights, and in countries that are less polarized along lines of class or ethnicity." They conclude that there is an atmosphere of stable expectations and mutual confidence that promotes commercial transactions in high trust and civic-minded countries which means that collective action problems are more likely to be overcome and economic growth is more likely to occur. In a follow-up analysis that considered a larger number of countries, Zak and Knack (2001) again find a positive relationship between trust and economic growth. Granato et al. (1996a, 1996b), Tabellini (2008), Williamson and Mathers (2011) and others have similarly found that levels of trust and other "culture variables" such as respect and generalized morality can lead to economic growth.

Additionally, there have been several studies that highlight the positive relationship between entrepreneurship and certain cultural attitudes, beliefs and orientations.[10] Hofstede (1980), for instance, has argued that cultures that are more individualistic, more comfortable with uncertainty, more masculine and that have low power distance are likely to have higher levels of entrepreneurship. Using surveys that attempt to measure national or regional culture, Shane (1992, 1993) and Davidsson (1995) have similarly discussed the impact of culture on national rates of entrepreneurship. These studies corroborate Hofstede's contention that possessing a certain set of national and regional cultural characteristics is related to the national and regional levels of entrepreneurship (Hayton et al. 2002: 35). As Hayton et al. (ibid.: 34) argue, Hofstede's taxonomy of cultural values and their effects on entrepreneurship has inspired much of the behavioral research that exists on the relationship between national culture and enterprise.

Although most of these efforts simply attempt to establish the relationship between certain cultural traits and economic progress, there have been efforts to explain how entrepreneurs can draw on these traits as they engage in enterprise. Harper (2003), for instance, explores how entrepreneurship is partly determined by cognitive factors that are in turn partly influenced by culture. According to Harper (ibid.: 36), whether a person is alert to opportunities for entrepreneurial profit or not depends largely on that person's economic agency beliefs, which he defines as those

> subjective expectations about the extent to which one can produce effects (i.e. given outcomes) and exert power over what happens in one's life . . . [i.e.] beliefs about locus of control (or *contingency* expectations) and beliefs about self-efficacy (or *competence* expectations).[11]

These "contingency" and "competence" expectations can "switch on entrepreneurial discovery," enabling some to perceive opportunities that others are not able to see or are not open to seeing. As Harper (ibid.: 44) explains, there is a strong relationship between entrepreneurship and internal locus of control (similar to what Hofstede described as low power distance) because a belief in an internal locus of control (i.e. that our own actions rather than those of others determine our fate) makes people "more 'cognitively alert' and 'perceptually sensitive'; more attentive to environmental cues regarding opportunities; much quicker in noticing changes in conditions; superior in their ability to extract, assimilate and use information; and capable of making decisions more efficiently." Individuals with a strong internal locus of control are, thus, more likely to notice opportunities for entrepreneurial gain than individuals with a belief in an external locus of control (i.e. that the actions of others and not our own actions determine our fate).

Self-efficacy has a similar effect. "Persons with a strong sense of personal efficacy," Harper (ibid.: 48–9) writes,

> are quick to take advantage of opportunities. They are also adept at discovering how to bypass institutional constraints. Even in situations that offer few opportunities and serious barriers to their progress, they are creative and alert enough to find ways of exercising some degree of control over events. Conversely, people with a weak sense of self-efficacy are less likely to seize opportunities and are easily deterred by institutional obstacles.

A person's contingency and competence expectations, Harper explains, are largely culturally derived. As Harper (ibid.: 151) recognizes, "there is cultural differentiation in how people construe personal agency, so too . . . in meanings of locus of control and beliefs about the sources of internal control."[12] Nicola's decision to start a business, then, depends on whether she believes that her successfully starting and running a business is truly contingent upon her following certain steps, like drafting a business plan, finding investors, registering her business name, and obtaining a business license. And, also on whether she believes she is competent enough to follow through with the requisite steps. Both her locus of control and self-efficacy beliefs will be influenced by her culture. Culturally derived beliefs in an internal locus of control and self-efficacy are, thus, conceived of as resources that facilitate entrepreneurial discovery.[13]

The conclusion that certain cultural resources are positively related to entrepreneurship and economic growth have led some to attempt to catalog the relevant traits and to characterize cultures as growth-friendly or growth-resistant depending on how many of the requisite traits they possess. Grondona (2000) and Harrison (1992, 2006), for instance, have argued that societies are more likely to develop the more of some twenty identifiable cultural factors they possess.[14] "These factors," Harrison (2006: 35) explains, "constitute a typology in which cultures that are favorable to economic development are contrasted with cultures that resist it." To name only a subset of the values they highlight, cultures, they assert, favor economic development where people focus on the future; where they have an internal locus of control and are optimistic; where wealth is seen as a product of hard work, work is seen as a moral duty and religions explain and justify success; where education transmits orthodoxy; and, where competition is encouraged. As Grondona (2000: 46) explains,

> it is possible to construct two ideal value systems: one including only values that favor economic development and the other including only values that resist it. . . . Neither of these value systems exists in reality, and no nation falls completely within either of those two value systems. However, some countries approach the extreme favorable to economic development, whereas others approach the opposite extreme.

Those societies that possess most of the twenty cultural factors can be said to have progress-prone cultures and those that possess only a few of these factors can be said to have progress-resistant cultures.

Societies with progress-prone cultures possess the right kind of cultural capital (i.e. the requisite cultural toolkit for economic growth and development). Admittedly, most of the studies discussed above do not explicitly describe culture as capital even though they treat culture as if it were a resource.

Some economists do, however, talk explicitly about cultural capital

There have been a few economists who have explicitly talked in terms of cultural capital.[15] The term cultural capital, however, has at least two competing (albeit similar) uses; one in sociology (following Bourdieu) and another in economics (where Throsby has presented the clearest articulation). Bourdieu (2002: 280) seeks to reintroduce "capital in all its forms" in order "to account for the structure and functioning of the social world." For Bourdieu, cultural capital acts as an endowment of views, attitudes and dispositions that (like other forms of capital) increases our effectiveness as we pursue our goals. Originally conceived of as a way of explaining why academic achievement differs across social classes and class fractions, cultural capital describes the benefits that individuals can gain because they are members of particular families, clubs, classes or societies.[16] According to Bourdieu (2002: 282), for instance, academic success or failure has less to do with natural aptitudes and monetary investments in education and much more to do with investments of cultural capital; "scholastic yield from educational action depends on the cultural capital previously invested by the family."[17] An individual's cultural capital, then, helps him/her to identify and exploit opportunities.

Cultural capital in the "embodied" state, "in the form of what is called culture, cultivation, *Bildung*," Bourdieu (ibid.: 282) explains, is its fundamental form.[18] In the embodied state it is "external wealth converted into an integral part of the person, into a habitus" (ibid.: 283). Of course, it makes sense that Bourdieu would seek to link his notion of cultural capital with his understanding of the habitus. The habitus, in Bourdieu's (1977: 76) thought, "is a socially constituted system of cognitive and motivation structures." It is "the product of history" that "produces individual and collective practices" (ibid.: 82). Bourdieu (ibid.: 82) has also described the habitus as a "system of dispositions" that is the root cause of whatever "continuity and regularity" we are able to "discern in the social world." The habitus is, thus, "a past [that] survives in the present and tends to perpetuate itself in the future by making itself present in the practices structured according to its principles" (ibid.: 82).

As Bourdieu (2002) explains, we get our initial endowment of cultural capital by virtue of our belonging to a particular class and we grow it through efforts at self-improvement. "The work of acquisition," Bourdieu (ibid.: 283) writes,

> is work on oneself (self-improvement), an effort that presupposes a personal cost . . . an investment, above all of time, but also of that socially constituted form of libido . . . with all the privation, renunciation, and sacrifice that it may entail.

Like other forms of capital, then, acquiring cultural capital beyond your initial endowment requires sacrifice.

"The accumulation of cultural capital in the *embodied* state," Bourdieu (ibid.: 283) suggests, "presupposes a process of embodiment, incorporation, which, insofar as it implies a labor of inculcation and assimilation, costs time, time which must be invested personally by the investor." You are not born knowing how to pick out the salad fork, what side of the street to walk on when walking with a lady, how to choose the appropriate wine for a particular dish, when to wear white or how to be a pleasant dinner guest. These are lessons that you learn over time and that can be used to capture symbolic and material profits; possessing cultural capital sets you apart from others. "Any given cultural competence (e.g. being able to read in a world of illiterates)," Bourdieu (ibid.: 283) explains, "derives a scarcity value from its position in the distribution of cultural capital and yields profits of distinction for its owner."

Cultural capital in the embodied state, then, is fairly viewed as a set of skills, a group of assumptions about the world and a system of dispositions as to how to behave in the world that we employ as members of particular classes and class fractions to help us further our ends, to capture symbolic and material profits. Moreover, Bourdieu's overall project can fairly be described as an attempt to construct an economics that can explain the structures that we observe in the social world by extending economic concepts such as capital to non-economic aspects of social life (Wilk 1996: 144).

Throsby (2001) has a similar ambition. He (ibid.: 44) hopes to bridge "the gap between economics and culture." Cultural capital, Throsby (ibid.) argues, "can provide a common basis [for both disciplines] from which the analysis of both economic and cultural aspects of cultural goods, services, behavior and other phenomena can proceed." According to Throsby (ibid.), the notion of cultural capital is a way of "representing cultural phenomena that captures their essential characteristics in a manner comprehensible within both an economic and a broadly cultural discourse." It is "a means of representing both tangible and intangible manifestations of culture" (ibid.: 15). Cultural capital treats both cultural products and phenomena "as long-lasting stores of value and providers of benefits for individuals and groups" (ibid.: 44). As such, Throsby, like Bourdieu who spoke of both embodied and objectified capital, is able to capture cultural products like paintings, music and buildings, as well as cultural phenomena such as beliefs, customs, practices and language with his formulation. Throsby (ibid.: 44) believes that the notion of cultural capital gives economists a way to talk about culture without having to step too far outside our familiar terrain and gives cultural theorists a way to talk about both the cultural and economic value that flow from cultural assets.

Throsby (ibid.: 46) defines cultural capital as "an asset which embodies, stores or provides cultural value in addition to whatever economic value it may possess." Because cultural value is what distinguishes cultural capital from other kinds of capital, understanding his definition of cultural value is critical to understanding his notion of cultural capital. While primarily economic values are embodied in and flow from physical capital (plants and machines), human capital (embodiment

of skills) and natural capital (resources provided by nature), cultural values live
in and flow from cultural capital. By cultural value, he simply means the worth,
importance or usefulness of a cultural asset or phenomenon that is not captured
by traditional definitions of economic value and that cannot readily be converted
into an economic price or even measured.[19] Throsby (ibid.: 29) has in mind here
sources of value that flow from the aesthetic, spiritual, social, historical and
symbolic qualities of cultural objects and processes. Of course, Throsby recognizes
that, though distinct, cultural and economic values are certainly related to one
another and assets can have both cultural and economic worth. As he (ibid.: 47)
suggests, the cultural content of tangible assets tends to "augment" their economic
value and, although intangible cultural capital has no economic value per se, "it
is the flows of services to which these stocks [of intangible cultural capital] give
rise which yield both the cultural and the economic value of assets."

Throsby (ibid.: 51) draws several parallels between his understanding of
cultural capital and the concept of natural capital (as employed by ecological/
environmental economists); "the definition of cultural capital has much in common
with the definition of natural capital." Both natural capital and cultural capital
are thought of as free gifts "inherited from the past . . . provided to us as an endowment," by nature, in one case, and by our ancestors, in the other. Just as nature
has given us large deposits of minerals, forests full of lumber and oceans full of
seafood, our ancestors have left us a cache of cultural assets (buildings, original
artwork, respect for the rule of law, a strong work ethic, etc.). And, according to
Throsby (ibid.: 51),

> a similarity can be seen between the function of natural ecosystems in
> supporting and maintaining the "natural balance" and the function of what
> might be referred to as "cultural ecosystems" in supporting and maintaining
> the cultural life and vitality of human civilization.

An ecosystem not only describes the environment where organisms live but the
interrelationships between different entities in a particular system and their
relationships with their physical space. Healthy ecosystems are valuable because
they provide a wide variety of services including climate stabilization, food
control, mitigation of droughts and floods, the purification of water and air and
the maintenance of arable soil, in short, because they provide the services necessary
for life. The "cultural ecosystem" (value systems, language, beliefs, customs, and
practices), Throsby suggests, operates in the same way—girding social institutions
and providing a context where human society can thrive. There is a set of cultural
resources in the Bahamas (perhaps the Junkanoo work ethic that thrives there or
the religiosity of Bahamians), to use an example that I will explore using a different
approach in Chapter 4, that is as vital to (living a prosperous) life in that country
as the sun, sand and sea that Bahamians have traditionally claimed as their chief
resources.

Interestingly, unlike the studies that implicitly treat culture as a form of capital,
the studies that explicitly treat culture as a resource tend not to identify certain

cultural traits as being essential for economic progress. Instead, they tend to highlight the relative cultural advantages that all societies necessarily possess. Indeed, this way of thinking about culture—treating it as a resource, as if it were capital like land or oil or the environment—is at the root of Berger's (2010) concept of "cultural comparative advantage." As Lavoie and Chamlee-Wright (2000: 64) explain,

> each society has within its grasp a unique repertoire of "cultural resources." Nature endows some societies with rich oil deposits and others with fertile soil. Similar to these natural resources, culture provides some societies with a kinship network conducive to building complex credit markets and other societies with a strong work ethic.

Societies possess certain cultural resources (i.e. particular endowments of cultural capital) and should, thus, "work on identifying which elements of their culture are most promising for them to cultivate in order to achieve what they would consider to be prosperity" (ibid.: 65).

From this perspective, every "culture *must* have a relative cultural advantage" (ibid.: 65). As such, the countries that prosper will not only have cultivated and exploited their comparative advantage but will also have taken advantage of their cultural comparative advantage. Indeed, the logic of comparative advantage applies to relative not absolute differences. If a Director of Information Technology, for instance, is better at both project management and software development than a particular programmer working for him, it is not necessarily the case that he should fire that programmer and perform both functions. Even with the difference in skill levels, the department is probably better off if the manager manages and the programmer programs; they should both specialize in their relative strengths. There are gains to be had from specialization.

The same is also true when we are discussing different cultures. Jin (1995: 265), for instance, has argued that Confucian culture has a cultural comparative advantage over individualist cultures in the use of certain governance structures that are useful for economic development. Similarly, Grant et al. (2005: 398) have argued that the best way for Aborigines in Australia to succeed economically is to "cultivate their cultural comparative advantage." Shane (1992) has likewise argued that cultural comparative advantage can explain cross-country differences in the number of inventions. While some countries appear to have a relative cultural advantage in inventiveness, he explains, other countries appear to have a cultural comparative advantage in organized, repetitive behavior. Those countries that invent new technologies, then, are unlikely to be the countries that bring them to market most efficiently. As Shane (ibid.) writes,

> some cultures have a comparative advantage in inventive activity that leads them to develop new technologies, ideas, and products. Those nations that do not have this comparative advantage, but have a comparative advantage in organized, repetitive activity, will often take these inventions and innovations

and produce them more efficiently—eventually wresting control of the markets for these goods from the innovators, who move on to new products and processes.

That (self-consciously) treating culture as a resource makes it possible to develop concepts such as cultural comparative advantage to explain why some societies are adept at certain productive economic activities and not others constitutes a very real advantage of this approach to discussing the relationship between culture and economic outcomes.

There are actually several good reasons to describe culture as a set of resources

Swidler (1986) has argued that we should conceive of culture as a toolkit containing recipes, narratives, symbols, rituals and beliefs that individuals utilize to solve the problems that they confront. As she (ibid.: 275) explains, "culture in this sense is much more of a style or a set of skills and habits than a set of preferences or wants." The cultural components contained in this toolkit, she explains, go into the construction of "strategies of action" that constrain and shape people's behavior as they pursue their goals. These strategies are "general ways of organizing action" derived from an individual's cultural toolkit such as relying on hard work, or trusting in a small cadre of close associates, or tapping into a broad array of loosely affiliated associates in order to get things done. As she (ibid.: 284) writes,

> the symbolic experiences, mythic lore, and ritual practices of a group or society create modes and motivations, ways of organizing experience and evaluating reality, modes of regulating conduct, and ways of forming social bonds, which provide resources for constructing strategies of action.

And, "culture provides a repertoire of capacities from which varying strategies of action may be constructed." It is through limiting the sorts of strategies that can be constructed, Swidler (ibid.) explains, that culture affects economic as well as other kinds of behavior.

Conceiving of culture as a toolkit, Swidler (ibid.) argues, offers social scientists a more sophisticated way to discuss the relationship between culture and behavior than pointing to culture as shaping desires.[20] Since expressed wants can be similar across cultures and can also vary within cultures, thinking of culture as being the source of wants, she contends, is problematic. Instead, people should be conceived as only being able to pursue goals for which they have the requisite cultural equipment. Dana, from the United States, and Sigrid, from Sweden, for instance, can both share the same desire for a particular kind of life (e.g. to be a social entrepreneur working in poorer communities) but Dana might be able to effectively pursue it because she has the right sort of cultural resources (e.g. a cultural legacy of volunteerism) whereas Sigrid's cultural tools (e.g. a dependence on the welfare state to tackle social ills) might be inappropriate for pursuing the goal that they have in common. Differences in the observed pursuits of groups from different national, ethnic and class backgrounds, then, have more to do with their different cultural competencies than any differences in their underlying desires.

Another possible advantage to conceiving of culture as a set of resources is that it reminds us that cultures are not unalterable. Recall, neither a country's nor a company's capital stock remains fixed over time. It can, for instance, be altered and added to through investment. Change in the absence of investment, however, is also inevitable. Capital stocks can both depreciate in value and deteriorate in form over time unless the requisite upkeep is undertaken. Swidler (ibid.) has made a similar observation regarding a community's cultural resources. Although cultures can and do persist over time, she contends, in unsettled times cultures can prove to be less stubborn to change. Likewise, as Throsby (2001: 68) writes, "neither culture nor economy is a static thing but . . . each is constantly changing." And, as Lavoie and Chamlee-Wright (2000: 18) suggest, culture "is not a static thing but an ongoing process."

Focusing on culture as a form of capital also reminds us that culture, though alterable, is not easily alterable. Recall, it is costly to change a country's or a company's capital stock (i.e. it requires investment or allowing it to lose value) even though it is possible to change it. It is, likewise, difficult to change a society's cultural capital stock. As Jones (1995: 273) has argued, however, most economists adopt a position of cultural nullity which assumes that culture adapts rapidly to economic changes. This is perhaps best illustrated by an allegory.[21] Imagine, for instance, an individual who grows up in a community where it is safe to drink the tap water. This person would rationally develop the habit of going to the tap, filling it with water and drinking it without reservation. Suppose now that that person moves to a community where the tap water is contaminated. Incentives are such that they will quickly abandon the habit of heedlessly drinking the tap water. Cultural habits, then, will only be maintained so long as the costs associated with changing them are lower than the benefits. This assumes, of course, that systematic errors in the assessment of the costs and benefits of adopting new cultural habits will not persist.

There is reason to believe, however, that in some contexts systematic errors in assessing the costs and benefits associated with behaving in new rather than traditional ways might be long lasting. Imagine, instead, an individual who grows up in a context where the tap water is contaminated. This person would have rationally developed the habit of filtering or otherwise attempting to purify the tap water before drinking it. If this person now moves to a context where the tap water is safe to drink there is no reason to be confident that he will ever learn that he can safely drink the water without attempting to purify it. Observing someone drinking the tap water without filtering it, for instance, he may very well dismiss what he sees as an anomaly or interpret it as saying something about the character of the drinker he observes and not of the water (e.g. he might assume that the drinker has developed immunity to contaminated water). Unlike the person who once drank the tap water without reservation who moves to a context where he will get sick if he continues his thoughtless behavior, the person who grew up where the water was contaminated might never be confronted with the fact that his efforts to purify the water in his new setting are wasteful. The cultural habit, though inappropriate given the current circumstances, might nonetheless persist.

Economists have referred to this persistence of beliefs and habits even when they seem to be costly to maintain as path dependence (i.e. the notion that current choices are constrained by past choices so that the path of institutional change is limited by existing institutions). As David (1985: 332) explains, "a path dependent sequence of economic changes is one of which important influences upon the eventual outcome can be exerted by temporally remote events, including happenings dominated by chance elements rather than systematic forces." The persistence of the QWERTY keyboard is a classic example of path dependence.[22] Although other types of keyboards exist and have proven to be superior on a variety of margins, the QWERTY keyboard has remained locked-in as the dominant keyboard arrangement for several reasons. Network effects are such that the more keyboard manufacturers produce QWERTY keyboards, the more companies deploy QWERTY keyboards and the more typists are trained to use QWERTY keyboards, the more expensive it is for manufacturers, companies and typists to adopt a new standard. That economic change is often path dependent, however, does not mean that economic change is impossible. New technologies are adopted (e.g. 8-track cartridges gave way to cassette tapes which gave way to CDs which are being replaced by MP3 players). Rather, the conclusion that economic change is often path dependent is meant to suggest that the past influences the direction of change. As North (2005: 52) writes, "path dependence is not 'inertia,' rather it is the constraints on the choice set in the present that are derived from historical experiences of the past." And, as North (1990: 98) asserts elsewhere, "path dependence is a way to narrow conceptually the choice set and [to] link decision-making through time."

Institutional change also tends to be path dependent.[23] Although formal institutions (e.g. legislation) can often be changed quite rapidly, informal institutions (e.g. beliefs, habits, practices) tend to be more stable and, when they do change, it tends to be slow and incremental. The belief systems held by people today, North suggests, are inherited from and are, therefore, dependent upon belief systems that their ancestors relied on to make decisions and navigate their lives. A society's existing cultural capital stock, which is comprised of a society's beliefs, habits and practices, then, can be the source of path dependence. As North (1994: 364) explains,

> it is culture that provides the key to path dependence . . . The current learning of any generation takes place within the context of the perceptions derived from collective learning. Learning, then, is an incremental process filtered by the culture of a society which determines the perceived payoffs.

Of course, a society's existing cultural capital stock may not provide its members with the cultural equipment that they need in order to deal with their current challenges.

Indeed, the belief systems of past generations may be passed on even when they are not relevant to the circumstances of the current generation and even when they are harmful to the progress of the current generation. As such, it is entirely possible for cultures to get "stuck in an institutional matrix" that, for instance, "rewards piracy" (North 1990: 110) or that "did not evolve into . . . impersonal exchange" (North 1994: 363) or one that impairs entrepreneurial discoveries and impedes entrepreneurial efforts (Storr 2002). "There is . . . no guarantee," North (ibid.) writes, "that the cumulative past experience of a society will necessarily fit them to solve new problems. Societies that get 'stuck' embody belief systems and institutions that fail to confront and solve new problems of societal complexity." Groups of people may experience a *lock-in* of inefficient institutions and erroneous beliefs since objective circumstances can change even when beliefs and perceptions do not. Unfortunately, as North informs, this lock-in of inefficient (erroneous) beliefs happens frequently. For the economist, then, path dependence offers a useful way of explaining the persistence of harmful beliefs and why some countries do not prosper.

As with other forms of capital, in this view, individuals are said to utilize cultural resources as they pursue their goals; societies are said to possess different stocks of cultural capital, which means that each will enjoy a comparative advantage in at least one type of activity (i.e. they will have the appropriate cultural equipment to do something productive); and changes to the cultural capital stock are viewed as possible but also as incremental and requiring investment. There are, thus, several advantages to conceiving of culture as a toolkit. It offers a clear link between culture and economic behavior. It also forces economists to consider the relative cultural advantages that all societies possess. And it reminds us that cultures can and do change but that change is likely to be costly and path dependent.

But treating culture as capital is somewhat misleading

Although there is something appealing about this way of discussing culture, particularly for economists, there are also disadvantages to thinking of culture as a form of capital. To be sure, there is something to the notion that each culture has strengths that can help it to progress. It is admittedly possible to profitably think of culture as a resource. But culture is not really a resource that we use and then put away. The real problem, then, with conceiving of culture as a resource, as I have stated elsewhere, is that it is misleading and inadequate (Storr 2004: 33).

Neither capital nor culture is well served by the analogy. Capital has traditionally been thought of in physical terms: as the existing stock of assets that can be used to produce other goods. It, thus, includes everything from factories and equipment (fixed capital which tend to be quite durable) to stockpiles of raw materials and semi-finished goods (circulating capital which is generally exhausted during the production process). More important, though, than its physical qualities is capital's role in production and the deliberate sacrifice of present income for expected future benefits (i.e. investment) that is necessarily involved in its accumulation. Although culture is a somewhat broad term, used to describe high art, good manners, attitudes, etc., as I discussed earlier, it is most appropriately used to describe the "webs of significance" in which man is suspended and which "he himself has spun" (Geertz 1973: 5). "As interworked systems of construable signs," Geertz (ibid.: 14) explains, "culture is not a power, something to which social events, behaviors, institutions, or processes can be causally attributed; it is a context, something within which they can be intelligibly—that is, thickly—described." Culture, then, is an environment, a backdrop where certain events are rendered intelligible and understandable, while others are not.

To talk about culture as if it were analogous to capital, thus, reveals a misunderstanding of both concepts. Arrow's (2000) observations about "social capital" are certainly relevant here. As noted earlier, social capital has been used to describe social networks and to make the point that phenomena such as trust relations and social clubs can promote economic progress. For Arrow (ibid.: 4),

> the term "capital" implies three aspects: (a) extension in time; (b) deliberate sacrifice of future benefit; and (c) alienability. . . . The aspect defined as (a) above may hold in part; we speak of building a reputation or a trust relation. But these are not like physical investment; a little trust has not much use. But it is especially (b) that fails.

Social networks, Arrow points out, are not typically entered into with the hopes of any future material pay-off. And, as Arrow (ibid.: 3) asserts, "the motives for interaction are not economic. People may get jobs through networks of friendship or acquaintance, but they do not, in many cases, join the networks for that purpose." Similarly, we may gain access to credit or a loyal clientele because we are the member of this fraternity or that congregation, but usually that is not why we pledge a fraternity or attend a church service. Joining a social club or a religious organization cannot, fairly, be characterized as an investment; there are usually more immediate, more proximate benefits that we derive from our involvement (e.g. enjoying fellowship). Similarly, many aspects of social capital are acquired without our deciding to acquire it. Learning our first language and being born into a particular family, caste or ethnicity does not involve any deliberate act on our part and, moreover, neither learning to speak nor being born can meaningfully be said to involve sacrifice (Sobel 2002: 144). The same critiques would apply to the concept of cultural capital.

Culture is, simply, not a resource that is "acquired" through prudence or thrift. To be sure, individuals can invest in the production of "cultural goods" such as paintings or the acquisition of some so-called "cultural skills" such as a second language (i.e. cultural objects that take time to produce and do yield income streams in the future).[24] But many aspects of culture simply cannot be acquired by deliberate investment. And, more often than not, individuals acquire "cultural skills" without even being aware that they are acquiring them. As Bourdieu (2002: 283) has admitted, for instance, "cultural capital can be acquired, to a varying extent, depending on the period, the society, and the social class, in the absence of any deliberate inculcation, and therefore quite unconsciously." Moreover, learning about a culture and coming to understand, appreciate and even adopt a part of its belief and value systems does not necessarily make someone a part of that culture. Neither the tourist, nor the actor, nor the anthropologist can, for instance, ever become authentically Canadian. They can certainly describe, or mimic, or even understand Canadians but time spent visiting Canada, watching Canadians, or studying Canadian history, attitudes and practices does not convey Canadianness. Similarly, time spent by Canadians abroad does not strip them of their Canadianness. Perhaps, their accents may become less pronounced or even undetectable but at heart they remain Canadians.

Consequently, cultural capital, because it so clearly fails the deliberate sacrifice test, is not capital.[25] It is also unclear if culture is appropriately thought of as merely a thing that we use. Again, central to any definition of capital is the notion that it describes tools or resources that are employed in production. As Ricardo (1821: 325) writes, "capital is that part of the wealth of a country which is employed in production, and consists of food, clothing, tools, raw materials, machinery, etc., necessary to give effect to labor." And, as Lachmann (1978: 53) explains,

> all capital goods are, directly and indirectly, instruments of production. Not all of them are man-made (e.g. mineral resources are not) but all of them are man-used. It is indeed characteristic of such "natural" capital resources that but for the existence of man-made capital designed to be employed in conjunction with them, they would not even be economic goods. The theory of capital is thus primarily a theory of the material instruments of production.

As discussed above, there is obviously a sense in which culture can be thought of as a tool. It is true, for instance, that entrepreneurs rely on culture to "discover" profit opportunities. Indeed, as we noted earlier, Lavoie (1991: 36; emphasis added) has made the point as eloquently as anyone that

> the profit opportunities entrepreneurs discover are not a matter of objective observations of quantities, but a matter of perspectival interpretation, a discerning of the intersubjective meaning of a qualitative situation. Profits are not measured; they are 'read.' *Entrepreneurship . . . is primarily a cultural process. The seeing of profit opportunities is a matter of cultural inter-pretation.*

But an entrepreneur being able to successfully interpret her circumstances because she is embedded in a particular culture is not the same thing as her using culture to read profit opportunities. Her reliance on culture, as Lavoie understood, is entirely different than, say, the carpenter's reliance on hammers and nails to build tables and chairs. Culture is not something that entrepreneurs use for this or that purpose and then put away when it is no longer needed. Rather, individuals lug around their cultural baggage, often unaware that they are even carrying it.[26] And it comes into play entirely against or, more accurately, outside of their will.

Gadamer's (1976) discussion of language also proves relevant here. As Gadamer (ibid.: 62) asserts,

> language is by no means simply an instrument, a tool. For it is in the nature of the tool that we master its use, which is to say we take it in hand and lay it aside when it has done its service.

But, as Gadamer contends, something different is going on when we choose a word or set of words from our store of possible words and expressions, use them to convey some sentiment and then let them return to our cache, our vocabulary, ready-at-hand for use another day. Indeed, as Gadamer (ibid.) points out,

> such an analogy is false because we never find ourselves as consciousness over against the world and, as it were, grasp after a tool of understanding in a wordless condition. Rather, in all our knowledge of ourselves and in all knowledge of the world, we are always already encompassed by the language that is our own.

The same can be said of culture. We are never able to simply take it off, to set it aside, to be completely free from its affect and influence.[27] As Reed (2002: 792) argues, we cannot pick and choose our culture like we might pick up an axe, as our very understanding of social reality is mediated "by patterns of understanding that are culturally given."

While it is possible to conceive of culture as either a set of skills that we use to further our ends or as a deeply embedded set of assumptions that we may or may not be aware of (i.e. as a habitus or in a manner closer to Geertz's definition), it cannot be simultaneously conceived of as both. As Bourdieu (1977: 18) describes, "agents are possessed by their habitus more than they possess it . . . it acts within them as an organizing principle of their actions." The habitus acts as a "*modus operandi* of which he is not the producer and has no conscious mastery" (ibid.: 79). It is not something that we master; instead it masters us. "As an acquired system of generative schemes objectively adjusted to the particular conditions which it is constituted," Bourdieu (ibid.: 95) explains, "the habitus engenders all the thoughts, all the perceptions, and all the actions consistent with those conditions, and no others." Ironically, cultural capital does not even capture culture as Bourdieu understands it.[28]

There is, arguably, another reason why culture should not be thought of as a form of capital. For culture to be meaningfully conceived of as a form of capital it must be possible to distinguish it from other forms of capital. Physical and human capital, for instance, are helpful categories because it is possible to distinguish between physical objects (such as a typewriter) and skills (such as the ability to type). It is likewise possible to possess one without possessing the other. It is unclear, however, how a typewriter or the ability to type are any less an expression of a society's culture than its artwork or rituals. It is also unclear why an office would be seen as any less a center for cultural expression than a society's museums or cathedrals. Under Throsby's articulation of cultural capital, if it is to remain a meaningful category at all, it must allow economists to sort between a typewriter and a painting, between the ability to type and to perform rituals. If typewriters and paintings, the ability to type and to perform rituals can all be considered cultural capital, then all resources are cultural resources. Recall that cultural capital yields cultural value and perhaps economic value as well (if they are tangible goods), while other forms of capital only yield economic value; that is how we are to distinguish them (Throsby 2001: 45). It is difficult, however, to imagine any capital asset that does not give rise to cultural value (as he defines it) and so it is difficult to imagine any capital that is not always also cultural capital. In the same way that the hoe, the whip and the cotton gin are deeply significant symbols of the Antebellum South, the cellular phone, the Internet and the automobile are among the important symbols of the modern United States of America; they are all sources (to one degree or another) of aesthetic, spiritual, social and historical value.

Treating culture as a resource also encourages us to try to "score" cultures (i.e. to catalogue their absolute or relative strengths and weaknesses; to employ phrases such as "more cultural capital"; to talk about "the size of cultural capital"). Indeed, this is what economists who theorize that levels of trust or respect or any number of culture variables are positively linked to economic growth are implicitly doing. This is also exactly what Bourdieu (2002: 284) and Throsby (2001: 58) seem to be advocating at times. And, it is what Harrison (2006) explicitly endorses.

Moreover, even social scientists that would otherwise be critical of conceiving of cultures as being progress-prone or progress-resistant end up talking in those two terms when they conceive of culture as a form of capital. Although Swidler (1986: 277), for instance, is quick to point out that "a culture is not a unified system that pushes action in a consistent direction" and that "cultural resources are diverse . . . and normally groups and individuals call upon these resources selectively, bringing to bear different styles and habits of action in different situations" (ibid.: 280), she (ibid.: 275) nonetheless believes that we can lack the cultural equipment to perform certain tasks. Similarly, Harper (2003: 133) both "rejects that individualism or communalism . . . is either categorically pro- or anti-entrepreneurship" but maintains that having an internal locus of control (be it personal or group-oriented) is categorically pro-entrepreneurship (ibid.: 152).

Conceiving of cultures as being inherently progress-prone or progress-resistant, however, has been roundly criticized. Pye (2000: 255), for instance, has argued that "it is unscientific to try to draw up a universal list of positive and negative cultural values for economic development. What may be positive in some circumstances can be quite counterproductive under other conditions." Similarly, Lavoie and Chamlee-Wright (2000: 61) explain, "outside any context, we cannot know if any particular [cultural value] . . . will inhibit or enable prosperity."

To summarize, conceiving of culture as a form of capital is an analogy that, arguably, obscures more than it reveals.[29] To be sure, it reminds us that culture is at work in many areas where we might have forgotten to look for it. But it implies that there are areas of economic life that are not impacted by culture. If we accept that there is such a thing as cultural capital, then we have to also accept the possibility that we may find non-cultural capital out there somewhere. Similarly, by describing culture as capital we treat it as a resource (something we use to accomplish our ends) rather than as a context where goals and the means to be employed are shaped and given meaning. And treating culture as capital opens the door for conceiving of cultures as possessing or failing to possess the requisite tools for some tasks. Cultural capital, thus, reveals itself to be a deeply troublesome concept and conceiving of culture as a resource appears to be a problematic move.

If we must discuss culture using traditional economic concepts, there are possibly better ones than capital

To my mind, culture is much more like a constitution than it is like capital.[30] Recall that a constitution outlines the formal rules that govern a society and, as such, sets up the context within which (economic) activity takes place. Brennan and Buchanan (1980: 5), for instance, define a constitution as "the set of rules, or social institutions, within which individuals operate and interact with one another." Hayek (1960: 178) has, similarly, noted that a constitution assigns "specific powers to different authorities," while limiting "their powers not only in regard to the subjects or the aims to be pursued but also with regard to the methods to be employed." A constitution, thus, describes the rules of the game for the referees and the players, the authorities and individual citizens, and, consequently, defines and delimits the range of opportunities that an individual can legitimately exploit. As Brennan and Buchanan (1980: 5) explain,

> a game is described by its rules—its constitution. These rules establish the framework within which the playing of the game proceeds; they set boundaries on what activities are legitimate, as well as describing the objects of the game and how to determine who wins.[31]

Certain strategies are allowed under a constitution and others are forbidden. Similarly, political and legal institutions evolve within constitutional systems that create incentives for some activities and discourage others. Constitutional rules, thus, serve as points of orientation, shaping human interaction and providing structure to everyday life (North 1990: 4).[32] Recall, also, that constitutions are not static; they usually have procedures by which they can be amended. Nor, however, are they completely fluid; constitutional change tends to be incremental rather than revolutionary.

Like constitutions, cultures can be thought of as shaping human interaction and are neither completely malleable nor are they completely resistant to change. Still, there are reasons why even this analogy (i.e. thinking of culture as a constitution), though preferable to conceiving of culture as a form of capital, is problematic.[33] First, cultures shape the meaning attributed to and the effectiveness of constitutional orders while constitutional orders define the (political and legal) environment in which cultural practices take place and evolve. Treating cultures as constitutions would obscure the interesting interplay between the two.[34] Indeed, treating cultures as constitutions collapses the important distinction between institutions (i.e. points of orientations) and culture (i.e. patterns of meanings).[35] Second, cultures travel while constitutions do not travel. To be sure, it has proven extremely difficult to export constitutional orders to foreign soils (see Coyne 2004). But I am making here the more pedestrian point that when individuals move to a new country their worldviews and values move with them while the formal laws that they previously lived under do not move with them. Ironically, this metaphor, thus, lacks a key advantage of the culture as capital metaphor, namely, that individuals can and do travel with their (cultural) baggage. Finally, while we can describe certain constitutional orders as being inconsistent with economic growth, we cannot, as argued above, describe certain cultures as being inconsistent with economic growth.[36]

Conclusion

Unfortunately, attempts by economists to study the impact of culture on economic outcomes, though welcome, have been somewhat dissatisfying. Most treat culture as a set of resources. Whether they attempt to identify certain cultural tools as being essential for economic progress or they specify that every culture enjoys a comparative advantage that it can exploit, economists who think of culture as a resource incorrectly specify how culture affects economic behavior. Culture is, simply, not a form of capital. Culture is not like a set of tools that individuals can pull out of their toolkit and use whenever they need them to achieve some particular end. Culture is not an item in our production functions. Culture, instead, colors our decisions regarding which tools (strategies) are available to us and which tools we should utilize as we pursue our goals.

This way of conceiving of culture has certain methodological implications for how economists might attempt to understand the relationship between culture and economic behavior. It would, for instance, rule out studies that try to identify cultures by certain dominant cultural values and then link those dominant cultural traits to particular economic outcomes. It is unclear, however, if this would be a great loss. As even the scholars behind those studies confess, it is difficult to identify and isolate the dominant cultural values of a community using the methods that they have adopted. Moreover, it is difficult to be certain that any of the measures that are adopted actually measure what they claim to measure. As Beugelsdijk (2006: 377) has found, "the measure [of trust that most of these studies employ] is not a good proxy for the theoretically assumed causal links. It does not measure trust. Instead, we may be measuring the well-functioning of institutions." And recall Tabellini (2008: 262) has acknowledged that "not only are [trust and respect] measured with error, but their interpretation is also somewhat ambiguous. . . . besides measuring individual values, these variables might also capture social conventions or beliefs about others."

Admittedly, the critique that I offered above has also been somewhat dissatisfying. In this chapter as well as the preceding ones, I developed an argument for why economists should pay more attention to culture than they do currently and critiqued some of the approaches employed by economists in their (all too rare) efforts to study how culture affects economic activity. Implicit in those critiques was an argument in favor of a particular approach to studying the relationship between culture and markets that does not leave the study of economic culture to non-economists but also avoids some of the pitfalls that have plagued many previous efforts by economists to study the impact of culture on economic behavior. Except for my insistence that economists should embrace Weber's social economics, however, I have not yet attempted to develop the approach that I would recommend for studying how culture affects economic activities.

In Chapters 4 and 5, however, I tease out some of the methodological implications of recognizing that culture is not a resource but that focusing on culture is, nonetheless, important for understanding economic activity. Rather than treating culture as a form of capital, the approach that I recommend suggests that economists focus on the culturally constituted spirits that animate markets. Ironically, though exploring the culture of markets by focusing on the economic spirits which give life to markets seems less concrete than conceiving of culture as a set of tools, the effect of culture on economic behavior becomes less ethereal and much easier to grasp when looking for economic spirits than when trying to conceive of culture as a collection of tools.

4 Economists ought to be looking at the spirits that animate markets

Although culture impacts economic behavior, economists do not pay a great deal of attention to culture. Most appear to think that it is too nebulous a concept to incorporate into economic analysis; or think of cultural questions as the purview of one of its sister social sciences; or think of culture as resulting from actors' past economic decisions rather than influencing their present and future economic decisions. Those economists that do pay attention to culture tend to treat it as a resource. Culture, for them, becomes a form of capital. It becomes a tool that actors employ as they attempt to further their ends. As with all types of tools, it is assumed and argued that some cultural tools are better than others. Those individuals from the right cultures (e.g. cultures that promote self-efficacy) are more likely to succeed than those individuals from the wrong cultures (e.g. cultures with a narrow radius of trust). Those societies with the right cultures (e.g. cultures that are more individualistic) are more likely to prosper than societies with the wrong cultures (e.g. cultures that promote predation). Moreover, as with all types of tools, some cultural tools, it is assumed and argued, are better for some types of activities than others. Individuals and societies can be said to have a cultural comparative advantage in some kinds of activities (e.g. small-scale manufacturing) and not others (e.g. large capital-intensive production). This way of thinking about the relationship between culture and economic behavior, as I have argued, both misunderstands culture and mischaracterizes how it impacts economic behavior. Rather than individuals and societies possessing a cultural toolkit, culture influences how individuals identify and conceive of the tools that they have at their disposal. Rather than individuals and societies possessing certain cultural comparative advantages, culture determines how individuals identify and conceive of their opportunities and the resources they might utilize in trying to take advantage of those opportunities.

Conceiving of culture not as a tool but as something that guides and shapes though does not determine economic behavior poses a serious challenge for economists. Specifically, it makes paying attention to culture important and even necessary but it does not offer any guidance as to how economists should operationalize culture (i.e. how it should enter into their theoretical and applied efforts).

One strategy for dealing with this challenge is to focus on the spirits that animate markets. Not surprisingly, economists are unaccustomed to talking about animating spirits. Keynes and subsequent discussions of "animal spirits" is perhaps the only exception.[1] Recall, Keynes (1973: 161) argues that many of our positive actions "depend on spontaneous optimism rather than on a mathematical expectation, whether moral or hedonistic or economic." Because individuals do not possess knowledge of the future and it is difficult (if not impossible) for them to form reasonable hypotheses as to how the future will turn out, actors often have to rely on something other than rational calculation if they are to act at all. Rather than carefully weighing expected benefits and costs before acting, Keynes (ibid.) contends,

> most . . . of our decisions to do something positive, the full consequences of which will be drawn out over many days to come, can only be taken as a result of animal spirits—of a spontaneous urge to action rather than inaction.

This basis for action, Keynes (ibid.) explains, must supplement and support "reasonable calculations" if entrepreneurs are to engage in enterprise. And, if this "spontaneous optimism" is "dimmed," he (ibid.) asserts, then "enterprise will fade and die." The existence of and the key role played by animal spirits "means, unfortunately, that slumps and depressions are exaggerated in degree, but that economic prosperity is excessively dependent on a political and social atmosphere which is congenial to the average business man" (ibid.).

Several studies have suggested that there is some theoretical and empirical support for Keynes' claim that our economic actions rely on animal spirits. Azariadis (1981), for instance, has discussed animal spirits conceived of as self-fulfilling prophecies. Additionally, Howitt and McAfee (1992) have developed a model where low animal spirits leads employers to hire fewer workers because they expect low aggregate demand and where high animal spirits lead to increased employment and an economic boom. Similarly, Farmer and Guo (1994) have found that their model of animal spirits, defined as the self-fulfilling beliefs of investors, is a reasonable predictor of the fluctuations in the US economy since the 1950s. And, Akerlof and Shiller (2010) have likewise discussed how animal spirits drive the economy.

In discussing the spirits that animate markets, however, I am not principally concerned with Keynes' animal spirits. Instead, building on Weber's discussion of the spirit of capitalism, I argue that markets are animated by one or more culturally derived economic spirits which shape the economic calculations and behavior of the actors who inhabit them.[2] According to Weber (2002, 2011), different economic spirits animated the different forms of capitalism which existed in different places and in different eras. As such, we would expect the spirit of capitalism in one place and time to differ in important respects from the spirit of capitalism in another place or time. And we should expect entrepreneurs in one place and time to behave differently than entrepreneurs in another place or time.

For instance, Weber (2002, 2011) has argued that modern capitalism in Western Europe and North America was animated by an economic spirit that promoted a worldly asceticism, an eschewing of worldly pleasures with an emphasis on acquisition as an ultimate end. Like Keynes' animal spirits, Weber's economic spirits not only offer a basis for action in the face of uncertainty but also inform rational calculations (i.e. how individuals weigh their prospects). And, thus, importantly, they shape how market participants behave.

This chapter defends the notion that every market is animated by particular economic spirits.

As Weber argued, every market is animated by a particular spirit

The Protestant Ethic and the Spirit of Capitalism (2002, 2011) is typically and somewhat simplistically understood as Weber's attempt to demonstrate how Protestantism (particularly Puritanism) *caused* modern capitalism.[3] Weber, however, made at least five distinct claims in *The Protestant Ethic and the Spirit of Capitalism* and his various responses to his critics. He argued (among other things) that

(a) capitalism can take on a variety of forms;
(b) each form of capitalism is animated by a particular economic spirit;
(c) the spirit of modern capitalism can be described as a worldly asceticism;
(d) the particular ethos of modern capitalism and the attitudes toward work that emerge from Protestantism (particularly Puritanism) are (in many respects) identical; and
(e) the spirit of modern capitalism in the West found a consistent ethical basis in Protestantism.

Weber (2002, 2011) has argued that capitalism can take on a variety of forms. It is, of course, possible to construct a sufficiently abstract ideal type of capitalism that would characterize all economic systems that relied on the utilization of capital. This ideal type would speak to the common features of capitalism regardless of its particular form and would apply to traditional and modern forms of capitalism, to politically oriented and market-oriented forms of capitalism, to capitalism as it existed in all places and at all times. Capitalism as it existed in particular places and epochs, however, differed in important respects. It is, thus, possible to construct more concrete ideal types that contain those features of capitalism that are unique to the specific instance(s) under study. As Weber (2002: 263) explains, "we either analyze everything that was common to such economic systems at all times, or we analyze the specifics of a particular historical system of this type."

In *The Protestant Ethic*, for instance, Weber (2002, 2011) is chiefly concerned with modern capitalism, that is, the kind of capitalism that originated in Western Europe in the seventeenth and eighteenth centuries. Elsewhere, he examines the capitalism of antiquity, market-oriented versus politically oriented capitalism, and the capitalisms of India and China.[4]

Others have echoed this claim that there are a variety of capitalisms. Hall and Soskice (2001), for instance, argue that it is possible to distinguish between two types of capitalism: liberal market economies and coordinated market economies. As they (ibid.: 8) explain,

> in *liberal market economies*, firms coordinate their activities primarily via hierarchies and competitive market arrangements. . . . In *coordinated market economies*, firms depend more heavily on non-market relationships to coordinate their endeavors with other actors and to construct their core competencies.[5]

Although all firms rely on both market and non-market relationships, they (ibid.: 9) explain, "the incidence of different types of firm relationships varies systematically across nations." Dore et al. (1999), similarly, focus on the "particularity" of the evolution of capitalist institutions in Britain, the United States, Germany and Japan. Specifically, they point to how economic institutions in this group of countries, especially corporate control structures, were quite similar in the 1920s, diverged quite dramatically after the Great Depression, and appeared to be converging again at the end of the twentieth century. Additionally, Whitley (1999) discusses why differences in the central characteristics of business systems in the Americas, Asia and Europe are likely to persist even as the level of internationalization grows.

According to Weber (2002, 2011), each of these forms of capitalism is generally animated by a particular economic spirit. "An historically given form of 'capitalism'," Weber (2002: 263) explains, "can be filled with very different types of 'spirit'; this form can, however, and usually will have different levels of 'elective affinities' to certain historical types of spirits."[6] Stated another way, in the actual world, a given economic spirit (e.g. one that stresses creativity) will either fit comfortably or uncomfortably within a particular capitalist form (e.g. in a liberal market economy versus in a socialist economy). There can, for instance, be a modern capitalist economy peopled with characters that embrace traditionalism. Or, there can be a market-oriented economy where an ethic of rent-seeking has come to thrive. As Weber (2011: 89) explains, "of course, it may happen that 'spirit' and 'form' do not come together at all." Although the relationship between a particular kind of capitalism and the spirit that is said to animate is not one of "mutual dependency governed by any law," it is more than just coincidental. As Weber (2002: 19) explains, "the 'capitalistic' form of an economy and the spirit in which it is run do indeed stand in a generally *adequate* relationship to each other." Although a particular form of capitalism can exist where the spirit that shares a high level of affinity does not exist, because the economic form and the economic spirit adapt and reinforce one another, there tends to be a high degree of adequacy or correspondence between them (ibid.: 264). The spirit most appropriate for modern capitalist economic arrangements, for example, tends to animate modern capitalist economic systems. And, market-oriented economies tend to be predominantly peopled with market-oriented entrepreneurs. For Weber, then, a particular form of capitalistic enterprise is generally linked to a particular economic spirit.

The spirit of capitalism that he discusses in *The Protestant Ethic* is just one of any number of economic spirits that might exist. As Weber (2011: 79) concedes,

> the expression "spirit of capitalism" will be used here in just this specific manner—naturally the spirit of *modern capitalism*. . . . the Western European and American capitalism of the last few centuries constitutes our concern rather than the "capitalism" that appeared in China, India, Babylon, the ancient world, and the Middle Ages. As we will see, *just that peculiar ethic was missing in all these cases.*

Weber (2002: 19) employs the term "the spirit of [modern] capitalism" to describe the set of attitudes and orientations that find "their most adequate expression in the [modern] capitalist enterprise" and that give the modern capitalist enterprise "its most adequate *spiritual motivation.*" The different capitalisms that existed elsewhere or during different periods, Weber (ibid.) explains, had spirits that were quite different than the spirit that existed in modern Western capitalistic contexts.

In *The Religion of India* (1958) and *The Religion of China* (1951), Weber went on to explore the different forms and spirits of capitalism that existed in those countries.[7] In *The Religion of India*, for instance, Weber (1958) argues that, although India possessed many of the institutional and cultural pre-requisites for a modern form of capitalism, various aspects of Hinduism acted as a barrier to it developing indigenously.[8] In particular, the caste system that specified which occupations caste members could pursue and regulated interactions between members of different castes, including business dealings between members of different castes, prevented individual advancement beyond one's status group. The *economic spirit* of Hinduism, then, was one that was traditionalist, resistant to change, and so unlikely to lead to the development of modern capitalism.[9] Similarly, in *The Religion of China*, Weber (1951) argues that both institutional obstacles (primarily the structure of the state) and cultural/religious barriers (especially the *economic spirit* of Confucianism) blocked the development of modern capitalism in China. According to Weber (ibid.: 228), the Chinese businessmen sought self-control and dignity above all else, ascribed success to divine powers, inhabited a world where distrust was endemic and adjustment to existing social conventions and circumstances was stressed. The economic spirit of Confucianism was, thus, different in important respects from the spirit of enterprise that characterized modern capitalism.

Others have echoed Weber's claim that different forms of capitalism are animated by different economic spirits.[10] Often, however, the discussion is not in terms of the economic spirits that animate markets but in terms of the metaphors and models that color economic life in various contexts. Recall, for instance, that North (1994: 362) recognizes that "ideas, ideologies, myths, dogmas, and prejudices matter." And, that economic life can differ significantly from context to context depending on the economic models at play there. Similarly, as Lavoie and Chamlee-Wright (2000: 53) argue, "if you want to get a sense of whether a community is apt to grow wealthier, we are suggesting you find out what stories they tell, what myths they believe, what heroes they admire, what metaphors they use." These stories, myths, heroes and metaphors suggest to members of the community which economic activities are likely to be successful and which to avoid. Likewise, as noted previously, Bird-David (1990) has argued that different societies organize their economic lives on the basis of different "primary metaphors." These metaphors (fundamentally) shape how an individual in this or that context views her activities, her economic relationships, and her environment.

Gudeman (1986) has also argued that individuals rely on local models to both make sense of the world and guide their actions. As Gudeman (ibid.: 37) explains,

> humans are modelers . . . the human is a self-constituting, fully reflexive being, whose behavior is characterized both by hindsight and foresight, so that past activities are at once the objects of critical reflection and models for action. Humans are products of their past . . . yet this past is also drawn upon when making plans for the future.

Specifically, local (economic) models guide economic action, including how to secure a livelihood and how to distribute goods and services across society as well as how to achieve and explain economic success and to avoid and understand economic failure. Stated another way, local models become "embodied" in economic practices, relationships and institutions. Gudeman (ibid.: 37–43) has explained that these local models are culturally constructed (i.e. different cultures view the world through different models), are often built around primary metaphors (of the sort Bird-David highlighted) and usually require an ontological commitment (i.e. a belief that the model describes the world as it really is).[11]

Consider, for example, the local models constructed by the Bemba and Bisa of northern Zambia.[12] These groups have close historical ties and share the same primary metaphor but have constructed somewhat different local models and so organize economic activities somewhat differently. As Gudeman (ibid.: 90) explains,

> for both groups the work of the ancestors lies at the center of the economy. Their primal metaphor is that of nature as the ancestors. In the world of the Bemba and the Bisa, . . . nature is constituted as an ancestral performance in relation to live humans. To have a successful hunt or abundant harvest is to receive a blessing from the forebears of society.

Chiefs are believed to be the living embodiments of their ancestors and, so, the Bemba and Bisa believe that persuading the ancestors to bless them with economic success requires that they make offerings to their chiefs (ibid.). Although the

Bemba and Bisa have much in common, there are differences in their local (economic) models. For instance, the Bisa local model emphasizes hunting over agriculture while the Bemba primarily engage in agriculture (ibid.: 91). Additionally, the Bemba believe that the ancestors taught all of them agricultural techniques but the Bisa believe that hunting skills are selectively inherited by those whose ancestors were hunters (ibid.: 103). Similarly, the Bisa employ a much more complicated but immediate system for distributing economic goods than do the Bemba (ibid.: 104). Because the goods that the Bemba distribute (e.g. raw grain, porridge and beer) are homogenous and can be stored, goods are allocated on the basis of social positions with greater quantities going to those who are better positioned (e.g. chiefs receive more than village elders who receive more than ordinary villagers). Because the Bisa must allocate game, which is both heterogeneous and difficult to store, however, differently positioned villagers receive different animals and different parts of animals (e.g. hippo, pig, waterbuck and ant bear are distributed among a hunter's family while lions go entirely to chiefs who also have rights to the more durable parts of eland and elephants).

Modern capitalism in Western Europe and America, Weber (2002: 12) asserts, was animated by a spirit of capitalism that combined the penchant for the "*making of money* and yet more money, coupled with a strict avoidance of all uninhibited enjoyment."[13] The spirit of (modern) capitalism is characterized by what Weber described as a "worldly asceticism" and a rationalization of business practices that did not exist in other places and epochs. This is not to suggest that the spirit of capitalism encouraged an unprecedented *level* of acquisitiveness on the part of entrepreneurs in early modern Western Europe and America. Indeed, it is likely that the desire for gain and even greed are universal phenomena.[14] Instead, Weber's argument is that entrepreneurs do not possess the *kind* of acquisitiveness possessed by entrepreneurs in early modern Western Europe and America. Under the sway of this worldly asceticism, Weber (ibid.) states, "the aim of a man's life is indeed moneymaking, but this is no longer merely the means to the end of satisfying the material needs of life." Moreover, this ethic is "completely devoid of all eudaemonistic, let alone hedonistic, motives, [it is] so much purely thought of as an end *in itself* that it appears as something wholly transcendent and irrational, beyond the 'happiness' or the 'benefit' of the *individual*" (ibid.). As a result of this ethic, individuals pursue wealth not because they enjoy the act of pursuing wealth nor because they enjoy the kind of life that increased wealth brings but because they feel compelled to "make money and yet more money." Additionally, as Weber (2002: 88) explains, the spirit of capitalism also describes "the particular frame of mind that . . . strives systematically and rationally *in a calling* for legitimate profit." The spirit of capitalism describes a kind of economic rationalism where impartial calculations as opposed to tradition or superstition are the basis of economic decisions. "Work in the service of a rational production of material goods for the provision of humanity," Weber (2011: 96) explains, "has without question always been hovering over the representatives of the 'capitalist spirit' as a directing purpose of their life's labor."

The spirit of capitalism transformed accumulating capital into a virtue. Weber (2002: 85) contrasts the *spirit of capitalism* that he found in the West with the *spirit of traditionalism* that he explained it had to contend with and eventually overcame.[15] The traditionalist ethos was one that was resistant to change and did not identify the striving for gain as an ethical endeavor. As Weber (2011: 85) explains, motivated by the spirit of traditionalism, "a person [simply] does not . . . want to make more and more money but simply to live—to live in the manner in which he is accustomed to live, and to earn [only] as much as is necessary for this." Moreover, "in ancient and medieval times," Weber (2002: 14) explains, the modern attitude toward moneymaking, rather than receiving social acceptance, "would have been denounced as an expression of the most filthy avarice and of an absolutely contemptible attitude." The quest for more and more money as "a certain norm-bound style of life," that is, the rational pursuit of profits conceived of as an ethical calling, was what distinguished the *spirit of modern capitalism* from the economic spirit which preceded it.

Stated another way, being a merchant and an entrepreneur came to be considered dignified under modern capitalism. McCloskey (2010) has similarly argued that a change in the liberty and dignity afforded to the bourgeoisie not only accompanied but lead to the Industrial Revolution. A change in institutions (from less to more liberal institutional regimes), she argues, was not the proximate cause of the Industrial Revolution. Instead, the tremendous economic growth associated with the Industrial Revolution was spurred by a change that could be seen in the way first the Dutch and then the British came to regard and talk about entrepreneurship. The word "honest," for instance, came to describe individuals who were upright rather than those who possessed a high social rank. Merchants, similarly, came to be described as gentlemen, which was a term that was once reserved for aristocrats. As McCloskey (ibid.: 403) summarizes, "the initiating changes" of the Industrial Revolution "were sociological and rhetorical—that is to say, they were about habits of the lip, what people thought and said about each other." The Dutch, then the British and then the rest of the West began to admire merchants and to respect their efforts and achievements. And, again, this change in attitudes toward bourgeoisie led to the dramatic explosion in economic growth in the West which took place in the seventeenth, eighteenth and nineteenth centuries.[16]

Weber claims this ethos which elevated work to the status of an ethical calling was (in many respects) identical to the attitude toward work that emerged out of Protestantism (particularly Puritanism); "the essential elements of the attitude which is there termed the 'spirit of capitalism' are precisely those which we found to be the content of Puritan asceticism of the calling" (Weber 2002: 120). Calvinism, for instance, stressed that natural man is in a state of total depravity and can do nothing to change his condition. As the 1647 *Westminster Confession* explained, however, unlike those who are "foreordained to everlasting death," those that were called were "predestined unto everlasting life" (ibid.: 70). The elect have been transformed and reoriented. Weber (ibid.: 76) argues, however, that this doctrine created a serious challenge for Calvinists: "one question inevitably very soon arose for every single believer, and forced all other interests into the background: 'Am I one of the elect? And how can I be certain of my election?'"[17] Calvinist pastors adopted two strategies for dealing with this difficulty. One strategy held that it was the obligation of every believer to assume that they were one of the elect and to dismiss any doubts. In the other (of relevance to us here), "*tireless labor in a calling* was urged as the best possible means of *attaining* this self-assurance. This and this alone would drive away religious doubt and give assurance of one's state of grace" (ibid.: 78).

For the elect, then, work became an ethical duty. "According to God's unambiguously revealed will," Weber (2002: 106) summarizes, "it is *only* action, not idleness and indulgence, that serves to increase his glory." The division of labor, the use of profit and loss accounting, the rationalization of economic life, in short, the salient characteristics of the modern capitalistic enterprise, thus, achieves a moral force. Similarly, the productive investment of capital is encouraged while the consumption of luxuries is discouraged. The Puritans believed, Weber (ibid.: 160) explained, that

> for everyone, without distinction, God's Providence has prepared a calling, which each person must recognize and work within, and this calling is not . . . a destiny to which one must submit and resign oneself, but a command of God to the individual to work to his glory.

Weber saw much more than an incidental link between the Puritan ethic and the spirit of capitalism; "a constituent part of the capitalist spirit, and not only this but of modern culture, namely, the rational conduct of life on the foundation of the *idea of the calling*, was born . . . out of the spirit of *Christian asceticism*." The particular ethos of modern capitalism is not only (in many respects) identical to the attitudes toward work that emerge from Protestantism (particularly Puritanism) but the spirit of modern capitalism in the West found a consistent ethical basis in Protestantism. According to Weber (ibid.: 115), "it was only in the ethics of ascetic Protestantism that [certain aspects of the spirit of capitalism] found a consistent ethical foundation." And, as he (ibid.: 116) explained,

> a religious value was placed on ceaseless, constant, systematic labor in a secular calling as the very highest ascetic path and at the same time the surest and most visible proof of regeneration and the genuineness of faith. This was inevitably the most powerful lever imaginable with which to bring about the spread of that philosophy of life which we have here termed the "spirit" of capitalism.

This had dramatic implications, in Weber's view, for the development of modern capitalism. Although the religious foundations of this worldly asceticism have withered away, when it was alive, it played a significant role in bringing about modern capitalism.[18]

To recap, Weber made (at least) five important claims in *The Protestant Ethic and the Spirit of Capitalism*: (a) capitalism can take on a variety of economic forms; (b) each kind of capitalism has a matching ethic that gives it its life-force; (c) a worldly asceticism animates capitalism in the West; (d) this ethic is the same as the Protestant ethic; and (e) the Protestant ethic gave birth to the spirit of modern capitalism. Although these claims are related and appear tightly woven together in *The Protestant Ethic*, they are not wholly dependent on one another. They do not operate as the legs of a stool or the pillars of a temple. Indeed, only two of Weber's claims in *The Protestant Ethic* are foundational: his notion that different kinds of capitalism exist and that there is an economic spirit that impacts the particular brand of economic life that exists in each society. The others can be removed without tipping over the stool or destroying the temple.

And Weber's central claims survive his critics, with a few corrections

Using analogies to describe aspects of economic life is a common and, ultimately, an essential rhetorical device. Note, however, that even if the images employed in those analogies are unlike the real phenomena they are said to portray, we can still benefit from the effort.[19] To the extent that *The Protestant Ethic and the Spirit of Capitalism* was an attempt to describe the spirit that animated modern capitalism and to explore its historical roots (as Weber claimed it was) and not an attempt to prove that modern capitalism was a product of Protestantism (as his critics and proponents sometimes claim), then we dismiss his effort too quickly if we do so just because there are problems with one or even a few of the claims that he made in that essay. Indeed, Weber could have gotten the theology completely wrong and still have maintained that something like the worldly asceticism he identified is present in modern capitalist economies, since no Puritan ethic need exist to support that claim. Similarly, the link that he tried to establish between the spirit of capitalism and what he described as the Protestant ethic can still be viewed as a useful explanatory/expository move even if nothing like that ethos could be found in Protestantism. In emphasizing (even if mistakenly) those aspects of Protestantism that he thought of as economically relevant, Weber taught us quite a bit about the spirit of capitalism.

Likewise, it is possible to maintain that a spirit such as the one that Weber described both animated modern capitalism and flowed from Protestantism without accepting that one gave birth to the other or that the relationship was in the direction that Weber implied. As Weber (ibid.: 115) concedes, "some of the roots of this style of life go right back to the Middle Ages, like so many elements of the capitalist spirit." The Protestant ethic and the spirit of capitalism may, in fact, be twin children of the same father; the same historical circumstances may have given rise to both attitudes. Both the spirit of capitalism and the Protestant ethic could have a basis in, say, nationalism (see Greenfeld 2001) or ethnicity (see Chow 2002) or in some shared historical experience like slavery, colonialism, or communist rule (see Storr and Butkevich 2007). Or, Protestantism might also have been economically conditioned. Again, as Weber (2002: 122) notes at the end of *The Protestant Ethic*, "it cannot, of course be our purpose to replace a one-sided 'materialist' causal interpretation" of the relationship between Protestant asceticism and the spirit of capitalism "with an equally one-sided spiritual one."[20] Weber saw *The Protestant Ethic* as only a first step. It was meant to serve as a "preliminary work" for a larger sociological project.[21] He understood that the relationship between the Protestant ethic and the spirit of capitalism was never as strong or as one-sided as some suggest that he argued in that monograph.

Also, even if Weber misidentified the spirit of modern capitalism and no worldly asceticism can be found in modern capitalistic contexts, it is still possible to maintain (his central thesis) that many different kinds of capitalism exist and that each is animated by a particular spirit. That we walk into the cathedral, look up at the roof, and mistake the decorative posts for support beams, does not mean that there is not a ceiling overhead or that there is not something holding it up. Recall that, for Weber, the spirit of modern capitalism was just one of several possible rationalizations of economic life and that he recognized that his explanation of the spirit that he believed animated modern capitalism as well as his exploration its historical roots could be mistaken. Indeed, he realized that "it is possible to 'rationalize' life from extremely varied ultimate standpoints and in very different directions" (Weber 2002: 27) and that "we understand the 'spirit' of capitalism in terms of what we deem 'essential' from our point of view, [it] is by no means the *only* possible way of understanding it" (ibid.: 9).

Arguably, understanding the relationships between Weber's claims in *The Protestant Ethic and the Spirit of Capitalism* in this way allows us to view the many negative critiques of his work and the one hundred plus years of controversy surrounding that book in their proper perspective. Marshall (1982: 67), for instance, has complained that,

> Weber offers little or no independent evidence concerning the motives and world-view of either modern or medieval businessmen and labourers. His evidence concerning the former, apart from the "provisional description" offered by Franklin's advice, is drawn exclusively from Protestant teaching. This, of course, suggests a . . . tautology whereby the Protestant ethic and the spirit of modern capitalism are defined in terms of each other.

Hamilton (1996) has levied a similar charge against Weber. According to Hamilton (ibid.: 60), Weber provided "no serious evidence" for many of his claims about Calvinism, the doctrine of predestination and the duty to engage in "intense worldly activity" that resulted from that doctrine. Weber should, therefore, signal his conclusions, in Hamilton's (ibid.: 63) opinion, "as hypothetical options rather than confirmed findings." Although these critiques are fair, Weber was aware of the tentative nature of his discussion in *The Protestant Ethic*. Recall, Weber referred to his effort as necessarily preliminary. He was also careful to point out that the "evidence" he provided was meant to be illustrative not definitive.[22]

There is also some evidence that Weber got his theology wrong; that the theologians that Weber employed were not representative of the broader thrust of Puritanism; that Weber presented a biased interpretation of Protestantism where he culled only those principles and themes that supported his thesis; and, that Weber exaggerated the differences between Puritanism and other Protestant faiths and between Protestantism and Catholicism.[23] MacKinnon (1988a, 1988b), for instance, has argued that Weber exaggerated the role played by Calvin's particular conception of predestination as well as Calvinism's uniqueness. Although Weber's thesis "rests on the assumption that Calvin's absolute conception of predestination was dogmatically preserved by seventeenth-century English Calvinism," MacKinnon (1998a: 144) argues that

> Calvanism abandoned Calvin's predestinarianism via the introduction of covenant theology. No longer are the redemptive aspirations of the faithful blocked by the impenetrability of God's purpose. Now, the infallible promise of assurance is issued to "all" who are prepared to sincerely labour for it.

This realization, MacKinnon (ibid.: 169) argues, robs the Protestant ethic of its basis within Protestantism. Moreover, according to MacKinnon (ibid.), the Calvinists were not anymore oriented to this-worldly concerns than their Lutheran or Catholic counterparts. "Calvinism," MacKinnon (ibid.: 170) states,

> is not unique in its this-worldliness as Weber would have us believe. Accordingly its prevalence in England did not promote capitalist accumulation by directing the ultimate value to seek success in an ordinary calling, though it may have done so in other ways. Conversely, the continental dominance of Catholicism and Lutheranism did not retard capitalistic development in the way that Weber claims but, again, may have done so by other means.

If MacKinnon is correct and Calvinism retained the otherworldly focus of its counterparts (instead of encouraging an "intense worldly activity"), then it would be impossible to maintain that either a specifically "Protestant" ethic exists or that Puritanism (as opposed to Lutheranism or Catholicism) had anything to do with producing the capitalistic spirit.[24]

There remains a great deal of debate about the Weber thesis.[25] Admittedly, several of Weber's claims—in particular, that the Protestant ethic gave rise to the spirit of modern capitalism—have been seriously damaged by these critiques. Notice, however, that although Weber's assertions about the strength and the direction of the link between the Protestant ethic and the spirit of modern capitalism and between Protestantism and the evolution of modern economic development have been seriously challenged, his contention that capitalism comes in a variety of flavors and his claims about the importance of the capitalistic spirit to economic progress have escaped these critiques unscathed. Similarly, although Weber's critics are right that he did not prove his case, this is not the same thing as saying that Weber was wrong. A spirit such as the one Weber called the Protestant ethic might very well have existed and may very well have animated modern capitalism.

Unfortunately, many of Weber's critics misunderstood his project at a fundamental level. To condemn him for failing to do what he did not set out to do and never believed that he accomplished is to distort his effort. Weber (2011: 178) understood that *The Protestant Ethic* was a preliminary "sketch" and, as such, was incomplete in many respects.[26]

The most common critiques against Weber are not, then, devastating to his whole schema, as some have claimed. A large amount has survived, much of it quite useful for any discussion of the relationship between culture and markets.[27] Though Weber may have gone down the wrong path (the Protestant ethic may not have given birth to the spirit of modern capitalism), the manner in which he drove, arguably, still exists as a model for conducting culturally aware economic analysis. His approach (with one addendum to be offered later) offers a strategy for getting at the spirit that animates the economic form in a particular context: (i) identify the particular economic spirit, (ii) sketch out its probable historical and cultural roots, and (iii) describe how it impacts economic life.

There are, however, several modifications that might be made to the approach that Weber adopted in *The Protestant Ethic*. First, modern capitalism and the spirit of modern capitalism are still quite abstract constructs. A great deal of variety can be accommodated within these ideal types. Pretending otherwise obscures key differences between the economic spirits and economic forms that exist within different societies (that are nonetheless similar in some important respects). Weber tended to focus on the spirit of capitalism and the form of Puritanism that existed in England. Additionally, he rarely highlighted any differences between modern capitalism and the economic spirits in the Western Europe and the United States. Second, multiple economics spirits can (simultaneously) shape the economic practices that exist in a particular context. Although Weber (ibid.: 19) is likely right that for every economic form there is one and only one economic spirit with which it has a high degree of affinity, it is also the case that more than one economic spirit can and often does coexist with every economic form. Focusing on the dominant economic spirit that exists within a society runs the risk of overstating the link between the dominant economic spirit in a society and that society's economic form and can obscure how competing economic spirits in a given context interact. In fact, as Weber (2002: 19) conceded, the spirit of capitalism and the spirit of traditionalism both pre-date and survive the emergence of modern capitalism.[28]

So, there is reason to adopt a (modified) Weberian approach to examining how culture impacts economic behavior and outcomes. This approach would seem to call for identifying the economic spirits that animate a society's markets, examining their cultural and historical roots and describing how they impact economic life.

In the following sections, I offer a brief application of the (modified) Weberian approach outlined above followed by an extended application of that approach. First, I describe the economic spirit that animates economic life in St Bernard

Parish, Louisiana. St Bernard is a predominantly white middle-income community just east of Orleans Parish. Next, I describe the economic spirits that animate economic life in the Commonwealth of the Bahamas. The Bahamas' economy is often described as a boom and bust economy and the pattern of entrepreneurship that currently exists in that country is arguably explainable by the economic and political structures that it inherited from its British colonizers as well as the cultural patterns that developed during slavery and colonialism.

For example, it is possible to use this approach to describe the attitudes toward work in St Bernard Parish

In Chamlee-Wright and Storr (2011b), my co-author and I argue that residents of St Bernard Parish think of themselves as "blue-collar" and that a definite spirit of hard work and independence exists in that community.[29] For instance, both Michael Fontana[†] and Al Delaney[†] described St Bernard as "a blue-collar community." Barbara Chase[†], likewise, described St Bernard as "a good parish" comprised of "people not afraid of hard work." Similarly, Frank Williams[†] states, "You know, we're not lazy people. We work." Residents of St Bernard also tend to think of themselves as "self-reliant" (ibid.). David Belacose[†], for instance, remarked that "people down here are just a very self-sufficient, industrious sort of people. And, if they can't get something done, they're just gonna do it themselves." Similarly, Doris Voitier described St Bernard residents as "a very resilient self-aligned people. It's not a community that has a sense of entitlement, always looking for a handout or something." And, Michael Fontana[†] claimed that "we in the Parish, we are a self-sufficient type of community." Comments along these lines dominated the interviews that were conducted by our team. When asked to describe their parish, residents of St Bernard Parish tended to emphasize that theirs is a "working class," "middle class," community populated by "independent," "self-reliant," "hard working" people who "pay their bills" and are "not afraid to get their hands dirty." "The key thrust of these comments," Chamlee-Wright and Storr (ibid.: 278) conclude, "was not to emphasize a particular socio-economic status or to offer a demographic description of the community but to suggest a particular orientation toward life and work that tends to characterize them and their neighbors."

These attitudes toward work, arguably, shaped economic life in St Bernard Parish. Our purpose in that study was to explore how those attitudes toward work shaped the response of St Bernard residents to the devastation of Hurricane Katrina. Katrina devastated this community. The storm, which left most of the parish under eight feet of standing water for nearly three weeks, caused almost $3 billion in property damage. And, as a result of Katrina and its aftermath, 163 residents of the community died. "In response to this disaster," Chamlee-Wright and Storr (ibid.: 274) argue, "community members who returned within two years of Katrina tended to adopt a self-reliant strategy depending primarily on their own efforts and informal support from kin and other community members rather than formal support from external sources."

It is also possible to adopt the approach outlined here to explain the Bahamas' economic culture

In *Enterprising Slaves and Master Pirates* (2004), I noted that there were high levels of self-employment and a preponderance of low-capital intensive industries in the Bahamas but that customer service tended to be poor and business dealings in the country were often politicized. These stylized facts, I argued, were (at least partially) explained by the country's economic culture. Businessmen in the Bahamas exhibit a strong work ethic and a tremendous creativity but also possess narrow radii of trust and have high discount rates. Thus, I concluded, two primary metaphors, two distinct and competing economic spirits, can be said to color economic life in the Bahamas.

One, call it the "spirit of Rabbyism," promotes piracy over enterprise, celebrating "the trickster (that is, the person who gets something for nothing) while ridiculing the hard worker" (Storr 2004: 56). The essential elements of this spirit can be gleaned from even a cursory read of Bahamian folklore. Indeed, the Bahamas is a country that once had a vibrant storytelling tradition and the preeminent figure in that orature was B' Rabby, "the archetypal hero-trickster character" (Kulii and Kulii 2001: 46; see also Glinton-Meicholas 1993).[30] B' Rabby is a figure who hopes to gain much more than a full day's pay for much less than a full day's work. Often pitted against his friend and foil, the dimwitted B' Bouki, Rabby's cunning, his quick thinking, his ability to manipulate and deceive—in short, his wiles and his wits—are his chief assets, operating as both defensive and offensive weapons. Rabby's cunning wins him a great deal of admiration and his figure emerges out of the Bahamian tradition of "talking ol' story" as a model for "entrepreneurship" in the Bahamas.

There is, however, another economic spirit—a competing set of attitudes and proclivities—which animates economic affairs in the Bahamas. In addition to the spirit of Rabbyism, the "spirit of Junkanoo" also colors economic life in that nation of islands. Junkanoo is a popular semi-annual cultural event that is, arguably, the *quintessential* Bahamian cultural experience and is the *essence* of what it means to be a Bahamian. Indeed, it has variously been described as the heartbeat, the pulse, the spirit, and the soul of the Bahamian people. Craton and Saunders (1998: 488), for instance, have called Junkanoo "the essential expression of Bahamian identity" and Nash-Ferguson (2000: 2) affirms that "Junkanoo is tightly plaited into the Bahamian psyche." The extensive and almost year-long planning and preparation for the Junkanoo festivals teach Bahamians that success and hard work are inextricably linked. Junkanoo also rewards creativity and cooperation. These attitudes are very much like and are, arguably, the source of the enterprising spirit that animates economic life in the country.

Consequently, while celebrating B' Rabby's penchant for getting something for nothing, Bahamians have also adopted a Junkanoo ethic where success is possible through hard work, even in the face of obstacles. Applying the (modified) Weberian approach outlined above in order to understand the Bahamas' economic culture means teasing out the characteristics of these spirits and tracing their historical and cultural roots.

The spirit of Rabbyism

Again, B' Rabby's chief asset is his cunning. Cunning is an important part of B' Rabby's arsenal; it is both an offensive and defensive weapon. He is an excellent liar, using his "quick tongue" to both get what he wants and to get himself out of trouble. He is the classic trickster-hero figure. Rabby's cunning, as demonstrated in one B' Bouki and B' Rabby tale after another, means that Rabby always gets the better of his friend and, while Bouki "c[an] hardly find food for his family," Rabby's household "look[s] plump and prosperous" (Turner 1998: 52). Not surprisingly then, Bahamians tend to admire B' Rabby because, using only his wits and his wiles, he is able to sidestep every roadblock, overcome every obstacle, escape every trap, win every bet and battle and attain any and everything that he needs or wants.

The theme of cunning being an admirable quality occurs in *B' Rabby Makes B' Boukee his Cart Horse* (Burrows 1990). Burrows begins his account by reminding us that "Whereas B' Rabby is the trickster, B' Bouki is the foolish one, greedy, always getting himself into trouble. And, B' Rabby, he never pass up an opportunity to get at B' Bouki." In this story, Bouki and Rabby are living together like brothers. Somehow Bouki has found himself a girlfriend who he visits every day and brags about every night. Eventually, Rabby, who is overcome with jealousy, decides that he will steal Bouki's girlfriend. One day when Bouki is off somewhere fishing, Rabby goes to Bouki's girlfriend and tries to convince her that her beau Bouki is not boyfriend material. "B' Boukee," Rabby tells her, "ain' no man. I bet he ain' tell you that he's my father's cart horse and I does ride him every day."

That evening when Bouki goes to visit his girlfriend he finds her cold and distant. "What's wrong?" he asks her. She is coy at first but eventually tells him Rabby's fantastical tale: "He tell me say you is his father's cart horse and he does ride you every day." Bouki, of course, denies it vehemently and promises to bring Rabby back with him right away to clear up the matter. When Bouki reaches his house, however, he finds Rabby moaning and wailing in bed. An upset and unsympathetic Bouki grills Rabby, "Why you tell my girlfriend that I is your cart horse and you does ride me every day?" Rabby denies telling Bouki's girlfriend anything but tells Bouki that although he would like to help that he is too sick to move. "B' Rabby you gern move," Bouki exclaims, "if I gatta carry you."

So, Rabby climbs onto Bouki's back. After only a few steps, Rabby starts to complain that he is "bouncing up and down" too much and that he needs something to sit on. By this time, Bouki is more than anxious to have Rabby explain things to his girlfriend, so he is willing to agree to just about anything. He puts a saddle on his back and lets Rabby mount him. After a few more steps Rabby starts to complain again, "B' Bouki I sitting fine but my legs swinging too much." He convinces Bouki to get stirrups. Rabby goes on like this until Bouki agrees to put on the full gear of a cart horse: saddle, stirrups and reigns. Rabby has also dressed himself in full riding gear, complete with whip and spurs. When they approach

Bouki's girlfriend's house, Rabby, instead of getting off as he promised, jams his spurred heels into Bouki's side and begins whipping Bouki repeatedly with the whip. A surprised Bouki gallops all the way to his girlfriend's front door. "Ain' I tell you that B' Bouki is my father's cart horse," Rabby exclaims, and with that he jumps off Bouki, ties him to the gate and bounds up the stairs to the porch.

Arguably, the almost universal refrain "fool me once shame on you, fool me twice shame on me" has been rewritten in Bahamian lore; in the Bahamas getting tricked, even if it is the first time, is typically seen as entirely your fault. Similarly, Bouki is not a figure to be pitied he is a figure to be scorned. Recall, "B' Bouki is the foolish one, greedy, always getting himself into trouble. And, B' Rabby, he never pass up an opportunity to get at B' Bouki." Not surprisingly, "low cunning" or an inability to be cunning is frequently mocked in these narratives. Glinton-Meicholas (1993: 125), for instance, has described Bouki and his son Borin as "stupid, greedy and full of low cunning." Being full of low cunning appears last on the list of character flaws but, for Bahamians, it is the most damning. Indeed, being a "babe to the trade" of trickery was ultimately the cause of Borin's demise in the tale of *The Master Trickster*, an adaptation of a Haitian tale retold by Patricia Glinton-Meicholas in *An Evening in Guanima* (1993).

While "cunning" is consistently celebrated in these stories, greed is as consistently condemned. It is how the thief gets himself into trouble. Glinton-Meicholas (ibid.: 128), for example, disparagingly called Bouki, "Bouki-of-the-Bottomless-Belly," who "ate what he was given and asked for more." And, though it was "low cunning" that allowed them to be tricked, it is Bouki and Borin's greed that ultimately stung Rabby's sensibilities in *The Master Trickster*. Similarly, it is Rabby's greed that gets him caught by the farmer he was stealing from in *The Cane Field* (Hurston 1930), which is also called the *False Message: Take My Place* (Finlay 1925) or *Getting the Other Fellow to Take Your Place* (Cleare 1917).

This folk value of cunning as a virtue and greed as a vice is also clearly evident in Glinton-Meicholas' (1993) adaptation of *The Sperrit House*. Glinton-Meicholas begins her treatment by comparing the two friends. Rabby, we learn,

> was so sharp, he could teach a wasp a better way to sting. He could smell the [odors] from a pot and tell whether the cook had added goat peppers or bird peppers. Being a thief, Bouki's friend could look at a field of ripened corn and estimate to the last grain how much he could steal without getting caught.
> (ibid.: 59)

Rabby was truly a figure to admire. Bouki, however, "was different. On a good day, one and one could be three or four or, on a bad day as many as sixteen" (ibid.: 60). And, while Rabby was able to *control his passions* and was as *brave as a lion*, Bouki was both greedy and a coward. Again, Turner captured the consequences of these differences quite succinctly in *The House in the Sky* (1988), her adaptation of the same tale; "B' Bouki," she tells us, "could hardly find food for his family. On the other hand, B' Rabby's household looked plump and prosperous" (Turner 1988: 52). In spite of these differences, they were still friends, "united in their love of food and the desire to do as little as possible to get it" (Glinton-Meicholas 1993: 60).

One day, Rabby mentions to Bouki that he knows a good place where they can find food and so the two set out on their quest the very next day at the crack of dawn. When they reach the appropriate spot, a clearing in the middle of the forest, Rabby tells his friend, who by now is quite confused, what is going on. Apparently, a couple of days before Rabby had been in this same clearing when he heard someone singing a song and then saw a "*sperrit*" (spirit) house descend from the heavens to the ground. Rabby, not one to miss an opportunity, had committed the song the *sperrit* sang to memory and so is able to sing it again on the day when he comes with Bouki to search for easy plunder. As he sings it, the house comes down as expected and the pair go inside. The door closes behind them and the house returns to the heavens. A mouthwatering *sperrit* feast has been prepared and laid out on the dining room table; "juicy sides of beef, legs of mutton and huge hams, all roasted and ready to eat" (ibid.: 64). Bouki, Glinton-Meicholas (ibid.) tells us, "ran here and there . . . grabbing handfuls of this, a bowlful of that, trying manfully to stuff a quart of food at a time into a mouth, which was made to hold no more than a half pint." Rabby, on the other hand,

> found an empty sack and carefully packed it with small portions of all the things he liked. He was neat about it, cutting and sampling in such a clever way that nobody but another Rabby could tell that the dish had been disturbed.

When he is finished packing his sac, Rabby grabs it up, sings the appropriate words (to bring the house out of the heavens) and leaves. Bouki, unable to tear himself away from this windfall, does not follow. Instead, he eats and dances to the point of exhaustion, collapses, rolls under a bed and falls asleep.

When dusk comes, the *sperrits* come home and, realizing that someone has broken into their home, begin searching for the intruder. When they find Bouki under the "baby *sperrit*'s" bed, "the papa *sperrit* grab[s] his kukumakai [magic] stick and poke[s] at Bouki under the bed. Still drowsy, Bouki stumble[s] out to be greeted by a rain of blows" (Glinton-Meicholas 1993: 67). Though Bouki pleads for his life, "the *sperrit* pa[ys] no heed to Bouki's pleas. He might have been beating him still, if the sperrit child had not taken pity on Bouki and sung the house down" (ibid.). Bouki escapes out of the house into the night.

The Rabby that appears in *The Cane Field*, *The Master Trickster*, *B'Rabby Makes B'Boukee his Cart Horse* and *The Sperrit House*, indeed the Rabby of *How Brer Rabby Tricked Brer Lion*, *Starvation*, *B'Rabby*, *B'Whale and B'Elephant*, and the countless other Rabby narratives (and versions of familiar B' Rabby narratives) that float around the Bahamas, is a figure who, while rejecting greediness, nonetheless believes that he is entitled to whatever he can steal (and get away with), that it is alright to have a casual relationship with the truth, and that cunning is a necessary tool for survival.

It is perhaps not surprising that B' Rabby was a popular figure in the Bahamas during slavery and colonization where black Bahamians could not hope to overcome the tremendous odds that they faced if they tackled them directly (McFarlane 1998). Rabby tales spoke to the predicament that black Bahamians found themselves in prior to emancipation, prior to majority rule, prior to independence. Slavery and colonization were damnable institutions. Indeed, blacks in the Bahamas were horribly oppressed before 1967 when the majority black Progressive Liberal Party was elected to power. Prior to 1967, then, B' Rabby, who bested much stronger foes, was a source of inspiration and hope to the disenfranchised Bahamian black population.[31] Like Rabby, they did not have many resources at their disposal. And, like Rabby, they could use cunning, and trickery and lies when necessary, to resist, temper and escape their oppression. Like Rabby, they could outwit and outmaneuver, albeit surreptitiously, the mighty B' Elephant, B' Lion and B' Whale, as well as the machinations of their slave masters and the colonial state. It makes sense that B' Rabby was a figure that many Bahamian blacks embraced and sought to emulate.

These folktales, thus, teach us quite a bit about the values celebrated by Bahamians and about Bahamian attitudes and beliefs. It, for instance, makes sense that government corruption would be a major problem in a country whose folklore celebrates getting more than a full day's pay for less than a full day's work. In 1990, for instance, the Bahamas was listed as one of the six most corrupt countries in the world by the *International Credit Risk Guide* (Easterly 2001: 245) and reports of corruption (even at the cabinet level) were quite common during the twenty-five years that Sir Lynden Oscar Pindling was Prime Minister of the Bahamas.[32]

It is also not surprising that the most successful industries in these communities which applaud B' Rabby because he has been a master trickster would be illegal or extra-legal enterprises. "Piracy," as I argued elsewhere, "has been a definite model for economic success in the Bahamas ever since the seventeenth century, when Nassau on Providence Island (now New Providence) was a favorite harbor for West Indian pirates" (Storr 2004: 44). During the latter years of the seventeenth century and the first few decades of the eighteenth century, the Bahamas was the chief base of operations for thousands of pirates in the West Indies. Similarly, for a time, "wrecking," which involved luring unsuspecting ships to their ruin on the coral reefs that surround the Bahamas and "salvaging" their cargo, was the chief "industry" in the colony. The Bahamas was also a base of operations for blockade runners, who smuggled guns to the Confederate Army during the American Civil War, rum runners, who smuggled alcohol into America during prohibition, and drug dealers who smuggled illicit drugs into the US during the 1980s. These industries were at best ethically if not legally dubious.[33] These industries were also a tremendous boon to the Bahamas' local economy.

As noted above, I argued in Storr (2004) that this spirit of Rabbyism (i.e. the ethos of attaining something for nothing that was transmitted through the countries folktales and evidenced in many of its successful major industries) was one of at least two competing economic spirits that animated economic life in the Bahamas.

The other was the spirit of Junkanoo that emerged during the planning and preparation of the semi-annual Junkanoo festivals in the Bahamas and, arguably, gave rise to the *spirit of enterprise* that also characterized business dealings in the country.

The spirit of Junkanoo

Again, Junkanoo is the quintessential Bahamian experience. Thousands of Bahamians and their visitors dance through downtown Nassau in the early morning hours of Boxing Day and New Year's Day dressed in colorful costumes made of crepe paper and cardboard, shaking cow bells, blowing whistles, bugles or (more recently) brass instruments, or beating out rhythms reminiscent of African rhythms on large drums made by stretching goat skin over metal barrels. Thousands more come to watch and to dance. "Junkanoo is a phenomenon," as Wood (1995: 34) states, "that demands the full involvement of those who are either witnessing or participating in the event." As Wood (ibid.: 49) continues,

> in the case of Junkanoo ... the spectators of the parade co-perform by dancing, chanting and shouting, and thus enter the inner flux of the music ... The nature of the Junkanoo event is such that spectators share emotionally, verbally and kinetically in the performance.

Consider, also, Nash-Ferguson's (2000: 30) moving description of the excitement that Junkanooers feel in the days leading up to a Junkanoo parade as they collected their costumes. As she reports,

> it was like coming home again after a long absence. And everyone coming through the door said the same thing: "I come to get me!" They meant that they had come to get their costumes. ... With those words, the door to our heritage had slowly opened again, and our forefathers were reaching out across the centuries, bequeathing a proud and indomitable heritage through the power of Junkanoo. ... The real "me" would emerge in our costumes ... in our costumes, we would feel complete.

A definite ethos evolves and several habits and attitudes are developed during the preparation for the semi-annual celebrations. Certainly, the most important lesson that Bahamians learn from Junkanoo is that success and hard work are inextricably linked. Parades are not only about pretty costumes and powerful music. They are also highly contested competitions between as much as a dozen Junkanoo groups. The larger groups begin preparing for the next set of parades almost as soon as the results of the New Year's Day parade are announced. There are costumes to design and build. The cowbellers, the drummers and the choreographed dancers have to practice their music and their dance routines. By mid-year, when preparations are in full swing, Junkanooers are spending hours upon hours at the parks (where they hold practice) and in the shacks (the warehouses where Junkanoo costumes are built and housed). As Wood (1995: 19) reports, "each year from June to the close of the New Year's Day parade Junkanooers direct their energies fully toward the production of costumes and music for the parade." And, as Glinton-Meicholas (1994: 103) states,

> bands of men and women expend astonishing energy and artistry, from about midyear to the last moments of Christmas Day, designing and constructing costumes and huge, mobile sculptures of cardboard and wire, all covered with finely fringed, brightly coloured crepe paper.

Revelers know full well that their success in a given parade has as much to do with the time they spend in the shacks back in June as it has to do with their performances on Bay Street (downtown Nassau) in December and January.[34]

Additionally, Junkanoo recasts the relationship that Bahamians have with the fruits of their labor. Marx (1994: 59), you may recall, has complained that under capitalism, "the object which labor produces, its product, stands opposed to it as an *alien thing*, as a *power independent* of the producer." This objectification of labor's product, this estrangement of workers from the things that they produce, has resulted, Marx asserts, in laborers being alienated from the sensuous external world about them, the act of production, themselves and other laborers. Junkanoo, however, transforms the relationships that Bahamians have with the fruits of their labor and teaches them that economic relationships are not necessarily alienating. Although Junkanoo is big business in the Bahamas (a lot of money changes hands during the year-long preparation for the two parades), none of the products of Junkanoo are alien to Junkanooers. Rather than alienating Bahamians, Junkanoo, instead, brings them closer to themselves and each other. The Junkanoo costume is a symbolic expression of Bahamainess and the Junkanoo beat is the heartbeat of the Bahamian people; neither confronts Bahamians as "hostile" or "alien" externalized objects. Recall that when people come to pick up their completed costumes (that they, in some instances, have paid others to help them build) they remark that they have "come to get me" and that they believe that "the real 'me' would emerge in our costumes, the colours of our character, the design of our personalities, the pattern of our tastes, our pride, and our signature" (Nash-Ferguson 2000: 30).

Similarly, Junkanoo dissolves what Marx thought of as the "inevitable" class divisions, the supposedly necessary separation that results under capitalism between the rich and the poor, the entrepreneur and the wage earner, the owners of capital and the exploited workers. According to Marx (1994: 159), "society as a whole is more and more splitting up into two great hostile camps, into two great classes directly facing each other—bourgeoisie and proletariat." In the shacks, however, the store owner is often putting the final touches on her costume inches away from the sales clerk who is finishing his. In the park, the doctor may be taking orders from his band major who by day works as a janitor. On Bay Street, the main commercial thoroughfare in Nassau, the members of the so called bourgeoisie and the proletariat are dancing and beating their drums and blowing their whistles and shaking their cowbells next to one another. As Glinton-Meicholas (1994: 103) states, "in this society, Junkanoo is the great leveler, where . . . the rich make merry with the poor, the magistrate dances with the felon he may later prosecute, and members of the Government make brief accord with parliamentarians in opposition."[35]

Another significant lesson that Bahamians learn from Junkanoo is to trust in their own creativity. Junkanoo costumes have become large, elaborate, colorful creations where everything from insects, to fish and wildlife, to natural phenomenon, to national and international figures, to world events, have been constructed out of a combination of cardboard, metal wire, plastic, wood and Styrofoam and are "fringed" with strips of varied colored crepe paper "pasted" in complex patterns like a kaleidoscope. Although aspects of Junkanoo are reminiscent of Trinidadian Carnival, Jamaican Jonkonnu and Belizean John Canoe celebrations, Junkanoo grew out of the Bahamas' particular cultural milieu. The Junkanoo artists, designers, engineers, builders, and decorators are almost all Bahamian and the sound of Junkanoo is unlike anything else. To be sure, the beat of Junkanoo has African roots. The eclectic mix of drums, cow bells, whistles, horns, and brass instruments, however, is uniquely Bahamian.

The spirit of Junkanoo, thus, describes a set of beliefs and attitudes about work, success, class and creativity, which are embedded in and find their clearest expression in Junkanoo. This spirit is very much like the spirit of modern capitalism that Weber developed (Storr 2004: 97). That is, with one major exception. Recall that Weber (2002: 24) describes the modern capitalist entrepreneur as someone who

> shuns ostentation and unnecessary show, spurns the conscious enjoyment of his power, and is embarrassed by the outward signs of the social esteem in which he is held. His conduct of life, in other words, is often characterized to a certain degree by a form of *asceticism*.

There is nothing ascetic or austere about Junkanoo or the ethos that accompanies it. There is an aspect of Junkanoo and, indeed, of Bahamian identity that is all about flashiness. Junkanooers delight in decorating their already elaborate costumes with feathers, and glitter, and pieces of colored glass and even battery powered lights. Similarly, Bahamians are not (to put it politely) a modest people. "In this country," as Glinton-Meicholas (1998: 40) states, "you are not considered upwardly mobile unless you are demonstrably, visibly and even vulgarly so." Bahamians do, however, believe that success through hard work is possible even in the face of obstacles. And, as mentioned earlier, this spirit informs economic life in the Bahamas.

Indeed, the lessons that arise during Junkanoo about the importance of creativity, the possibility of success through hard work, and the fluidity of class divisions also color business life in the Bahamas. There is certainly a vibrant *spirit of enterprise* in the Bahamas. As Glinton-Meicholas (1994: 64; *emphasis added*) explains, "Bahamians have *an extraordinary yen and flair* for entrepreneurship and all the necessary optimism." Much of the Bahamas' economic success has been based on the strength of tourism, its leading industry, and the "yen and flair" of so many Bahamian entrepreneurs is often oriented towards earning dollars from the over four million tourists that pass through that country annually.[36] The porters in the airports or at the cruise ship docks, the neatly dressed taxicab drivers often wearing brightly colored neckties, the fruit vendors along the roadside, the straw market vendors who shower you with "hi darlings" and "come here sweeties" as you pass by their stalls, the hagglers that litter some of our beaches and offer to braid hair "a dollar a plait" or to rent you jet skis or scooters are all in the business of chasing tourist dollars. Many are quite successful.[37] Although "there was no going home for straw vendors" (Knowles 1998: 16) as one market woman put it, "there are many [Bahamian professionals and parliamentarians] whose school and college fees were paid for by the hard work of their straw vending parents" (ibid.: 43). Similarly, the neatly dressed taxicab drivers who chauffer tourists about the islands are "among the most aggressively enterprising . . . Bahamians" (Craton and Saunders 1998: 204) and—when willing to work twelve or thirteen hours a day, six or seven days a week (as many of them do)—can earn middle-class incomes.

That the spirit of Junkanoo would animate economic life in the Bahamas makes sense given the other aspects of the country's unique cultural milieu. In the Bahamas, for instance, hundreds of thousands of blacks lived and died as slaves. They lived under the constant threat and sting of the whip. Their movements were severely circumscribed. Their ankles and wrists were bound by cold, metal shackles. Slavery in the Bahamas, however, was different than slavery in the other West Indian colonies. While most countries in the West Indies were plantation hinterlands, the plantation economy never really developed in the Bahamas. The "thin, scattered, and easily exhausted" soil in the Bahamas was never able to sustain the production of sugar, the major commercial crop in the rest of the West Indies during the slavery era (Craton and Saunders 1992: 196). And, though cotton was tried and thrived in the Bahamas for a time, as Johnson (1996: 28) notes, "the commercial industry barely survived the eighteenth century." Bahamian slaves "benefited" from this failure.

A common feature of slavery in the West Indies was to give slaves "use rights" to a portion of the plantation to grow rations and to give them time in the evenings and on the weekends to tend to these provision plots. They were also allowed to sell whatever surplus crops they produced in weekend markets. The precipitate collapse of the cotton industry in the Bahamas, however, meant that

> Bahamian slaves ended up with a great deal of time to devote to their subsistence and market activities. And, as a result, they were able to both improve their standard of living and develop the skills and practices necessary to maintain a market economy.
>
> (Storr 2004: 88)

Stated another way, a key factor in the development of the spirit of Junkanoo that thrives in the Bahamas is the opportunity that Bahamians had even during slavery to engage in entrepreneurial activities, to grow their own crops and to sell them in the market.

The Bahamian slave's experience with the practice of *self-hire* also contributed to the peculiarity of the system of slavery in the Bahamas and, undoubtedly, the spirit of Junkanoo that still thrives. Slave owners in the Bahamas, mostly in Nassau,

> allowed their slaves to seek their own employment in return for a sum, mutually agreed upon, that was paid to them at regular intervals. By that arrangement, labor services that were due to the slave owners were commuted into cash payments.
>
> (Johnson 1996: 34)

This was a mutually beneficial arrangement. The slave owners were able to get a return for their investment (in their slaves). The slaves were able to achieve an unprecedented degree of freedom and economic success. As Johnson (ibid.: 36) informs, "by the late 1790s, slaves on self-hire controlled important areas of the urban economy." And, "In 1799, for example, [there were complaints] that slave middlemen were monopolizing the supply of fruits, ground provisions, and vegetables in Nassau and forcing up prices" (ibid.). The practice of self-hire should, thus, be credited with not only easing the transition of blacks in the Bahamas from slavery to freedom (see Johnson 1996) but "with laying the foundation for an economic system altogether different than the plantation economics found throughout the West Indies" (Storr 2004: 93). Through the self-hire system, Bahamian blacks gained valuable experiences negotiating wages and marketing their skills (i.e. manning a service economy) even when they were slaves.

It, thus, makes sense that the spirit of Junkanoo that lives in the Bahamas emerged out of this particular history. Indeed, one of the most important formative features in the development of Junkanoo, as Craton and Saunders (1998: 488) argue, was "the absence of a prolonged and intensive plantation economy and the consequent opportunities for the black majority to sustain and develop their own traditions." Junkanoo has African roots and evolved out of the peculiar experiences of African slaves in the Bahamas. As Wood (1995: 3) explains, "it grew out of the celebrations of enslaved people in the eighteenth and nineteenth centuries, when they had three days off at Christmas, and were relatively free during that period to pursue their own entertainment." Originally, these events included slaves dressing up in costumes and parodying their white slave masters, safely ensconced behind masks. After emancipation, however, these festivals developed into the organized competitions that we see today with large groups of revelers dancing down Bay Street to the sound of cow bells and goat skin drums in the large and colorful costumes that they have spent almost a year designing and building. "The uniqueness of the Bahamas' system of slavery," as I stated previously, "should be credited with cementing the belief that *enterprise could lead to economic success* into the Bahamian consciousness. And, with creating a festival (the semi-annual Junkanoo celebrations) and culture (the Junkanoo ethos) where hard work and creativity are celebrated" (Storr 2004: 93).

Conclusion

Every market is animated by multiple economic spirits. These spirits shape economic behavior and, in so doing, affect economic outcomes. These spirits are also cultural phenomena. Different cultural milieus give rise to different economic spirits. "The spirit of enterprise," as Lavoie and Chamlee-Wright (2000: 69) summarize,

> comes in many different flavors. Each culture creates a unique entrepreneurial pattern; each culture articulates its own genre of stories in which economic leaders achieve wealth-generating success within the specific institutional and customary contours of the society in which they live.

In the next chapter, I argue that focusing on the economic spirits that animate particular markets does not require economists to abandon economic analysis. Individuals can still be said to engage in purposeful behavior and even to seek to satisfy their preferences. They still respond to incentives. Individuals, however, cannot be assumed to be social morons with simplistic and static preference orderings. Individuals are neither isolated actors nor are they robots who respond automatically to stimuli. Instead, they are cultural creatures and the markets that they generate through their activities are cultural phenomena. The strategies they employ as they pursue their objectives are culturally derived. The way they interpret and respond to incentives is influenced by culture.

Similarly, focusing on the economic spirits that animate particular markets does not require that we downplay the role of institutions. Institutions can still be conceived of as points of orientation that individuals rely on to guide their actions. They can still be viewed as being critical in explaining why some societies prosper (i.e. those with an institutional matrix characterized by private property and the rule of law) and those that do not prosper (e.g. an institutional matrix that rewards piracy). Institutions, however, cannot be viewed as operating independent of culture. Institutions are both culturally derived and culturally mediated.

Focusing on the economic spirits that animate particular markets, however, does require that economists extend their empirical toolkits to include qualitative methods. Econometric efforts to study the relationship between culture and economic behavior must rely on imprecise and misleading measures of culture and seek only to establish whether or not a relationship, in fact, exists. Questions about how culture affects economic behavior and why economic actors made certain choices and not others do not readily lend themselves to quantitative empirical approaches. Instead, if the goal is to get at the meanings that individuals attach to their actions and, so, at the spirits that animate their behavior, then ethnography, archival research, and in-depth case analysis become the preferred methods.

5 This does *not* mean that economists have to abandon economics

Understanding a society's economic culture is a matter of identifying the critical characteristics as well as examining the cultural and historical roots of the economic spirits that shape economic behavior and color economic life in that context. Max Weber attempted to do just that when he identified the spirit of modern capitalism as the animating spirit of the type of capitalism found in Western Europe and in the United States. Although his effort failed on several margins, it succeeded in giving economists a model for studying how culture shapes economic decisions and outcomes. Instead of thinking of a society's economic culture as a form of capital and of a society as either possessing or failing to possess the appropriate manner or magnitude of cultural capital needed to attain economic success, Weber viewed the nature of economic life in a society as being partially the result of the economic attitudes and values that exist in that society. And, then, he attempted to identify the origins and to trace out the effects of those attitudes and values.

At first blush, this approach to examining economic culture seems a radical departure from contemporary economic theory and empirical methods. It would seem to require that economists talk a lot more about eerie concepts such as economic spirits and talk a lot less about concrete concepts such as prices, profits and property rights. It would seem to require that economists become more like their siblings in the neighboring social sciences and their cousins in the humanities and that they reject the powerful weapons in their scientific arsenal such as rational choice theorizing and institutional analysis and empirical testing. In fact, it would seem to require that economists abandon economics in order to study economic culture.

Admittedly, very few economists worth the title would buy an appreciation for economic culture if it meant that they had to give up the theories and tools of economics (as they understand the term) in exchange. At that price, the quantity demanded would be extremely low.

Arguably, this concern (i.e. that advancing culturally informed explanations of economic phenomena would necessarily crowd out economic theorizing about economic phenomena) partially explains why economists have been so reluctant to incorporate cultural considerations into their inquiries. Recourse to cultural explanations, they believe, is unwelcomed and unnecessary. This concern that cultural and economic explanations are at some fundamental level incompatible also explains the strategies for incorporating cultural considerations into economics that are adopted by those few economists who are concerned with how culture can impact economic behavior and results. By treating culture as a form of capital (and so misrepresenting the relationship between culture and economic choices and outcomes) they avoid any potential conflict between studying economic culture and continuing to practice economics.

Ignoring or misrepresenting the impact of culture on economic affairs, however, are not the only two nor are they the best solutions to the challenge of studying the culture of markets from within economics. Moreover, the approach to studying the culture of markets adopted here is not at all incompatible with economics. Indeed, acknowledging that every market is animated by a set of competing spirits does not require that we abandon economics. It does require, however, that economists are more thoughtful about how they pursue their analysis. And, that they are more thoughtful about how culture *as culture*, as opposed to culture *as a resource*, actually affects economic life. Arguably, focusing on culture and so the meanings that people attach to their actions and their context is an interpretive task that is not only wholly compatible with economics but necessary if economics is to be a useful tool in explaining economic behavior and outcomes in the real world.

Adopting this approach does require a departure from contemporary economic theory and empirical methods. But the required departure is more important, as I have argued, than most economists suppose and is not as radical, as I will argue below, as it appears on first blush.

This approach does not require that we reject rational choice

There are those who worry and even argue that focusing on how culture affects economic behavior is incompatible with a rational choice approach to studying economic behavior.[1] Recall, for instance, that Stigler and Becker (1977) have suggested that tastes do not differ significantly between individuals. In their view, all differences or changes in people's choices can be traced to differences in prices and incomes. Tastes, Stigler and Becker (ibid.: 76) argue, can be viewed as "stable over time and similar among people . . . widespread and/or persistent human behavior can be explained by a generalized calculus of utility-maximizing behavior, without introducing the qualification 'tastes remaining the same.'" As such, cultural differences, such as they are, can and ought to be endogenized; they are to be explained by economics not used to explain differences in economic outcomes.[2] "All changes in behavior," Stigler and Becker (ibid.: 89) insist, "are explained by changes in prices and incomes, precisely the variables that organize and give power to economic analysis."

Jackson (2009) has, similarly, suggested that cultural arguments are incompatible with (neoclassical) economics. According to Jackson (ibid.: 202), "neoclassical theory is [necessarily] ahistorical, claims universal relevance, plays down institutions, understates human creativity, has no sense of culture as process, evades social evolution, and models economic development in terms of equilibrium or adjustment towards equilibrium." Although disagreeing with Stigler and Becker on the degree to which economics is impoverished by the exclusion of cultural explanations, Jackson (ibid.) agrees with them that a focus on how culture affects economic behavior is incompatible with neoclassical economics. According to Jackson (ibid.),

> a cultural perspective does not forbid instrumental rationality but sees it as one particular, socially specific mode of behavior among others . . . unless orthodoxy drops its fascination with neoclassical theory and stops identifying neoclassicism with the economic way of thinking, the chances for a culturally informed economics are minimal.

Not surprisingly, rational choice explanations of social phenomena are often contrasted with cultural explanations.[3] Cultural considerations, however, need not be viewed as being inconsistent with (neoclassical) economics. Indeed, if a rational choice perspective is to be viewed as being capable of explaining *all* purposeful human behavior then it must make reference to culture. As I argued earlier, the choice before economists is not between employing culture and not employing culture. Instead, it is a choice between implicitly and explicitly employing culture.

Although acknowledging the impact that culture has on economic behavior does not require that we reject rational choice, it would involve abandoning conceptions of economic man as a rational fool.[4] Consider, for instance, Sen's (1977) critique of the behavioral assumptions of neoclassical economic theory. According to Sen (ibid.: 317), the notion that human beings are self-seeking egoists, that every actor is animated only by self-interest (sometimes but not invariably defined quite narrowly) has dominated economics since the nineteenth century. Its dominance, as Sen (ibid.: 322) explains, has much to do with economists' ability to "define a person's interests in such a way that no matter what he does he can be seen to be furthering his own interests in every isolated act of choice." The investor pursuing ever greater returns on his investment, the athlete pursuing ever greater success on the playing field, the brave soldier attempting to kill as many of the enemy as possible, the religious zealot attempting to win as many converts as he can and the committed altruist who spends every waking moment attempting to make the world a better place can all be described as self-seeking egoists. The trick, as it were, is to properly define their self-interests. In this sense, being rational simply means being consistent. "A person's choices," Sen (ibid.: 323) explains,

> are considered "rational" in this approach if and only if these choices can all be explained in terms of some preference relation consistent with the revealed preference definition, that is, if all his choices can be explained as the choosing of "most preferred" alternatives with respect to a postulated preference relation.[5]

Admittedly, if rational choice is to be conceived of in this way then cultural considerations are necessarily outside of the scope of rational choice theorizing.[6]

Unless, of course, culture's impact on choices is left implicit or culture is reduced to an object of choice (i.e. treated as a form of capital). But, as Sen (ibid.) explains, this way of conceiving of rational choice

> presumes both too little and too much: too little because there are non-choice sources of information on preference and welfare as these terms are usually understood, and too much because choice may reflect a compromise among a variety of considerations of which personal welfare may be just one.

Specifically, Sen (ibid.: 326) insists that commitment is an important ingredient in many types of human behavior but that rational choice defined solely as internal consistency cannot make sense of it. Unlike sympathy, which could be reconciled with egoism by simply treating regard for others as being in an individual's self-interest, because commitment involves individuals acting counter-preferentially it cannot be easily reconciled with rational choice. As Sen (ibid.: 327) explains, "one way of defining commitment is in terms of a person choosing an act that he believes will yield a lower level of personal welfare to him than an alternative that is also available to him." Commitment may also be said to be at work in the more difficult to ascertain "cases in which the person's choice, while maximizing anticipated personal welfare, would be unaffected under at least one counterfactual condition in which the act chosen would cease to maximize personal welfare" (ibid.). Sen has in mind here choices that people in actuality make out of concern for duty or a sense of right and wrong that do not necessarily lower their personal welfare.[7] Think of the religious devotee who offers prayers soon after waking every morning and gets some personal satisfaction from praying but engages in prayer because she views it as a moral obligation and not because she enjoys doing it. Of course, in this example, we might suggest that she is concerned with the net present value of the welfare that accrues from prayer including the riches that she believes will accrue to her in the afterlife from her living a devout life.[8] However, if she would pray regardless of whether or not the anticipated costs outweighed the expected benefits then she can still be said to be acting out of commitment and not in pursuit of her self-interest. "Commitment," Sen (ibid.: 329) summarizes,

> drives a wedge between personal choice and personal welfare, and much of traditional economic theory relies on the identity of the two. . . . The basic link between choice behavior and welfare achievements in the traditional models is severed as soon as commitment is admitted as an ingredient of choice.

Again, this is because commitment implies counter-preferential choice.

Sen (ibid.: 336) has, thus, argued that any description of human beings that leaves out the potential for commitment to sway choices and insists on there being "no inconsistencies in [his] choice behavior . . . must [view him as] a bit of a fool." According to Sen (ibid.), "the purely economic man is indeed close to being a social moron."

Actual human beings, Sen (ibid.) suggests, are far more complex. Accounting for human beings as they are, however, does not require that economists abandon rational choice or stop conceiving of humans as rational agents but it does require that they abandon conceiving of human beings as rational fools (ibid.: 342).[9] As Sen (ibid.: 336) summarizes, "to make room for the different concepts related to [economic man's] behavior we need a more elaborate structure." Sen (ibid.: 337) suggests that this more elaborate structure involves economists also considering individuals' "rankings of their preference rankings."[10] Individuals can and do have multiple preference orderings, can and do consider the consequences of adopting any of their various preference orderings, and can and do rank those various preference orderings. As Sen (ibid.) explains, these "meta-rankings" (i.e. rankings of preference rankings) can be used to explain the adoption of a particular political ideology over another, or a particular set of moral precepts over another, or to express preferences that individuals do not currently hold but wished that they did.[11]

Actual human beings are, thus, not rational fools but are also cultural creatures. Their cultures offer them a bundle of different preference orderings that they must decide between (i.e. competing economic spirits). Understanding economic life would, thus, seem to require economists to attempt to unearth the various economic spirits that can animate economic life (in a particular context) and then explain how those economic spirits can and do affect economic behavior. Recognizing this does not require that economists jettison rational choice but it does auger for a more thoughtful approach (i.e. one perhaps reformulated along the lines that Sen suggests).

In the final section of this chapter, I describe which empirical approach is likely to be most effective if the goal is to identify and describe the economic spirits that animate economic life in a particular context. In the next section, however, I argue that examining the culture of markets does not require that we downplay the role of institutions.

This approach does not require that we downplay the role of institutions

Since the role carved out for the culture of markets (i.e. as a system of attitudes and values that shapes how individuals identify, evaluate and choose between alternatives) is so similar to the role typically ascribed to institutions (i.e. "humanly devised constraints that shape human interaction" and "structure incentives in human exchange" [North 1990: 3]), it may make sense to treat them as substitutes within economic analysis and to adopt the one that offers the most empirical oomph. Indeed, my insistence that economists focus on the culture of markets (as something independent from the institutional environment in which markets are embedded) can be read as a privileging of the role of culture over the role of institutions. It is, thus, possible to argue that a foregrounding of the role that culture plays in shaping economic behavior and coloring economic outcomes along the lines that I propose here shrouds the important role that institutions play in determining economic choices and results.

There are, of course, those who reject cultural explanations in favor of institutional arguments on the grounds that it is institutions and not culture that are doing the meaningful work in the actual world. As North (1990: 3) explains,

> institutions reduce uncertainty by providing structure to everyday life. They are a guide to human interaction, so that when we wish to greet friends on the street, drive an automobile, buy oranges, borrow money, form a business, bury our dead, or whatever, we know (or can learn easily) how to perform these tasks. . . . institutions define and limit the set of choices of individuals.[12]

This way of defining institutions either treats culture as a subset of institutions or leaves very little scope for culture to play a role, independent of institutions, in shaping an individual's choices and actions.[13] If culture matters at all, it works through institutions and only indirectly influences economic behavior and outcomes. As such, it is institutions and not culture that should be doing the meaningful work in any economic analysis.

Culture, goes this view, only need enter into an economist's analysis, if at all, as an explanation for why certain institutions come to be adopted and/or continue to be effective.[14] North (1990, 2005), for instance, has argued that institutions embody, are determined by and are an external manifestation of a society's cultural beliefs and moral codes.[15] Formal institutions, North (2005: 49) asserts, express the worldviews and values of those who possess political power. "The structure of an economic market," North (ibid.: 50) writes,

> reflects the beliefs of those in a position to make the rules of the game, who enact rules that will produce the outcomes (that is, the sort of market) they desire, whether those desires are to create monopoly or to create a competitive market (always with the caveat that their beliefs may be incorrect and produce unanticipated consequences).

Moreover, as North (1990: 37) has argued, culture is the source of informal institutions. "Culture," as North (ibid.: 42) explains, "defines the way individuals process and utilize information and hence may affect the way informal constraints get specified." The norms, practices and codes of conduct in an economic market are culturally derived.[16]

Similarly, Lavoie and Chamlee-Wright (2000) have made the point that economic practices and policies will only prove effective if they fit the society's culture.[17] As such, the "same practices" that fail in one context "might yield positive results if they reflect and accommodate the particular cultural context elsewhere" (ibid.: 74). Chamlee-Wright (2005: 15) has, likewise, argued that a society's institutions are more or less effective depending on how embedded they are within its culture. "People involved in codifying the rules," Chamlee-Wright (ibid.) explains, "are not *creating* rules of property or contract or norms of behavior, they are *discovering* and articulating what has already evolved." If, instead, the rules that they introduce are unrelated to their society's culture, those rules are unlikely to bring about social coordination. "If they are to work," she (ibid.) writes, "the rules of society must fit well within and must be supported by the cultural context."[18]

Utilizing a taxonomy of institutions that characterizes them as foreign-introduced exogenous (FEX) institutions, indigenously introduced exogenous (IEX) institutions and indigenously introduced endogenous (IEN) institutions, Boettke et al. (2008) also argue that cultural fit determines which institutions are likely to "stick" and, so, which institutions are likely to be successful. Exogenous institutions are created and imposed by formal authorities (either foreign agencies or national governments). Indigenous institutions are not imposed from above but instead reflect local norms, customs and practices. According to Boettke et al. (ibid.: 337), IEN institutions are likely to be more sticky than both FEX and IEX institutions because they are grounded in "mētis" (i.e. the society's cultural practices and expectations). Although not as grounded in mētis as IEN institutions, IEX institutions have a greater likelihood of being grounded in mētis and to stick than FEX institutions since they are developed by local authorities who are themselves grounded in the cultural context. Only where FEX institutions dovetail with mētis will they stick. Boettke et al. (ibid.) argue that their proximity to mētis explains why post-war reconstruction efforts succeeded in Germany and Japan after World War II but failed in Bosnia after the Dayton Peace Agreement.

As I have argued, however, culture plays a more direct role in influencing economic life than in simply determining which institutions are adopted and prove to be effective. Moreover, culture also plays a direct role in influencing how institutions come to be understood and experienced. To ascribe culture an independent and direct role in shaping economic behavior and outcomes as well as in mediating institutions, however, does not require downplaying the role of institutions; the formal and informal rules of the game do matter. It does, however, involve acknowledging that institutions are not only culturally derived and supported but are also culturally filtered; the rules are necessarily seen through culture. Stated another way, economists should simultaneously resist the temptation to collapse culture into institutions and the temptation to ignore cultural considerations as they pursue their institutional analysis.[19] They should, instead, view culture and institutions as separate but linked.

Billig (2000) has made a similar point. According to Billig (ibid.: 783), there is a "relationship between culture and legal, organizational, and political institutions" that is "mutual, interactive, and dynamic." Institutions, as Billig (ibid.: 771) explains, are animated by culture. "Culture," for Billig (ibid.: 772), is neither "a separate and isolated 'box' apart from social, political, and economic life" nor "a looming set of traditions and precepts immune to the innovative action of individual agents."[20] Rather, it gives content and character to institutions.[21] The "same" institutions are, thus, likely to have different meanings and to be given different moral weights in different cultures. For example, the moral meanings and import associated with failing to greet a subordinate as you enter your workplace, or with lying to a potential customer, or with stealing office supplies from your place of employment are likely to be culturally specific even if there exists very similar if not identical de jure and de facto rules around greeting strangers (even subordinates) in the morning, and against lying (even to potential customers), and against stealing (even from your own workplace) in many cultures. The culturally specific moral weights associated with violating certain formal and informal constraints (i.e. of real consequence in some cultures and forgivable in others) impacts the (subjective) costs of violating those constraints and so the likelihood that individuals will do so. Understanding the culture of markets, thus, does not require an ignoring of institutions in favor of culture but a "focus on the nexus between institutions (viewed at many levels) and culture (construed in this dynamic and non-reified way)" (Billig 2000: 780).

But empirical efforts to explore the spirits that animate markets ought to be qualitative

If the aim is to explore the economic spirits that animate real world markets, then thick descriptions (i.e. archival social history, ethnography and in-depth case analysis) become the favored approaches. Although focusing on the economic spirits that animate markets does not require economists reject economics, it does require that they embrace alternative empirical methods. There are reasons to believe that quantitative empirical methods (alone) cannot accomplish the task. First, the kinds of questions that lend themselves to quantitative empirical responses are (for the most part) quite different than questions about why certain economic spirits evolved and how those spirits shape economic life. Second, treating culture as a form of capital and scoring cultures is arguably a natural outgrowth of seeking to answer questions about how culture impacts economic behavior and outcomes using quantitative methods.

Arguably, quantitative empirical techniques are best suited for questions about whether or not there is a relationship between two (quantifiable) phenomena. Indeed, there are some questions that can only be adequately explored by using quantitative measures and employing statistical methods. For instance, whether or not there is a relationship between how well countries perform on certain areas and indicators of economic well-being is a question that begs for a quantitative examination. If, say, levels of entrepreneurship and the percentage of a population that report being comfortable with uncertainty are correlated, then there is some reason, albeit not a definitive reason, to believe that a relationship does exist. If, on the other hand, these measures are not correlated, then there is some reason, again not a definitive reason, to believe that a relationship does not exist. The same rationale holds for utilizing more advanced statistical techniques such as regression analysis, which reveals the relationship between one variable and the other variables that are believed to "explain" it.

Of course, there are several reasons why discovering a quantitative relationship of this sort can never (by itself) allow us to be certain of a relationship between two phenomena. Continuing with the example above, it is possible that the measures that we used for attitudes toward uncertainty and levels of entrepreneurship are poor measures of the actual phenomena. If our measures are imperfect, then the meaning of any statistical association between them is suspect. Moreover, even if our measures are perfect, the statistical relationship that we find can still be spurious. It is possible that a higher level of comfortableness with uncertainty does not lead to more entrepreneurship or that a higher level of entrepreneurship does not lead to higher levels of comfortableness with uncertainty, even though the two are correlated. A third, yet to be determined, variable might explain both. Although sophisticated statistical techniques have been developed to mitigate this danger, it can never be fully overcome.

Ultimately, recourse to a theoretical proposition that points to and argues for a particular (causal) relationship and interpreting the quantitative findings in light of other relevant (quantitative and qualitative) information is unavoidable if the social scientist is to make sense of his results. This has been a common critique of econometrics. Leontief (1971), for instance, has argued that many econometric efforts are more concerned with the application of ever more sophisticated statistical techniques to empirical problems than with how closely their assumptions and results track reality.[22] Econometricians, he suggests, are more likely to adopt more sophisticated techniques than to seek more varied and more accurate data sources. Leamer (1991) has, similarly, pointed to the poverty of useful data sources available to econometricians and the fragile nature of the inferences that can be made from the data they do utilize. Additionally, Hendry (1980) has openly questioned whether econometrics is more akin to alchemy than to real science. And, Mankiw (1995) has argued that econometric studies, particularly those studies that examine the causes of economic growth, tend to suffer from issues of simultaneity, multicollinearity, and degrees of freedom.

However, that there are very real challenges associated with adopting quantitative empirical approaches is not the sole reason why they are arguably inappropriate for the study of the culture of markets;[23] to be sure, qualitative methods have their own pitfalls.[24] Instead, privileging of quantitative over qualitative methods is problematic with regards to questions of how culture impacts economic behavior and outcomes because quantitative approaches tend to distort empirical research in this area. As Rizzo (1978: 53) writes, "not all issues of interest are quantifiable. If we try to explain complex phenomena only by reference to quantifiable variables, then we are likely to be throwing away some information that we do, indeed, have." Privileging quantitative over qualitative approaches encourages social scientists to pursue certain kinds of questions and to disregard others. It also limits them to offering certain kinds of answers when they attempt to answer those questions. And, in the worst cases, privileging quantitative over qualitative approaches pushes the social scientists to assign quantitative measures to phenomena that might not be measurable. As Hayek (1952: 89) argued, this insistence on assigning measures to phenomena that cannot be measured

> is probably responsible for the worst aberrations and absurdities produced by scientism in the social sciences. It not only leads frequently to the selection for study of the most irrelevant aspects of the phenomena because they happen to be measurable, but also to "measurements" and assignments of numerical values which are absolutely meaningless.

As noted earlier, even those who advance quantitative approaches for the empirical examination of the relationship between culture and economics are concerned about their ability to really "measure" culture. Recall, for instance, Tabellini's (2008: 262) confession that the measures of culture that he employs (taken from the *World Values Survey*) are at best "imperfect indicators" of the phenomena in question. And, recall his recognition that "not only are [values] measured with error, but their interpretation is also somewhat ambiguous" (ibid.). Notice also that these studies have tended to be efforts to establish that there is a relationship between culture and economic outcomes and not to explain how the two are connected. Again, as Tabellini (2010: 711) confesses, "culture" in his work "is still largely a black box." Additionally, statistical attempts to establish that there is a relationship between culture and economic outcomes (necessarily) treat culture as a form of capital.[25] Whatever measures of a country's cultural characteristics are adopted, they enter into the econometric models alongside and perform the same function as measures of that country's stock of financial, human, social, physical and other forms of capital.

If economics is a science that recognizes people's thoughts and beliefs as the essential data and is concerned with the culture of markets, then the privileging qualitative over quantitative methods of apprehending history is more appropriate. Stated another way, any empirical approach that hopes to illustrate and complement a social science that aims at recovering the meanings that individuals attach to their actions and environments would necessarily emphasize thick descriptions.[26] Indeed, Mises (1957: 280) has argued that "thymological analysis," which tries to discover how and why people at specific times valued and acted in different ways, "is essential for the study of history."[27] Similarly, Hayek (1952: 88) has criticized "the common tendency to disregard all the 'merely' qualitative phenomena and to concentrate, on the model of the natural sciences, on the quantitative aspects of what is measurable."

Although, as Hayek (1952: 26) suggests, even if it is possible to rely on introspection and then extrapolation to other minds when we are theorizing, we can do much better when we engage in empirical/historical studies. Rather than making guesses based on introspection, people's beliefs and thoughts are arguably better accessed by observing what they do and asking them what they believe and think, by looking closely at their social, political and economic environments, by examining their religious rituals and creeds, by listening to the stories that they tell one another, the poems that they recite and the songs that they sing. The economist who wishes to understand economic life in a particular context, for instance, might very well have to pay attention to phenomena that might influence or be influenced by economic factors in addition to purely economic phenomena.[28]

Geertz has described this process as attempting to "see things from the native's point of view." As he (1983: 57) explains, the aim is

> to produce an interpretation of the way a people live which is neither imprisoned within their mental horizons, an ethnography of witchcraft as written by the witch, nor systematically deaf to the distinctive tonalities of their existence, an ethnography of witchcraft as written by a geometer.

The applied social scientist does not uncritically (re)present what the native has expressed. Nor is his role to assume that his way of seeing is necessarily superior to the views of the individuals he is studying; he is not "endowed with a kind of supermind, with some sort of absolute knowledge, which makes it unnecessary for him to start from what is known by the people whose actions he studies" (Hayek 1952: 90). He does not merely voice their sentiments nor does he deign to speak on their behalf. Instead, "seeing things from the native's point of view" requires that we try to gain insight into how people see their own selves and situations by mining their archives, reading their literature, listening to their folklore and praise songs, conducting interviews, and living among them. But it also means that we should attempt to situate and explain what Geertz calls "experience-near concepts" (what people believe and think) with the aid of "experience-distant concepts" (the theoretical tools we have at our disposal like rational choice economic theory). The ethnographer's task is not to put "oneself into someone else's skin" but "to grasp concepts that, for another people, are experience-near, and to do so well enough to place them in illuminating connection with experience-distant concepts theorists have fashioned to capture the general features of social life" (Geertz 1983: 58).

Additionally, representing "experience-near concepts" with the help of "experience-distant concepts" suggests that (in our empirical work) we should be developing thick over thin descriptions. It should, however, be noted that to recognize that the facts of the social sciences are what people believe and think and so to privilege thick descriptions in empirical/applied enterprises in no way suggests that we should abandon thin descriptions of the social world in our theoretical endeavors. On the contrary, thick descriptions are only possible if they are informed by thin descriptions. As Boettke (2001: 253) writes,

> we need, in other words, both "thin" and "thick" description for our social theory to possess both meaning and relevance—coherence and correspondence so to speak. . . . The justification of the "thin description" of economic theory is that it affords us more compelling "thick descriptions" of the social experience of particular times and places.

Without a thin description of what distinguishes a twitch from a wink (i.e. one is an involuntary act and the other a conspiratorial gesture), thick descriptions of the situation would also fail to distinguish between the two. Stated another way, without theory/models that explain a phenomenon while abstracting away much of the social detail, without "experience-distant concepts" to use Geertz's formulation, the applied social scientist could not make sense of social life, he could not offer thick descriptions. At best, he would be able to offer detailed accounts of social phenomena that offered little to aid our understanding. Though detail is necessary for an applied social science that tries to capture what people believe and think, it is not sufficient. Specifically, an effort to explore the culture of markets in some context must rely on thin theoretical accounts of how culture affects economic behavior (i.e. economic life is everywhere animated by one or more culturally derived economic spirits) as well as rich empirical detail about that context (i.e. in place x the economic spirits y and z are at work).

Chamlee-Wright (2010b, 2011) has made a similar point. According to Chamlee-Wright (2010a), efforts to understand complex social phenomena are akin to an attempt to solve a gigantic three-dimensional puzzle where the pieces are not only being manipulated by outside forces but are moving of their own volition. Because of this dynamism, she explains, there exists no picture that can serve as a guide to solving the puzzle. Social scientists faced with the task of making sense of such complexity, as she offers, may decide that taking a somewhat "aerial" view of the puzzle helps them to see the picture more clearly, to determine the most important parts of it, and to compare it to other puzzles or the same puzzle over time. They often use econometric techniques in an attempt to simplify their task. Or, as she notes, they may use experimental methods in order to observe how parts of the puzzle behave under controlled conditions. These methods, Chamlee-Wright (ibid.: 324) argues, are not always sufficient. As she (ibid.) explains, "by itself, the aerial view does not tell us much about why the changes are happening and why the patterns we observe emerge." Additionally, not all questions can be explored in a laboratory setting.

Instead, Chamlee-Wright (ibid.) argues that qualitative approaches can be the most useful tools that economists have in their toolkits for understanding complex social phenomena. For some questions, she (ibid.: 325) writes,

> we need to come down from time to time and look at our puzzle up close. Qualitative research is like stepping inside our puzzle, so that we can understand what constitutes the environment in which our puzzle pieces (or people) are operating. We can observe individual behavior and the interactions between these living and interpreting beings. . . . Ideally we would want to talk to the people we seek to understand.

Chamlee-Wright (ibid.: 326) has in mind what she calls "interview talk" as opposed to "survey talk." Rather than simply allowing individuals to offer feedback on a set of questions for which the range of possible responses is known, interview talk "provides access to that interior life that frames problems in particular ways, allowing people to articulate their strategies relative to their mental models of how the world works" (ibid.).[29]

Chamlee-Wright (2011) further explains the advantages of qualitative methods over quantitative methods for asking questions about why and how certain things happened. "The overarching case favoring qualitative empirical methods," she (ibid.: 165) explains,

> is that they enable us to develop an economics of meaning . . . If we want to understand how people perceive their own circumstances and craft purposeful strategies of action in the face of those circumstances . . . we may find it extremely helpful to talk to them (or in the case of historical research, to read or hear what they said) in a way that is guided by the theoretical frames available to us.

Again, if the goal is to understand why individuals behaved as they did and how certain phenomena impacted their behavior, economists have to adopt qualitative methods.[30] Specifically, it would seem to require that they engage in "ethnographic field work, archival research, and in-depth case analysis" (ibid.: 166).

This is arguably particularly poignant advice for economists interested in the culture of markets; especially, since other approaches to studying the culture of markets are problematic. The student of the culture of markets should engage in ethnography, archival history or in-depth case analysis in order to discover the stories of economic success that are told in a particular community, the myths that are widely shared about the kinds of economic activities that are likely to be profitable, the individuals who are admired as heroes and the metaphors that are used to guide economic endeavors (Lavoie and Chamlee-Wright 2000: 53; Storr 2004: 35). The student of the culture of markets should construct ideal types of the economic spirits that animate economic life in a particular context, explain the origins of those ideal types and their effect on individuals' economic choices. The student of the culture of markets should be concerned with how the competing economic spirits that exist within every society shape individuals' economic behavior and those societies' economic outcomes.

Conclusion

Focusing on the culture of markets, then, does not mean that economists have to give up on economics. It does not mean that they have to reject rationality but it does require that they stop conceiving of man as a rational fool. It does not mean that they have to downplay the role of institutions but it does require that they recognize that particular spirits and institutional matrices not only have more than "an adequate relationship to each other" but that institutions are not experienced directly, and rather they are experienced through a cultural filter. And, it does not require that economists give up on doing empirical work but it does require that they embrace qualitative approaches. The concern that viewing culture as shaping economic behavior and coloring economic outcomes and foregrounding cultural explanations would somehow crowd out or overwhelm the economics in an economic analysis is simply not well founded.

Nor, to return to a discussion begun in Chapter 2, are the excuses that economists traditionally offer to explain their ignoring culture valid. Culture conceived of as worldviews and value systems is not too hazy a concept for economists to work with so long as they are prepared to engage in ethnography, archival history or in-depth case analysis. Similarly, culture need not be conceived of as the exclusive province of social scientists outside economics so long economists stop conceiving of economic man as a rational fool. And, finally, culture need not be seen as irrelevant to explanations of economic behavior so long as economists recognize that prices and institutions are culturally mediated.

Epilogue

Most economists are not concerned with how culture affects economic activity. If pressed to explain why, economists will typically argue that culture is too difficult to measure, or that considerations of culture are outside the domain of economics, or that culture does not shape economic behavior but is, instead, an artifact of economic activity. Although understandable, these reasons are not enough to justify our ignoring the role of culture in economic affairs. In fact, economists cannot really understand real world markets unless they understand the culture of markets.

Culture colors economic life and, as such, economists cannot help but make assumptions about how culture shapes economic behavior and influences economic outcomes. Of course, these assumptions can and often do remain implicit. But there are good reasons to make these assumptions explicit. First, adding culture to our models might improve their predictive power. Second, explicitly theorizing about how culture affects economic choices might improve our understanding of that relationship. Specifically, we might avoid mistakenly conceiving of culture as a form of capital and might appreciate its role in guiding people's decisions about which tools (i.e. capital goods) are available to them and which they should adopt. Third, focusing on the culture of markets might improve our understanding of economic phenomena. The meanings that actors attach to price change, profits and property are (partly) influenced by culture.

The approach to studying the culture of markets proposed here is self-consciously Weberian. Although some of Weber's central arguments in *The Protestant Ethic and the Spirit of Capitalism* have proven controversial, the method for studying the culture of markets that he develops in that book remains quite useful. That method calls for identifying the economic spirits that animate a particular market and then describing how those spirits shape economic life. Moreover, that method does not mean that economists have to reject rational choice, or downplay the role of institutions, or give up on empirical analysis. Studying the culture of markets does not overturn economics. Rather, it improves our understanding of real world markets.

Although I believe that focusing on the culture of markets yields a richer understanding of markets than is traditionally advanced by economists, it is only a partial step toward developing a complex theory of the market. Future economic research must also focus on the sociality of markets if we are to theoretically and empirically describe markets as individuals actually experience them.

As I argue elsewhere, the market is among other things a social space (Storr 2008). Despite our rhetoric regarding anonymous exchange, people, simply, do not experience the market process as an anonymous force. Of course, when our business goes under or we lose our job, we often complain that it was impersonal and cold forces beyond our control that decided our fate. But, even here, it is rarely if ever anonymous forces that are held to account. It is the banker who we have known for years who refuses to extend the loan. Or, it is the customer we have built a relationship with that is not renewing her order. Or, it is the company where we have worked for ten years that is laying us (and us in particular) off. The market is not an unknown thing that we are detached from. It is, if you will, up close and personal.

Our typifications of the market are not anonymous but are instead quite concrete. The baker and the brewer are usually not strangers but people that we deal with regularly. We may not rely on the beneficence of the butcher, the baker and the brewer to get our daily meals but we do expect to know their names and over time develop meaningful connections with them. In the real world, repeated dealings not one-shot games predominate. As such, the places we frequent do not exist for us as anonymous typifications. We do not go to "a barbershop." We go to "Jason's Barbershop." We do not go to "a grocery store." We go to "Giant Food" or "Whole Foods" or "Trader Joe's." Even when we are interacting with a new barber at Jason's Barbershop or a new cashier at Whole Foods, our frequent interactions with barbers and cashiers at these establishments means that we view them as more than strangers. The organizations that we deal with regularly (and their employees) become entities that we feel that we know, can trust and to whom we want to be loyal.

Moreover, there is a potential for market relationships to develop into social friendships. Indeed, individuals see the market as not just a space for dickering but also as a social space where social content often overlays economic relations and where social friendships are developed and maintained. We buy our weekly groceries from the same stores and through the course of our dealings come to be acquainted with the clerks, the cashiers, the managers and even the owners. We eat lunch every workday at the same few restaurants and so come to know the hostesses and the waitresses. We attend happy hour at the same bar every Friday night, get our haircut at the same barber every fortnight and use the same accountant at tax time every year and, as a result, we are on a first name basis and become quite friendly with our bartender, our barber and our accountant. It is quite normal for coworkers to eat dinner at each other's homes and for their kids to have play dates. Most of our experiences in the market are not with strangers. And, though they begin that way, like our interactions at church or in our clubs, the people we routinely interact with in the market do not remain strangers for long. Arguably, these relationships that develop in markets can be as meaningful as connections developed elsewhere. Market relationships can and do develop into relationships characterized by feelings of trust and, therefore, the potential of betrayal. A variety of social bonds do often develop in markets.

Social bonds can also be strengthened in and because of markets. By allowing individuals to resolve their differences without violence, by making it possible for transactions to be positive rather than zero sum games, the market creates fertile soil for the development of social friendships. Similarly, shopping and consuming can be social activities that provide an opportunity for friends to deepen their bonds. Geographically dispersed communities and friendships are also made possible by the communication and transportation services available because of the market. By making geographically dispersed communities possible, the market and the technological developments it spurs allow individuals to be more selective about whom they want to engage and to maintain the relationships that they value most if they become separated by distance.

As economists, we should make every effort to understand how individuals actually experience markets. The arguments developed here explore why and how economists should think about the culture of markets. The few hints offered above suggest that it is also important for economists to focus on the sociality of markets. Individuals certainly do not experience the market in a cultural vacuum nor do they experience the conversation of the market as a conversation with strangers. Instead, individuals experience the market as an extension of culture where relationships become overlaid with social content and social friendships develop. Because market relations do not remain unfamiliar with each other, market relationships have the potential to develop into social friendships. Similarly, by framing how individuals experience markets, how entrepreneurs perceive opportunities, how individuals determine which goals to pursue, culture deeply affects economic activity. As the brief discussion above suggests, economists should not deliberately abstract from the extra-economic relationships occurring in markets. Similarly, as discussed throughout this book, economists qua economists should be in the business of trying to understand the culture of markets.

Notes

Preface

1 "The Market as a Social Space: On the Meaningful Extra-Economic Conversations that Can Occur in Markets," was presented at the Colloquium on Market Institutions & Economic Processes, C. V. Starr Center for Applied Economics, Department of Economics, New York University, New York, NY, December 2006. Professor Kirzner's correspondence is dated December 27, 2006. The paper was published as Storr (2008).

2 Kirzner would tell me as much in his comments on my paper (with frequent co-author Arielle John) about the determinants of entrepreneurial alertness. In that paper, Storr and John (2011) argue that "rather than closing off inquiry, [Kirzner's] theory of entrepreneurship makes a fruitful analysis of the psychological characteristics of entrepreneurs and the determinants of alertness possible." These psychological characteristics, we argued, are mediated by culture. Kirzner, as the 2010 Upton Scholar at Beloit College, was given an opportunity to comment on my presentation of this paper, which was one of several efforts to engage his oeuvre.

1 Introduction

1 See Wilk and Cliggett (2007) for an excellent overview of the literature on how culture impacts economic life within economic anthropology. See Zelizer (2010) for an important recent contribution to the discussion of economic culture within economic sociology. Several recent studies within entrepreneurial studies have, similarly, explored how culture impacts how entrepreneurs discover and exploit profit opportunities. See, for instance, Freytag and Thurik (2010) for an overview. Much of the literature on culture and entrepreneurship builds on Hofstede's (1980, 2001) observation that cultures that are more individualistic, more masculine, more comfortable with uncertainty and that have low power distance (i.e. members of the society do not accept that power is distributed unequally) are more consistent with entrepreneurship; see, especially, Shane (1992, 1993), Davidsson (1995) and Hayton et al. (2002).

2 Elsewhere, Greif (1997) has described cultural beliefs as a common pool resource that helps individuals to coordinate their activities. Greif (ibid.: 239) argues that "cultural beliefs [are] . . . a common resource that affects the social and organizational development of societies and hence economic performance." And,

> when a game has a unique equilibrium, following the usual methodology in economics, one may assume that this equilibrium would be reached independent

of previous behavioral beliefs. When a game has multiple equilibria, however, behavioral beliefs affect the selection of an equilibrium.

(ibid.: 255)

3   Greif (1994: 917) explains that both groups of traders, however, were able to solve the merchant-agent commitment problem. As he (ibid.) explains,

the Maghribis and the Genoese faced a similar environment, employed comparable naval technology, and traded in similar goods. The efficiency of their trade depended, to a large extent, on their ability to mitigate an organizational problem related to a specific transaction, namely, the provision of the services required for handling a merchant's goods abroad. A merchant could either provide these services himself by traveling between trade centers or hire overseas agents in trade centers abroad to handle his merchandise. Employing agents was efficient, since it saved the time and risk of traveling, allowed diversifying sales across trade centers, and so forth. Yet without supporting institutions, agency relations could not be established since an agent could embezzle the merchant's goods. Anticipating this behavior, a merchant would not hire an agent to begin with. For agents to be employed, the organization of society had to enable them to commit themselves ex ante to be honest ex post, after receiving the merchant's goods. The societal organization of the Maghribis and the Genoese enabled them to mitigate this commitment problem.

They, however, solve this problem in different ways.

4   As Greif (1994: 922) writes,

When the Maghribis began trading in the Mediterranean early in the eleventh century and when the Genoese began trading toward the end of that century, they had already internalized different cultures and were in the midst of different social and political processes. Their cultural heritage and the nature of these processes suggest that among the Maghribis a collectivist equilibrium was a natural focal point, whereas among the Genoese an individualist equilibrium was the natural focal point.

5   See Greif and Tabellini (2010) for a similar discussion of how different initial value systems and social arrangements in China and Europe led to the adoption of different institutional arrangements to solve collective active problems. Collectivist cultures such as the Chinese, they argue, tend to rely on informal enforcement mechanisms and moral obligations to sustain cooperation. Individualist cultures such as the Europeans, they explain, however, tend to rely more on formal enforcement mechanisms and generalized notions of morality to engender social cooperation.

6   The Old Institutionalists and the Austrians are possible exceptions. Kreps (1990) is another possible exception. Kreps (ibid.), however, suggests that culture impacts economic behavior in a least two distinct ways: (a) where multiple equilibria exist culture allows the players of a game to predict which strategies the other players will pursue, and (b) culture can stand in when it is difficult to identify all the relevant contingencies in advance by giving players a lens through which to evaluate new circumstances as they arise (e.g. defining what counts as cooperation). See Hermalin (2001) for a useful reconsideration of Kreps' model that highlights the differences between these two functions that Kreps assigns to culture. This first task of culture is more akin to the role that economists typically ascribe to (informal) institutions which

act as points of orientation that help actors select between competing strategies when there are multiple equilibria. The first task of culture (i.e. as a coordinating device) is also very similar to the role that Dasgupta (2003: 56–9) assigns to culture. The second role is much closer to what I want to highlight here. Interestingly, Kreps' exposition of this second role of culture has proven vulnerable to criticism from (a certain group of) economists. As Hermalin (2001: 230) explains

> the second interpretation of culture offered by Kreps is that of culture as a way of categorizing future unforeseen contingencies for the purposes of sustaining cooperative play. Although Kreps's argument is clear, a proponent of formalism in economics might fault it on the grounds that there is too much "hand waving." In particular, there is no formalization of unforeseen contingencies. . . . Whether one can adequately formalize the culture-as-defining-cooperation interpretation is an open question. Certainly, partially adequate formalizations are possible, but even these require a certain amount of 'hand waving' vis-à-vis the impact of unforeseen contingencies. To the extent one is willing to put up with hand waving, progress is possible. To the extent one is unnerved by it, future economic research on this aspect of corporate culture is on hold until the profession develops acceptable models of unforeseen contingencies and, more generally, bounded rationality.

7 There are, of course, different ways of defining culture. Indeed, Geertz's definition of culture is by no means the only definition of culture employed by economic anthropologists let alone all anthropologists and, though widely embraced, it is not even the definitive one within anthropology. See Kroeber and Kluckhohn (1952) and more recently Kuper (1999) for discussions of the various ways that culture is conceived. My point is not that these other definitions are not valid just that they are different than the one Geertz advances. They are using the same word to describe (possibly very) different things. An attempt to explain how *culture-as-defined-by-others* influences economic behavior is, thus, not an attempt to explain how *culture-as-defined-by-Geertz* is impacting economic activity. Any overlap between them is, arguably, accidental.

8 Like social structure, it might make sense to describe culture as an emergent phenomenon and to ascribe to it emergent causal powers. I am grateful to Paul Lewis for alerting me to this similarity between culture and social structure. See also Lewis (2000, 2010) for a fruitful discussion of what casual properties we ought to ascribe to emergent social phenomena. As will be discussed in subsequent chapters, Geertz (1973: 14) was quick to claim that culture as he sees it does not cause anything; meaning for him it is not the "efficient cause" of anything. It is unclear, however, if he had in mind the concept of "emergent causal powers" when he claimed no causal powers for culture. In fact, it is quite likely that Geertz would agree with Lewis that culture, like "the pattern of vested interests laid down by antecedent social stricture[,] disposes people to act in particular ways but does not compel them to do so" (Lewis 2000: 259).

9 Geertz's definition is the one adopted here for several reasons: (a) it is at root Weberian and, as will become obvious, Weber factors heavily in the analysis that follows; (b) Geertz was an economic anthropologist and so was concerned with how culture impacted economic life; and (c) most importantly, his definition is closest to my own thinking on culture. My task in this book, then, is to argue that culture-as-defined-by-Geertz colors economic life and so economists ought to pay attention to it and, then, to outline an approach to incorporating culture-as-defined-by-Geertz into economics.

One way to read this book is, thus, to read the criticisms of the various approaches to looking at the culture of markets presented in Chapter 3 as arguments that economists ought to try to understand the relationship between culture-as-defined-by-Geertz in addition to their efforts to understand how culture-as-defined-by-others affects it.

10   Notice that the claim is that this is a "risk" of this approach not an inevitability of this approach. Moreover, there might be legitimate reasons to treat culture as homogenous and static. For instance, in order to do cross group comparisons we need to homogenize to some extent (e.g. selecting a certain set of beliefs and values to represent each culture). Additionally, when analyzing how culture impacts behavior in a single period or a few periods it might make sense to treat culture as static, especially since cultural choice tends to be slow and incremental. Stated another way, there is a trade-off between tractability and representing cultures as they exist in the real world. Still, if our purpose is to explain and understand how culture is shaping behavior in a particular context then, as I will argue in Chapter 3, we ought to err on the side of thick versus thin descriptions. I am grateful to Chris Coyne for getting me to focus on this point.

11   See Billig (2000) for a discussion of how anthropologists employ Weber as they explore the relationship between culture and economics.

12   See Swedberg (1999) for a discussion of Weber's contributions to economics. The claim that Weber's influence on modern economics is minimal deserves a caveat. While true of much of the discipline, Weber is an important figure in a number of heterodox fields, especially Austrian economics. As Lachmann (1951: 413) claims in his review of Mises' *Human Action* (1949), a seminal text within Austrian economics, "in reading this book we must never forget that it is the work of Max Weber that is being carried on here." See also Lachmann (1971), Boettke (1998) and Boettke and Storr (2002) for discussions of Weber's relationship with the Austrians. As Boettke and Storr (ibid.: 173) describe, the relationship between Weber and the Austrians is "deep and symbiotic . . . they share many of the same intellectual forebears and a commitment to the same methodological approach."

13   Building on this approach, Boettke and Storr (2002) envisage the social world as consisting of three overlapping spheres: economy, polity and society. Individuals, they argue, are necessarily and simultaneously embedded in (at least) all three spheres. As such, it is impossible to neatly isolate social activity from economic and political activity, or to neatly isolate political activity from economic and social activity, or to neatly isolate economic activity from social and political activity. As they (ibid.: 169) explain, in Weber's approach "the society, the polity and the economy are elevated, if you will, to the same level of prominence and dual, and treble notions of embeddedness are conceived of and utilized."

14   As Storr (2004: 15) notes elsewhere, "Weber's interpretive science was at its core an institutional economics. Weber knew full well that *institutions matter* and believed that *looking at institutions is critical* even when considering purely economic phenomena."

15   See, for instance, Horwitz (2008) for an interesting discussion of how the form and function of families have evolved over time.

16   See Chapter 2 for a discussion of the significance, with respect to the culture of markets, of viewing social science as being chiefly concerned with meanings.

17   Admittedly, this claim is not justified here. An attempt to justify it would have to show that meanings critical to understanding the social stock of knowledge are lost during the sort of simple categorization and aggregation that necessarily accompanies quantitative approaches. This argument is advanced, returned to and developed in Chapters 4 and 5.

18 As Ringer (1997: 110) notes, "Weber's methodology, and especially his theory of interpretation, can scarcely be imagined apart from his concept of the 'ideal type.'" Similarly, as Mommsen (1989: 121) writes,

> the development and systematization of an ideal-typical method of analyzing and presenting sociological and historical knowledge is one of Max Weber's enduring achievements. This is so despite the fact that disagreement persists about the logical status and epistemological function of this method, with the result that its value is still hotly debated.

And, as Eliaeson (2002: 46) explains, "Weber's methodology is primarily about conceptualization and the problem of producing intersubjectively meaningful selections from vast and infinite reality. The tool with which he addresses this problem and reflects on its difficulties is the ideal-type." See also Kalberg (1994) for a comprehensive discussion of the use of ideal types in Weber's comparative-historical sociology.

19 As Käsler (1988: 182) explains,

> again and again Weber refuses to see the "true content" of history or its "essence" in the ideal-types he develops. He warns repeatedly of the danger of hypostatizing ideal-types as the real, driving forces in history. . . . on the one hand . . . ideal-types must be extracted from historical reality, and on the other, that [in constructing an ideal-type] a cosmos of ideational contexts, internally lacking in contradiction, is created by accentuation, to the point of creating a utopian situation.

20 As Swedberg (1998: 193) writes,

> Weber emphasizes that all the different kinds of "cultural sciences"—history, economic theory, and so on—use these ideal types, whether they are aware of it or not. To phrase it differently: the ideal type, as Weber sees it, is something that all the cultural sciences have in common and that also unites them.

This assertion parallels the arguments advanced by Menger (1985) during the *Methodenstreit*. The choice, Menger explained, was not between theory and no-theory but between explicit and implicit theory.

21 As Mommsen (1989: 124) describes,

> basically, two categories of ideal types can be distinguished in Weber's methodological writings: (1) structural types—i.e. constructs which represent structures (they may be either ideal or material in kind); (2) types of social change—i.e. constructions which represent historical processes in time. In both cases the formation of ideal-typical concepts ranges over a wide spectrum and the ideal-typical constructs differ widely in the scope of their applicability. In other words, we are dealing with ideal types of very different degrees of aggregation and complexity.

22 As Weber (1978: 21) explains,

> the ideal types of social action which for instance are used in economic theory are thus unrealistic or abstract in that they always ask what course of action would take place if it were purely rational and oriented to economic ends alone. This construction can be used to aid in the understanding of action not purely economically determined but which involves deviations arising from traditional

restraints, affects, errors, and the intrusion of other than economic purposes or considerations.

Additionally, as Käsler (1988: 183) summarizes,

> the ideal-type is used in the *systematization* of empirical-historical reality, in that its distance from the typified construction is "measured" interpretatively. The ideal-type is a *construction*—but this construction is derived from reality and is constantly examined against reality, by using the "imagination" and the nomological knowledge of the researcher.

Similarly, as Eliaeson (2002: 49) explains, "the ideal-type is helpful in order to make us observant, aware of the peculiarities in the empirical reality we are about to explain." And, as Mommsen (1989: 123) writes,

> according to Weber, ideal types are basically nomological in nature; that is, they do not possess reality in any sense . . . nor do they have a normative status of any sort. In principle, ideal types can be constructed at random, although it is obligatory to make full use of all relevant empirical information; it is intended to achieve the greatest possible conceptual clarity by accentuating those aspects which are seen to have particular significance from a specific vantage-point.

23 It might also lead to a richer conception of what a market, in fact, is (see Fleetwood 2007).
24 Although by and large economists' efforts to explore the culture of markets have tended to adopt the view of culture that I criticize here, there have been a handful of studies within economics that have adopted the approach that I am hoping to develop here, studies of the culture of markets that employ thick notions of culture and aim at understanding what really occurs in markets. For instance, McCloskey's *Bourgeois Dignity: Why Economics Can't Explain the Modern World* (2010) describes how the economic culture that emerged in the seventeenth and eighteenth centuries in northwestern Europe gave rise to the Industrial Revolution. Similarly, Chamlee-Wright's *The Cultural Foundations of Economic Development: Urban Female Entrepreneurship in Ghana* (1997) and my *Enterprising Slaves and Master Pirates: Understanding Economic Life in the Bahamas* (2004) both treat entrepreneurs as cultural characters and delve into the historical and institutional details that influence economic culture in particular contexts. While acknowledging that culture can be both economically relevant and economically conditioned, this project focuses almost exclusively on culture as an economically relevant phenomenon i.e. how culture shapes economic behavior. See, for instance, Cowen (2002) for an interesting discussion of how economic phenomena can shape cultures.
25 Ironically, some of my earlier work on the relationship between culture and economic behavior would fit quite comfortably among the studies that I criticize here (see, for instance, Storr 2002 as well as, possibly, Storr and Butkevich 2007).

2   Economists should study culture

1 Schütz (1967) points to naming as a way of contextualizing another's behavior. Calling an eye twitch a wink, for instance, places it within what Schütz calls an "objective context of meaning."
2 "Primary metaphors" are concepts that some groups of people use to make sense of their environment and, so, to guide their actions. They are, thus, also concepts that

social scientists can sometimes use to make sense of the economic actions and arrangements of various peoples.

3 See Wilk and Cliggett (2007) for a review and critique of the efforts of anthropologists to discuss how culture affects economic life. "The problem with cultural economics," they (ibid.: 142) argue,

> is that once you make rationality relative and culturally embedded, you only have two choices in evaluating or analyzing people in other cultures. The easiest course is to portray some groups as more rational than others, with all the chauvinism such a judgment implies . . . The second is to relativize *all* rationality and conclude that *no* culture is more rational than another and that scientific, objective knowledge about other cultures is therefore impossible.

In Chapters 3 and 4, I engage a handful of these studies to demonstrate the efficacy of enlisting culture in order to explain economic phenomena and propose a third direction for cultural economics that avoids chauvinism but does not embrace relativism.

4 See also Bird-David (1992b) for her use of "primary metaphors" to explain economic practices in other contexts.

5 See Levin (2008) for a review and critique of these efforts. Although economic sociologists have been somewhat reluctant to discuss the role of culture (Zelizer 1988), at least since Parsons, however, sociologists have recognized the importance of culture. As Parsons (1937: 764) explained,

> the relations of culture systems to action are highly complex. Here it is necessary to state only that they may, on the one hand, be considered as products of processes of action; on the other, as conditioning elements of further action, as for instance is true of scientific and other "ideas." The sciences of action can no more avoid concern with them than they can with "physical" facts. But the logical relation is essentially the same. They constitute unproblematical data, knowledge of which is essential to the solution of concrete problems.

6 See Zelizer (2010) for a collection of her work on how culture shapes the economy.
7 In Chapter 3, I review and critique some of these efforts.
8 Jones (1995, 2006) has described these latter two reasons as "cultural nullity." As Jones (2006: 5) explains,

> strictly speaking, [cultural nullity] can take more than one form and is often adopted unconsciously. One version is vague about whether cultures really exist but assumes that, even if they do, they are so marginal to economic concerns that they may be safely ignored. Another version accepts that cultures do exist but hypothesizes that they are creatures of the economy, able to adjust so painlessly to changing incentives that in this case, too, they may be ignored. . . . the professional culture of economists prevents most of them from seeing that culture matters at all. The topic has been left to other disciplines.

Ironically, although he is critical of this position, Jones ends up adopting a form of cultural nullity. He concludes, for instance, that culture is not particularly important. "In many instances," he (ibid.: 259) writes, "the effects are likely to be small and will wash out over time." And, cultural explanations may still be valid but we should "not expect too much" (ibid.: 260). Billig (2000: 784) has similarly observed that

> the great majority of economists will go on completely ignoring culture or invoking it without actually incorporating it into their analyses. For them culture

represents the unimportant, irrational, messy noise that we must hold constant if we ever hope to get on with formal analysis.

Alternatively, Harrison (2006: 11, 13) has argued that "the thesis of culture matters makes a lot of economists uncomfortable. . . . The reluctance of many economists to confront culture reflects in part the difficulty of quantifying cultural factors and identifying clear patterns of cause and effect." Although I recommend qualitative approaches to studying the relationship between culture and economic behavior in Chapter 5, I believe that more fundamental barriers to the inclusion of cultural considerations into economics are at work.

Although very different in tone, Jackson's (2009) discussion of why economists avoid cultural explanations is more closely aligned with the reasons that I identify. Jackson (ibid.: 187) has argued that

> economics has followed core doctrines that exclude cultural thought. This cultural vacuum was a by-product of the desire to imitate natural sciences, rather than a deliberate disavowal of culture. Most economists were busy with increasingly specialized research and felt no need to ponder the doubts raised by cultural critics—cultural thought was nullified by being ignored. Economics has not been nakedly anti-cultural, but the gist of its theories and methods has been to debar culture.

Jackson (ibid.: 202) points to three barriers to incorporating culture into economics: neoclassical theory, disciplinary boundaries and quantitative techniques. According to Jackson (ibid.: 202–3),

> [1] Neoclassical theory is ahistorical, claims universal relevance, plays down institutions, . . . an economics built on these principles will never accommodate culture properly and epitomizes the mechanistic thinking that cultural critics have abhorred. . . . [2] The economics discipline, as presently constituted, regards cultural methods as non-economic and irrelevant. In a climate of extreme specialization, cultural arguments are beyond the purview of economics. . . . [3] A third barrier to cultural thought in economics has been the mathematization of the subject.

Jackson believes that these barriers are likely to prove stubborn in the face of any effort to employ cultural considerations in economics. While I agree that disciplinary boundaries do pose a challenge to introducing cultural considerations into economics and I recommend that economists interested in the role of culture embrace qualitative methods, I do not believe that the approach that I advance is necessarily inconsistent with neoclassical economics if by neoclassical economics Jackson simply means rational choice theory. The three reasons that I argue explain why economists have little interest in culture are, thus, similar but are not identical to Jackson's "three barriers."

Lavoie (1994: 52–5) has also argued that universalism, formalism, quantitativism and causalism have kept economics from dealing with culture. In Chapter 3, I discuss how some of these philosophical presuppositions of modern economic theory have (unfortunately) influenced many of the efforts to incorporate culture into economics but I do not believe that they explain why most economists ignore culture.

9 Critiquing cultural explanations of economic development in Asia, Fukuyama (2001: 3132) goes on to argue that

Asian underdevelopment could be explained not just by culture, but also by political conditions, poor economic policy, weak institutions, global economic conditions, and a host of other factors. Those promoting culturalist interpretations usually had no empirically convincing way of demonstrating that cultural factors were indeed as important as they claimed.

10 As I will discuss and critique in Chapter 3, a number of the studies that explore how culture impacts economic behavior and outcomes rely on measures constructed from the type of survey that Tabellini utilizes.

11 This conception of economics as being concerned with certain aspects of human behavior, which Robbins describes as an *analytical* conception, is a break from *classificatory* conception of economics that the classical economists embraced which considered certain kinds of behavior as being the subject matter of economics. For instance, Marshall (1890: 14) has described economics as the

> study of men as they live and move and think in the ordinary business of life. But it concerns itself chiefly with those motives which affect, most powerfully and most steadily, man's conduct in the business part of his life.

Economics, for the classical economists, was about human beings interacting in the business sphere. Notice, then, that Robbins' argument is quite different than the one offered by Marshall (ibid.). Marshall (ibid.: 20), instead, argued that

> the side of life with which economics is specially concerned is that in which man's conduct is most deliberate, and in which he most often reckons up the advantages and disadvantages of any particular action before he enters on it. And further it is that side of his life in which, when he does follow habit and custom, and proceeds for the moment without calculation, the habits and customs themselves are most nearly sure to have arisen from a close and careful watching the advantages and disadvantages of different courses of conduct. There will not in general have been any formal reckoning up of two sides of a balance-sheet: but men going home from their day's work, or in their social meetings, will have said to one another, "It did not answer to do this, it would have been better to do that," and so on. What makes one course answer better than another, will not necessarily be a selfish gain, nor any material gain; and it will often have been argued that "though this or that plan saved a little trouble or a little money, yet it was not fair to others," and "it made one look mean," or "it made one feel mean." It is true that when a habit or a custom, which has grown up under one set of conditions, influences action under other conditions, there is so far no exact relation between the effort and the end which is attained by it. In backward countries there are still many habits and customs similar to those that lead a beaver in confinement to build himself a dam; they are full of suggestiveness to the historian, and must be reckoned with by the legislator. But in business matters in the modern world such habits quickly die away.

Additionally, Marshall (ibid.: IV. VII. 3) argues that

> the causes which control the accumulation of wealth differ widely in different countries and different ages. They are not quite the same among any two races, and perhaps not even among any two social classes in the same race. They depend much on social and religious sanctions; and it is remarkable how, when the binding force of custom has been in any degree loosened, differences of personal character

will cause neighbours brought up under like conditions to differ from one another more widely and more frequently in their habits of extravagance or thrift than in almost any other respect.

Unlike Robbins, then, Marshall did not seem to think that there was an economic aspect to all human behavior. Instead, for Marshall, there were spheres of life where individuals acted economically (i.e. weighed costs and benefits) and spheres where they did not act economically. Economists did not need to pay attention to culture because the effects of culture were limited in the economic spheres of life.

12   Although I agree that this is what took place, Robbins' definition of economics because it is concerned with the relationship between the social environment and the economic aspect of behavior need not have been seen as ruling out any mention of culture within economics. It could, for instance, have been read as allowing for and even necessitating the study of the relationship between culture and economics.

13   In fact, I have advanced that very argument elsewhere (see Storr and John 2011).

14   See, for instance, Knack and Keefer (1997), Glaeser et al. (2000), Jackson (2009) and Tabellini (2008) for a handful of efforts to elucidate the connection between various aspects of culture and economic outcomes. Kreps (1990) and Greif (1994) did, of course, attempt theoretical advances vis-à-vis the role of culture.

15   Or, perhaps, changes in institutions which result in price changes.

16   This is a counter to the behaviorist move that, arguably, attempts to shrink the scope of pure economic theory.

17   I challenge this way of conceiving of culture (i.e. as a form of capital) in Chapter 3.

18   See also Bisin and Verdier (2000, 2011) and Bisin et al. (2004, 2009).

19   Friedman (1953), of course, is not without his critics. See Boland (1979) for a summary of the criticisms of Friedman's methodology and a response to those criticisms. See also Hayek's (1964) argument that pattern predictions are sometimes all that are possible.

20   That the meaning of a lived experience can be different depending on when and from what vantage point it is viewed, is perhaps the clearest indication that meaning has to do with reflection. As Schütz (1967: 74) writes,

the meaning of a lived experience is different depending on *the moment from which* the Ego is observing it. . . . its meaning is different depending upon the *temporal distance* from which it is remembered and looked back upon. Likewise, the reflective glance will penetrate more or less deeply into lived experience depending on its point of view.

21   Recall that Weber has argued that "in [the category] 'action' is included all human behavior when and in so far as the acting individual attaches a subjective meaning to it" (cited in Schütz 1967: 15).

22   Mises (2003: 88–92) has alternatively challenged Weber's categories of action on the grounds that all human action is purposeful, even habitual action which can seem automatic.

23   And, Schütz (1967: 19) explains,

there is one fact which shows that most of my actions do have meaning. This is the fact that, when I isolate them from the flux of experience and consider them attentively, I then do find them to be meaningful in the sense that I am able to find in them an underlying meaning.

24   See Weigert (1975) for a critical exposition of Schütz's theory of motivation.

25 Characterizing "genuine because-statements" as referring necessarily to past projects motivated by events that are even further past has huge implications for any delineation of the scope and aim of social science. Recall that Mises drew a sharp distinction between praxeology (theoretical social science) and history (applied social science). In Mises' (1949: 51) view, praxeology employs conceptual cognition and aims at explaining "what is necessary [and universal] in human action." History, on the other hand, aims at understanding specific historical events. Recast in Schützian language, providing genuine because-statements is, thus, the province of historical sciences. Praxeology is an interpretive frame that can, at best, reveal what Schütz called "pseudo-because-motives."

26 Schütz calls this tracing back a move from the objective meaning to the subjective. As he (1967: 217) writes,

> it is only when I begin to grasp the other person's point of view as such, or, in our terminology, only when I make the leap from the objective to the subjective context of meaning, that I am entitled to say that I understand him. . . . Now, we have already seen that all knowledge of the subjective experiences of others must be obtained signitively. . . . we can start out from the external sign itself and, regarding it as a product, trace it back to the original actions and subjective experiences of its inventor or user. This is how, within the world of signs, the transition is made from the objective to the subjective context of meaning.

I should note that "objective meaning," for Schütz (ibid.: 31, 33), can be defined both negatively (i.e. the meaning of an act that's different than the actors intended meaning) and positively (i.e. the meaning of a sign or the product of an act that is intelligible in its own right). See Storr (2010) for a discussion of Schütz's views on objectivity.

27 I should note that the book where this concept is developed was completed after Schütz's death by his co-author and former student Thomas Luckmann. As Schütz's biographer Barber (2004: 220) describes,

> On the basis of Schütz's manuscripts (in the form of notebooks) Thomas Luckmann brought *The Structure of the Life-World* to its final form . . . Luckmann . . . altered Schütz's plans, expanding a section on typifications in the third chapter on the subjective stock of knowledge [and] producing an entirely new chapter, the fourth, on knowledge and society.

The arguments presented in these sections, however, draw heavily on Schütz's work in this area and fit neatly into his body of work. See Schütz (1967: 78–83) for Schütz's own writings on the stock of knowledge.

28 Admittedly, the social stock of knowledge does not map neatly into culture. There are, indeed, times when the social stock of knowledge appears to be more akin to institutions as "points of orientation" than culture as "patterns of meaning." Schütz did not, however, seem to have this distinction in mind and he ascribed both functions to the "social stock of knowledge."

29 As Lie (1997) describes, "the neoclassical market is shorn of social relations, institutions, or technology and is devoid of elementary sociological concerns such as power, norms, and networks." Arguably, there are good reasons why economists pay such scant attention to the market. As Coase (1988: 7) explains,

> this [absence of the market in economic theory] is less strange than it seems. Markets are institutions that exist to facilitate exchange, that is, they exist in order

to reduce the cost of carrying out exchange transactions. In an economic theory which assumes that transaction costs are nonexistent, markets have no function to perform.

30   As I will explain in Chapter 5, this does not imply an acceptance of radical cultural relativism. It is instead an acknowledgement that, though rationality is universal, the culturally specific ways of interpreting those circumstances that influence our choices are not universal.

31   I have left aside issues such as whether or not the price change constitutes a significant enough change to warrant notice, which is more obviously culturally conditioned.

32   The problem, of course, does not go away if we allow her to make errors but assume that on average the group of individuals to which she belongs will interpret the price change correctly or that the group would not make systematic errors in making their assessments. We can argue that systematic errors are not a problem because the market corrects errors. But, we should remember, the market corrects errors by offering feedback to market actors (i.e. profits when people behave as they should and losses when individuals make errors). That feedback also has to be interpreted. And, to assume that those feedback mechanisms will be correctly interpreted is to assume that for the most part group members possess the appropriate cultural frame. The point here is not that assuming that group members by and large possess the appropriate cultural frame is an unreasonable assumption. Group members would soon die off if their cultural frames allowed for systematic errors across a wide range of activities. The point here is simply that assuming that group members by and large possess the appropriate cultural frame is a necessary assumption of this theoretical position.

33   Lavoie (1991: 36) has, similarly, argued that

> entrepreneurship necessarily takes place within culture, it is utterly shaped by culture, and it fundamentally consists in interpreting and influencing culture. Consequently, the social scientist can understand it only if he is willing to immerse himself in the cultural context in which the entrepreneurial process occurs.

Additionally, as Lavoie and Chamlee-Wright (2000: 72–3) write,

> one of the main things that directs the entrepreneur's vision is culture. Entrepreneurial decision-making is not some sort of pure calculation but a complex reading of the polysemic dialogue of the market. It is necessarily embedded within a cultural context. . . . culture provides a framework of meaning that allows entrepreneurs to make sense of all the various, often conflicting pieces of information [they have available to them]. Culture gives shape to the interpretive process that is entrepreneurship.

3   But economists often misunderstand the relationship between culture and markets

1   Rational choice has also made inroads into sociology, although its success there has been limited. See Coleman (1990), Hechter and Kanazawa (1997), Kiser and Hechter (1998), and Goldthorpe (1998) for discussions of how rational choice theory can and has be utilized within sociology and see Boudon (1998, 2003) for a critique of the use of rational choice theory in sociology. And, see Swedberg (1990) for several discussions of the relationship between economics and sociology.

2 See, for instance, Black (1948), Buchanan and Tullock (1962), Olson (1965), Brennan and Buchanan (1980) and Caplan (2001, 2007).

3 See, for instance, Becker and Stigler (1974), Basov et al. (2001), Leeson (2007, 2009), Levitt and Venkatesh (2000) and Leeson and Skarbek (2010).

4 See, for instance, Portes (1998) and Granovetter (1973, 1995) for discussions of how social capital aids individuals in getting in a job. And, see Aldrich (2010, 2011a, 2011b, 2011c) and Chamlee-Wright and Storr (2009, 2011a, 2011b) for discussions of how social capital can facilitate post-disaster community recovery.

5 See, for instance, Torsvik (2000), Poulsen and Svendsen (2005), Carden et al. (2009), Sønderskov (2009) and Chong et al. (2010).

6 See, for example, Folbre (2008) for a critique of the economics of the family. Additionally, Newman's *Sociology of Families* (2002) and Ermisch's *An economic analysis of the family* (2003) provide good overviews. See also Horwitz (2005, 2008, 2010). And, see the volumes written on the sociology of the family.

7 DiMaggio's (1979) critique of Bourdieu is also relevant.

8 Arrow (1972: 357), for instance, has argued that

> virtually every commercial transaction has within itself an element of trust, certainly any transaction conducted over a period of time. It can be plausibly argued that much of the economic backwardness in the world can be explained by the lack of mutual confidence.

9 See Beugelsdijk (2006) for a critique of studies which use this and similar measures of trust to explain economic progress.

10 Because entrepreneurship is positively linked to economic growth (Holcombe 1996; Wennekers and Thurik 1999; Baumol and Strom 2007; Acs 2006), these studies also speak to the relationship between cultural resources and economic progress.

11 Harper (2003: 39) further explains that locus of control may be internal or external. As he (ibid.) explains,

> belief in *internal control* means that one perceives a series of related events to be contingent upon one's own behavior or one's own relatively durable characteristics. "Internal" people thus believe that they have some control over events in their life and that they are, therefore, responsible for their own destiny.

In contrast,

> a belief in *external control* means that a person perceived an event "as following some action of his own but not . . . entirely contingent upon his action" (Rotter 1966: 1). "External" people are more likely to interpret events as the result of factors outside the self that they cannot influence.

12 Although several studies have linked belief in internal control with individualism and belief in external control with collectivism, Harper (2003: 133) argues that this connection is overstated. Beliefs in an internal locus of control and self-efficacy need not be individualized but can be beliefs in a group's ability to alter its fate. Consequently, the range of cultures in Harper's formulation that can be said to have an internal locus of control and sense of agency is much larger than is traditionally recognized. Harper, of course, is right to point out that collectivism need not be seen as being opposed to entrepreneurship. As he suggests, whether individualist or collectivist views are dominant will shape the type of entrepreneurship (group versus individual) that emerges, as there can be personalized and group notions of locus of

control and personalized and group notions of efficacy. It is important to note, however, that the economists who stress the division between individualism and collectivism and how the prevalence of those different views affect entrepreneurship do not focus (as Harper does) on how culture impacts the personality traits that are relevant for entrepreneurship but instead focus on how individualism and collectivism impacts the economic policies and practices that emerge (Greif 1994). The "problem" with collectivist cultures is that they tend to adopt collectivist policies and practices. These collectivist policies and practices retard entrepreneurship.

13   Admittedly, Harper's (2003) treatment of culture is a bit more nuanced than the summary presented here. He, for instance, acknowledges that there can be differing views within cultures. As he (ibid.: 136) writes,

> within societies and nations there might be significant cultural variation. In addition, there are people who hold interdependent values residing in individualist cultures, and people who hold independent beliefs living in group-oriented cultures, though the proportions of each in both cultures vary. Moreover, any particular person, whether in an individualist or group oriented culture, is likely to mix independent and interdependent aspects.

Still, as Harper (ibid.) confesses, he "unavoidably resorts to the nation-state as the unit of analysis, especially when reporting on the findings of others." Although aware that cultures are heterogeneous, Harper ends up treating them as homogeneous.

14   In recent iterations, Harrison (2006) identifies twenty-five rather than twenty cultural factors as being important for economic growth.

15   Recall, for instance, that Greif (1997: 239) has argued that "cultural beliefs [are] . . . a common resource that affects the social and organizational development of societies and hence economic performance."

16   A great deal of literature has explored the relationship between cultural capital and educational attainment. Education sociologists, in particular, have embraced the term and used it extensively in their efforts to explain how social group origin impacts educational success. See, for instance, the articles in *Cultural Trends* (2004) vol. 13 (2) and *The British Journal of Sociology* (2005) vol. 56 (1).

17   Usually, Bourdieu (2002: 282) explains,

> measurement[s] of the yield from scholastic investment takes account only of monetary investments and profits, or those directly convertible into money, such as the costs of schooling and the cash equivalent of time devoted to study; they are unable to explain the different proportions of their resources which different agents or different social classes allocate to economic investment and cultural investment because they fail to take systematic account of the structure of the differential chances of profit which the various markets offer these agents or classes as a function of the volume and the composition of their assets.

18   Cultural capital can also exist in the "objectified" state as cultural artifacts (such as books and paintings) and in the "institutionalized" state as in the case of educational qualifications.

19   Interestingly, that cultural capital is meant as a stand in for those aspects of a community's stock of resources that are difficult to measure has not stopped economists and others from attempting to measure cultural capital.

20   Like Stigler and Becker (1977), which I discussed in Chapter 2, Swidler (1986: 274) believes that focusing on how "culture shapes action by defining what people want"

is unsatisfactory. "What people want," she (ibid.) writes, "is of little help in explaining their action."

21 The initial set up for this allegory appears in Mises (1949) and is extended and modified in Storr (2002).

22 See, for instance, David (1985), Liebowitz and Margolis (1990, 2002) and Lewin (2001).

23 As North (2005: 62) explains,

> institutional change is typically incremental and is path dependent. It is incremental because large-scale change will create too many opponents among existing organizations that will be harmed and therefore oppose such change. Revolutionary change will only occur in the case of gridlock among competing organizations which thwarts the ability of organizations to capture gains from trade. Path dependence will occur because the direction of the incremental institutional change will be broadly consistent with the existing institutional matrix . . . and will be governed by the kinds of knowledge and skills that the entrepreneurs and members of organizations have invested in.

24 For instance, as Leeson (2008) describes, socially distant agents can adopt the cultural practices of their would-be trading partners to signal trustworthiness.

25 At least, not as it is conceived of by Arrow and other neo-classical economists. But there are other ways of conceiving of capital; ways that do not emphasize the physical aspects of capital, ways that do not focus primarily on capital represented as physical things. Although many of the Austrian definitions of capital, for instance, also highlight its material or physical character, they differ from traditional definitions because they also stress the knowledge aspects of capital. It is, therefore, possible that an Austrian conception of capital may lend itself more readily as an analogy to culture because of this emphasis on knowledge. Indeed, Chamlee-Wright (2008), for instance, was able to "repair" the concept of social capital by making a similar move. As Baetjer (1998: 10) explains, the Austrian view

> is more radical than simply that capital has knowledge in them. It is rather that capital goods are knowledge, knowledge in the peculiar state of being embodied in such a form that it is ready-to-hand for use in production. The knowledge aspect of capital goods is the fundamental aspect. Any physical aspect is incidental.

Baetjer uses the example of the hammer to elaborate the point. "A hammer," he explains,

> is physical wood (the handle) and minerals (the head). But a piece of oak and a chunk of iron do not make a hammer. The hammer is those raw materials plus all the knowledge required to shape the oak into a handle, to transform the iron ore into a steel head, to shape it and fit it, and so on. . . . Even with a tool as bluntly physical as a hammer, the knowledge component is of overwhelming importance.
>
> (ibid.; 10)

Although culture has been described of as a kind of knowledge—knowledge about how to respond to certain situations, how to interpret the actions of others, etc.—even Austrians who stress the knowledge aspects of capital, conceive of capital as a resource; capital is "knowledge in the peculiar state of being embodied in such a form that it is ready-to-hand for use in production." Moreover, as Lachmann (1978: xv) argued, the generic concept of capital without which economists cannot do their work has no measurable counterpart among material objects; it reflects the entrepreneurial appraisal of such objects. Beer barrels and blast furnaces, harbour installations and hotel-room furniture are capital not by virtue of their physical properties but by virtue of their economic functions. Something is capital because the market, the consensus entrepreneurial minds, regards it as capable of yielding income.

Capital is capital because entrepreneurs believe that it can be used to generate income. Cultural capital might then be meaningfully considered a form of capital by Austrian economists but it remains unclear if we should consider culture as a resource.

26 It is even somewhat misleading to employ the analogy to baggage that individuals carry about all of the time since one could imagine leaving behind baggage. One cannot leave behind their culture.

27 I am not suggesting here that we are slaves to our cultural heritages but that we do not live in abstracto; individuals are neither under- nor over-socialized (Boettke and Storr 2002). To be sure, viewing culture as an "Ancient Curse"—the dead hand of the past directing the present—is problematic for several reasons. As Lavoie and Chamlee-Wright (2000) argue,

> what the Ancient Curse approach to culture obscures is the very essence of culture: the fact that it is not a static thing but an ongoing process. Culture is not the dead hand of the past constraining our actions to traditions as contrasted with our Reason. It is the very site of our reasoning activities, shaping what we find persuasive, and being shaped by our participation in dialogue. It is not a single, unified thing but a complex of conflicting tensions and proclivities. It is the locus of, and the framework that gives meaning to, our efforts to change ourselves and our societies.

Change (ideological and institutional shifts) within cultures is not uncommon. Due to the actions of ideological entrepreneurs, individuals may alter their perceptions of their choice sets and began to see their current circumstances and their future prospects much differently than they had previously (Storr 2009). Alert ideological entrepreneurs can inspire a process of creative ideological destruction. They can alter paths, transforming virtuous to vicious circles and vice versa. Individuals are not enslaved by their cultures and, thus, defining culture in this way obscures the multiple meaningful ways in which a people's belief systems can be transformed.

28 As Wilk (1996, 144) complains, Bourdieu "ends up promising much more than he delivers, became his economics remains so vague and imprecise."

29 As will be discussed in Chapter 5, in addition to the problems discussed above, it also erases the difference between culture and institutions.

30 See John (2010) for a useful development of this view.

31 Brennan and Buchanan think of a constitution as a social contract. See, however, Lomasky (2011) for a discussion of why this is problematic. Rather than viewing constitutions as social contracts, Lomasky (ibid.) argues that they are much more fruitfully thought of as covenants. Arguably, for reasons that will become obvious, thinking of culture as a covenant is even more preferable than thinking of culture as a social contract.

32 Linking culture to constitutions proves to be particularly profitable when we remember that constitutions remain dead documents until their precepts become embodied in

culture. It is now common knowledge that it is not the de jure laws on the books that are operative in a society. Rather, the de facto rules that emerge are the ones that direct behavior. These de facto rules are surely culturally legitimated, transmitted and enforced.

33 I am grateful to Arielle John for helping me to think through a number of these concerns.

34 See Boettke et al.'s (2008: 340) discussion of mētis (i.e. culture) and how it relates to the persistence of institutions for an interesting discussion of the relationship between culture and institutions. As they concluded, the closer an institution is to mētis the more likely it is to stick.

35 In Chapter 5, I offer a more extensive discussion of this point.

36 Not surprisingly, constitutional rules have a significant effect on economic life. Indeed, it has been consistently argued, certainly since Smith, that commerce and manufacturing cannot flourish outside of a constitutional order that enforces contracts and protects private property. And, recent efforts in political economy have explored how different constitutional frameworks either promote economic progress or thwart economic growth. Weingast (1995), for instance, has argued that markets will expand under "market preserving federalism," a set of particular political institutions that try to limit the degree to which a political system can encroach on markets. Five conditions characterize the type of institutional arrangement: (a) a hierarchy of governments (each autonomous within their own sphere of authority); (b) subnational governments with primary authority over the economy within their jurisdictions; (c) a national government with the authority to police the common market; (d) governments who face hard budget constraints (each locality must have a balanced budget); and (e) an institutionalized degree of durability for this allocation of authority and responsibility (it cannot be altered by the national government). Implementing "market preserving federalism" in developing and transitioning areas might be a potential mechanism for growing markets in these contexts; jurisdictions would be able to experiment with markets and as a result some of the suspicion of markets that has built up during years of colonial and communist rule will be eroded. Market preserving federalism, Weingast argues, creates an environment where enterprise is promoted and predation is discouraged. Cultures, however, cannot similarly be described as progress-resistant or progress-prone.

4 Economists ought to be looking at the spirits that animate markets

1 See Koppl (1991) and Marchionatti (1999) for excellent introductions to Keynes' discussion of animal spirits.

2 Admittedly, it is possible to think of Keynes' animal spirits as being a particular type of economic spirit (i.e. as a spirit that inspires confidence to act under certain circumstances) and so as an example of the economic spirits that are being discussed here.

3 Unless otherwise noted, our references to the text refer to Baehr and Wells' 2002 translation of the original 1905 version of *The Protestant Ethic and the Spirit of Capitalism* or Kalberg's 2010 translation of the 1920 revised version rather than Parson's more problematic though much more popular translation of the 1920 revised version. See Gorski (2003) for a comparison of these translations.

4 See, for instance, Weber (1951, 1958).

5 This is, of course, similar to Weber's distinction between market-oriented and politically oriented capital (Weber 1978: 164–6).

6 This spirit, however, remains an empty concept until it is historically situated. As Weber (2002: 263) explains,

> both the concept of "capitalism" and, even more certainly, that of the "spirit of capitalism" are only conceivable as thought constructs of the "ideal type" variety. They can either be conceived of in the *abstract*, so that features that are *permanently* alike can be extracted in conceptual purity. In this case, the second of the two concepts becomes rather empty of content and almost purely a function of the first. Or they may be conceived of *historically*, so that "ideal type" thought images are formed of the features that are *generally* present are assumed to be likewise given and well known.

Only when the spirit of capitalism is historically situated does it make sense to talk about an economic spirit and form not fitting neatly with each other.

7 Admittedly, Weber's efforts within the sociology of religion are not without their critics. According to Allen (2004: 66), for instance,

> Weber's ultimate purpose in *The Religion of China* and in *The Religion of India* was to use both countries as counterfactual arguments for his central thesis about the role of Protestantism in giving birth to the capitalist spirit . . . this meant ignoring important aspects of social life in these colonized countries. . . . Weber has romanticized capitalism and painted India and China in dark colors to create a shining ideological image. He presents an image of stagnant, passive societies by often ignoring their long history of economic development. He constructs an image of "traditional" India and China by mainly reading off their social structure from religious texts. He ignores the impact of colonialism on their development and so effectively blames their religion for their stagnation.

Arguably, both books engage in the kind of cultural scapegoating that I have criticized in the previous chapters. Below, however, I suggest that Weber's method could be amended in ways that would allow practitioners to avoid this kind of cultural scapegoating.

8 As Weber (1958: 4) explains,

> Indian justice developed numerous forms which could have served capitalistic purposes as easily and well as corresponding institutions in our own medieval law. The autonomy of the merchant stratum in law-making was at least equivalent to that of our own [read Western European] medieval merchants. Indian handicrafts and occupational specialization were highly developed. From the standpoint of possible capitalistic development, the acquisitiveness of Indians of all strata left little to be desired and nowhere is to be found so little antichrematism and such high evaluation of wealth. Yet modern capitalism did not develop indigenously before or during the English rule. It was taken over as a finished artifact without autonomous beginnings. . . . Indian religion, as one factor among many, may have prevented capitalistic development (in the occidental sense).

9 As Weber (1958: 112) writes,

> it must still be considered extremely unlikely that the modern organization of industrial capitalism would ever have *originated* on the basis of the caste system. A ritual law in which every change of occupation, every change in work technique, may result in ritual degradation is certainly not capable of giving birth to economic and technical revolutions from within itself, or even of facilitating the first germination of capitalism in its midst.

10 Weber tended to stress religion as being the source of the economic spirit in various places. Arguably, this had more to do with the dominant role played by religion in the regions that he discussed rather than any essential role played by religion in shaping a society's economic spirit. Although "social action needs to be built on an ethical foundation," the spirits that "give motive force" to the various capitalisms that exist need not be linked to religion; it is not necessary that they have a continued relationship with the religious views which gave them life nor is it necessary, for that matter, that they have a basis in any religion (Greenfeld 2001: 16). As Weber also recognizes, even in his epoch what he characterized as the Protestant ethic was losing its religious connections. "Now one may be inclined to observe," Weber (2002: 23) confesses,

> that these *personal* moral qualities [that accompany the spirit of capitalism], in themselves, have nothing whatever to do with any ethical maxims, let alone religious ideas, but rather that the negative ability to *relinquish* old traditions . . . is an adequate basis for this conduct of life. And, in fact, today this is, in general, certainly true. Not only is there normally no correlation between the conduct of life and religious principles, but where a correlation does exist it tends to be, at least in Germany [during his day], negative in character. The kind of people who are inspired by the "capitalist spirit" today tend to be, if not exactly hostile to the Church, then at least indifferent. The prospect of the "holy tedium" of paradise holds few attractions for their active nature; for them, religion is simply something that stops people from working here on earth.

11 Gudeman (1986) also reminds us that local models are necessarily partial constructions. As Gudeman (ibid.: 39) explains,

> models are partial constructions. They are selective, offering a perspective without exhausting all the possible facets of an experience. Formal economic models, for instance, deal only with selected dimensions of what it means to secure a livelihood. Ricardo offered a model of the British economy, but he did not claim that it accounted for every aspect of that set of practices. The Physiocrats did not pretend to provide a model of all economic behavior. The same is true of the exotic models I shall examine.

12 Gudeman (1986) has also usefully discussed the local economic models of the Gogo in the Rift valley of central Tanzania and the Dobuans near New Guinea.

13 Weber (2002: 11) points to Benjamin Franklin's life and attitudes toward work as exemplifying this economic spirit. "At the beginning of such an investigation" as the *Protestant Ethic*, Weber (ibid.: 264) explains,

> one can only employ the most graphic *illustration* possible. The example I chose was drawn from a milieu which was still in many ways a barter economy, or at any rate (relatively speaking) a very *un*capitalist milieu, namely that of Benjamin Franklin.

As discussed below, his use of Franklin was illustrative rather than constituting proof for the existence of the spirit of modern capitalism.

14 As Weber (2011: 82) writes,

> the *greed* of the mandarins in China, of the aristocrats in ancient Rome, and of the modern peasant is second to none. And as anyone can experience for himself, the *auri sacra frames* [i.e. "the accursed greed for gold"] of the Naples cab driver, or *barcajuolo* [Venetian gondolier], representatives in Asia of similar

trades, and craftsmen in southern Europe and Asia is even unusually *more intense*, and especially more unscrupulous, than that of, for example, an Englishman in the same situation. The universal sway of *absolute* unscrupulousness in establishing one's own self-interest as the legitimate operating assumption for the pursuit of money has been specifically characteristic of precisely those countries where the unfolding of a middle-class capitalism—measured against the standards of Western development—has remained "backward."

15 According to Weber (2011: 82), "the capitalistic spirit . . . became prominent only after a difficult struggle against a world of hostile powers. The frame of mind [that characterizes the capitalist spirit] . . . would have been proscribed in the ancient world."

16 McCloskey (2010) has sought to distance both her approach and her explanation for the rise of modern capitalism from Weber's discussion. Specifically, she complained that "modern innovation [does not] have anything unusually 'greedy' about it" (ibid.: 140) and that

> what made us rich was a new rhetoric that was favorable to unbounded innovation, imagination, alertness, persuasion, originality, with individual rewards often paid in a coin of honor or thankfulness—not individual accumulation restlessly stirring, or mere duty to a calling, which are ancient and routine and uncreative.
>
> (ibid.: 144)

McCloskey's argument, however, is not as different from Weber's as she supposed. Weber never argued that modern capitalism had anything to do with modern capitalists being unusually greedy. In fact, as we show above, Weber (2011: 82) believed that greed is universal and did not believe that the West was especially greedy. Instead, like McCloskey, Weber believed that the capitalistic spirit held that entrepreneurship was honorable and promoted a particularly rational kind of profit seeking.

17 Calvin himself did not have this problem and did not think that it should be one. As Weber (2002: 76) explains, Calvin

> felt himself to be an "instrument" and was certain of his state of grace. Accordingly, his only answer to the question of how the individual could be sure of his election was basically that we should be satisfied with the knowledge of God's decree and with the trust in Christ which comes through true faith. He fundamentally rejects the assumption that one can tell from the behavior of others whether they are elect or reprobate, calling it a presumptuous attempt to penetrate the mysteries of God.

18 Influenced by this *worldly asceticism*, the successful entrepreneur is

> filled with the conviction that Providence had shown him the road to profit not without particular intention. He walked it for the greater glory of God, whose blessing was unequivocally revealed in the multiplication of his profit and possessions. Above all, he could measure his worth not only before men but also before God by success in his occupation, as long as it was realized through legal means.
>
> (Weber 1978: 1124)

19 This is perhaps worth further consideration. The market, for instance, has variously been described as an auction, a social contract, a beauty contest, and a conversation. The market, however, may still be like what the author (perhaps erroneously) calls a

conversation even if real-world conversations are nothing like the author's exposition. If we contend that the market is like an open ended conversation where speech partners do not talk off of a script but instead engage in a play of questions and answers and, that, consequently, the conversation that results is thus not the result of either participant's intentions, then the analogy still helps us to understand that markets are spontaneous orders—the result of human actions but not human design—even if all conversations in practice are really scripted dialogues. Indeed, we do still learn something about markets.

20 As Weber (2011: 178) writes, *The Protestant Ethic*

> has attempted, of course, merely to trace ascetic Protestantism's influence, and the particular *nature* of this influence, back to ascetic Protestantism's motives in regard to one—however important—point. The way in which Protestant asceticism was in turn influenced in its development and characteristic uniqueness by the entirely societal-cultural conditions, and especially *economic* conditions, must also have its day.

21 As Parsons (1967: 37) explained,

> in Weber's broad plan [*The Protestant Ethic*] was intended as no more than an *essay* in historical-sociological interpretation. It was a fragment which provided Weber a point of departure, not a culmination, for his main contributions to the sociology of religion. Now it clearly has attained the status of a classic, but it should be appraised as such within the context of its author's total contribution, not in isolation.

22 For instance, in discussing the examples that he was employing to tease out what he meant by the spirit of capitalism, Weber (2002: 51) writes that "for our purely illustrative purposes, it is, of course, immaterial that in none of the examples referred to were events played out in every detail precisely in the manner here depicted." This would also hold for Weber's use of Franklin as the exemplar of the spirit of capitalism. Despite charges from his critics (e.g. Dickson and McLachlan 1989), Weber was aware that his view of Franklin could have been wrong. But, again, the use of Franklin is illustrative and his words as an expression of the spirit of capitalism that Weber and not his actual life is what matters chiefly for Weber.

23 Stuijvenberg (cited in Hamilton 1996: 74), for instance, concludes after a review of Dutch Calvinist writings that "there never was this theological hinge around which everything turns in Weber's thesis. On this point the theological base which Weber lays under his thesis has never existed." This is not an uncontested point. Marshall (1982: 92) has suggested that there is reason to believe that Weber got the theology right or at least that his account is empirically plausible. See Marshall (ibid.: 69–96) for a detailed discussion of the debate around Weber's theology. Weber, however, can perhaps be forgiven for getting the theology wrong, if he did in fact get it wrong. Weber (2002: 129) confesses that he relied on secondary literature for some of his conclusions and recognized that

> a visit to English or American libraries is essential for any close study of many works [that he accessed primarily through secondary sources]. For the [*Protestant Ethic*] I have, of course, in general, had to make do with what was available in Germany.

24 Although MacKinnon's critiques would appear to be a death-blow to at least part of Weber's claims, Zaret (1992: 385) has argued that, "MacKinnon fails to sustain his

indictment of the Weber thesis because the evidence for that indictment is an implausible, insupportable interpretation of Puritan writings."

25 The discussion above of the debate spawned by the *Protestant Ethic* is admittedly brief. See, for instance, Marshall (1982) for an overview of the early debate surrounding the *Protestant Ethic*.

26 Others have defended him along similar lines. "For all its fame," Giddens (2001: xiv) explains, "*The Protestant Ethic* is a fragment." Weber knew that he was a long way from providing the kind of quantitative empirical evidence that Hamilton and Marshall have demanded. As Weber (2011: 178) understands,

> the further task is a different one [than the one he undertook]: to chart the significance of ascetic rationalism. The above sketch has only hinted at its importance. Its significance for the content of a community-building ethical *social policy* must now be outlined—that is, for the type of organization of social groups, ranging from the conventicle to the state, and their functions. Having done that we must analyze the relationship of ascetic rationalism to the ideals and cultural influences of humanistic rationalism. Further, we must investigate the relationship of ascetic rationalism to the development of philosophical and scientific empiricism, to the unfolding of technology, and to the development of nonmaterial culture . . . in general. Finally, beginning with the first signs of this-worldly asceticism in the Middle Ages and moving all the way to its dissolution in pure utilitarianism, we need to pursue the historical course of ascetic rationalism. That is, in its *historical* manifestations and through the particular regions of the expansion of ascetic religious devotion. Only after the completion of such investigations can the *extent* of ascetic Protestantism's civilizational significance be demarcated in comparison to that of other elements of modern civilization that can be changed and shaped in response to the actions of persons.

Beyond being mindful that the Protestant Ethic was only a sketch and did not prove any of the arguments that he advanced, Weber did not share Hamilton and Marshall's view of what counts as "empirical" evidence and what would constitute proof. Although Hamilton (1996: 60) concedes that Weber's "conclusions—which are simultaneously comparative, historical, and social psychological—are, for all practical purposes, beyond the reach of historical and social scientific method," he nonetheless criticizes Weber for not supporting his conclusions.

27 My view of the *Protestant Ethic* is similar to Billig's (2000). As he (ibid.: 785) writes, "I am not arguing here that Weber's 1904 perspective on the rise of European capitalism is correct or flawless. . . . Rather, I am explicating and endorsing his method of analyzing social and historical change." And,

> keep in mind that Weber was the most intellectually modest causal eclectic of any major theoretician. He never made, and he always denied, the assertion that capitalism was caused by Calvinist doctrine. Weber himself always expressed regret that anyone could infer this so-called "strong thesis" from his work. For him, the notion of elective affinity and the surprising revelation of capitalism as an unintended consequence were the major contributions of *The Protestant Ethic*.
>
> (ibid.: 779)

28 As Weber (2002: 19) describes,

> some economies are run by private entrepreneurs in the form of trade in capital (either money or goods with money value) for the purpose of profit, gained by

purchase of the means of production and the sale of the products (which makes them undoubtedly "capitalist enterprises"). Such economies can still be traditionalist in character. In the course of recent economic history, too, this has been the case not just exceptionally but regularly—though with constantly recurring interruptions by new and ever more violent manifestations of the "capitalist spirit."

29 The quotes below are taken from interviews conducted in St Bernard Parish. Where possible, aliases (signified with a [†]) were used to protect the identities of our subjects.
30 Although "talking ol' story" is something of a dying tradition in the Bahamas, the once popular tales are still a valuable source of insight into Bahamian identity and culture (Glinton-Meicholas 2000). The Bahamian storytelling tradition was a rich one, replete with colorful tales of gaulins and serpents and devils, often punctuated by proverbs and songs and told with the aid of "mimicry, onomatopoeia and gestures" (Glinton-Meicholas 1993: 13). The storyteller in Bahamian orature, however, was not just an entertainer. He was also "the news-bringer and historian of the clan, prescriber and disseminator of his people's culture, upholder of their religious practices and their moral values" (Turner 1988: viii).
    B' Rabby (the trickster) is the dominant character in Bahamian folk narratives (Glinton-Meicholas 1993; Turner 1988). I, for instance, can vividly remember sitting with my cousins at my grandmother's feet, enthralled for hours as she told us tale after tale of B' Rabby getting the best of his friend and foil B' Bouki. Brought over from the continent by enslaved Africans, B' Rabby and B' Bouki "are primarily a part of this country's African heritage" (ibid.: 12). B' Rabby, called Brer Rabbit in Black American communities (where he also thrived), is a "cunning" and "tricky" figure who "is the archetypal hero-trickster character" (Kulii and Kulii 2001: 46). Appearing as "Leuk, the hare and Bouki, the hyena in stories of the Wolof people of West Africa," links can also be drawn between B' Rabby and B' Bouki and the Antillean tales of Compere Lapi or Ti Malice and Bouki (ibid.). There is also a strong affinity between B' Rabby (or Brer Rabbit) and the "two major tricksters of Africa (Anansi or Anancy the Ashanti spider, and Ijapa, the Yoruba turtle)" (ibid.). Like Anancy (which is the dominant trickster character among the Ashanti in Ghana as well as in the Caribbean), whether B' Rabby is pitted against the likes of Brer Bear, Brer Wolf or Sly Brer Fox (in Black American narratives) or the powerful B' Lion and B' Whale or the dimwitted B' Bouki (his favorite adversaries in Bahamian orature), he "tries to nullify the plans of his [sometimes] stronger archenemies by using his superior intelligence and his quick thinking" (ibid.). B' Rabby usually gets the better of his rivals; his smarts are his chief asset and his major advantage.
    B' Rabby, however, is more than just the cunning protagonist taking advantage of B' Bouki in one tale after the other. He is also, I contend, a figure that we meet again and again in our history books, our folk songs, our poems, our novels and our plays. The pirates, smugglers and bootleggers of yesteryear, today's successful businessmen and political leaders, in short, the characters from our past and present who we admire and celebrate all seem to have something in common with the mythical creature. Similarly, contemporary novelists like Ian Strachan and satirists like Patricia Glinton-Meicholas represent the Bahamas as a nation peopled with B' Bouki and B' Rabby figures and depict Bahamian society as one dominated by what I call Rabbyism.
31 B' Bouki was, similarly, a cautionary figure.
32 In fact, a Bahamian Commission of Inquiry set up in 1986 to look at government involvement in the drug trade discovered that the then Prime Minister, Sir Lynden Oscar

Pindling, was spending more than five times his income every year (*Report of the Commission of Inquiry*, Nassau, Bahamas, 1984). See also the condemnation of corruption in Bahamian politics by a US diplomat in 2006 that appeared on *WikiLeaks*.

33   Interestingly, Bahamian history books have also tended to celebrate the Bahamas' pirate past. For instance, the pirate as hero is a dominant trope in Paul Albury's *The Story of The Bahamas* (1975), a history book that was taught in Bahamian junior high schools during the 1980s and 1990s. As Albury (1975: 60) confesses,

> the swashbuckling nature of these daredevils calls forth an admiration tinged with envy. We admire their sheer courage, the valor with which they faced greet odds, the defiance with which they fronted all the forces of law and order, and even death itself.

Albury (ibid.: 140) is, similarly, laudatory of the wrecking era: "the stories that can be told about the wreckers would entertain an audience for forty days and forty nights." Albury's tone is different when he is describing the more mundane alternatives to piracy and smuggling. Bahamian settlers, Albury (ibid.: 78) writes, "were confronted with land more stubborn than any they had ever tried to work before. In fact nothing looked very promising."

34   As a corollary to this, Junkanoo *teaches Bahamians to value competition*. They recognize that the costumes are more beautiful, the music is more intense and the camaraderie between members of their group is more pronounced because, in addition to whatever else it is, Junkanoo is also a "battleground."

35   This is certainly true of Junkanoo in the post-Independence, post-Majority Rule era. Before that time, however, Junkanoo was not an arena where class divisions melted but was instead an opportunity for the oppressed majority population to gain a temporary, if only symbolic, victory in their struggle to overcome oppression. As Wood (1995: 6) points out,

> By the 1930s, Bay Street was under the control of White-minority merchants. Because the Black majority did not hold economic or political power . . . Bay Street became the symbol of White economic and political repression. At Christmas, people would stream onto Bay Street from the Black residential areas known as *over-the-hill*. . . . Separated from Bay Street by a low hill, the over-the-hill area became the heart and soul of pre-Independence Black Bahamian culture. Consequently, the presence of Black Bahamians on Bay Street for the Junkanoo parades signified the taking over by Blacks of the White domain.

36   Thanks to tourism, the Bahamas is the richest independent country in the West Indies; Bermuda and the Cayman Islands are excluded because they remain (partially) under British rule. In the Bahamas, GDP per capita was $28,700 in 2010. In Barbados, the next richest, GDP per capita was $28,100 (CIA World Fact Book).

37   Even though it is sometimes difficult in the Bahamas to gain access to capital and credit for business ventures.

5 This does *not* mean that economists have to abandon economics

1   Recall, Weber (2011: 12) describes the spirit of capitalism as an irrational drive; "it appears as something wholly transcendent and irrational." Additionally, several anthro-pologists (i.e. the substantivists) have expressed this complaint regarding economists' insistence on characterizing all meaningful behavior as instrumentally rational behavior.

See Wilk and Cliggett (2007) for a discussion of how the substantivists would want social scientists to discuss the relationship between culture and economic behavior.

2 Stigler and Becker (ibid.: 77) endogenize cultural differences by introducing the notion of consumption capital that individuals accumulate as they are exposed to different things throughout their lives. Different stocks of consumption capital explain different economic outcomes. See also Bisin and Verdier (2001).

3 Whitefield and Evans (1999), for instance, contrast subjectivist political culture explanations for differences in the existence and evolution of democratic norms in Eastern Europe with rational choice explanations. As they (ibid.: 130) explain, a subjectivist political culture explanation would emphasize "shared values, beliefs and preferences in the political sphere that have been shaped by common historical understandings" in explaining existing political norms. A rational choice perspective, on the other hand, would stress "the importance of contemporary state context, individual endowments and opportunities for political voice" in shaping political responses (ibid.: 131). According to Whitefield and Evans (1999: 151), differences in Czech and Slovak attitudes toward economic and political liberalization have less to do with cultural differences and more to do with differences in their experiences, endowments and circumstances. Consider also Shapiro's (1998) discussion of whether or not the rational choice framework can cope with culture.

4 See, for instance, Green and Shapiro (1994) for an interesting critique of rational choice approaches in political science. Instead of suggesting that rational choice theorizing be modified to accommodate things like culture they suggest that the scope for rational choice theorizing ought to be limited. See, also, Smith (2008) for a related discussion concerning the scope of rationality. Smith (ibid.) has argued that human beings rely on both constructivist and ecological forms of rationality. Constructivist rationality is the form of rationality that models man as a rational fool (see the discussion of Sen 1977 in this section). Ecological rationality, on the other hand, is culturally derived or, rather, co-evolves with culture. "The behavior of an individual, a market, an institution, or other social system involving collectives of individuals is ecologically rational to the degree to that it is adapted to the structure of its environment." Smith (2008) argues that economists should pay attention to both forms of rationality.

5 It is important to concede that if this is what we mean by rational choice then cultural considerations are necessarily outside this view.

6 Lavoie and Chamlee-Wright (2000: 72), however, challenge the notion that culture is a counter-rational force (even if rationality is conceived of in this narrow sense). As they (ibid.) write, suggesting that

> if one is under the influence of culture one must not be 'acting rationally' . . . misunderstands economic decisions to be 'purely' calculating and atomistic, i.e. having nothing at all to do with culture. On the first point, clearly an individual does not wholly choose his culture as he would choose an item in the grocery store. The individual inherits a language community, values, and ethics. On the other hand, this does not mean that cultural influences lie outside of rationality. While we do not choose the cultural influences which shape our perspective, we have it within our grasp to challenge inherited cultural norms.

7 Sen (1977: 330–3) has in mind a wide range of economic decisions. Admitting that commitment is perhaps not that relevant when considering private goods, Sen (ibid.: 330) argues that "one area in which the question of commitment is most important is that of the so-called public goods." Additionally, Sen (ibid.: 333) writes that "the

question of commitment is important in a number of other economic contexts. It is central to the problem of work motivation, the importance of which for production performance can hardly be ignored."

8 But such devotion occurs even when there is no riches promised in the afterlife and the riches of the afterlife need not motivate the prayer. The point is not whether utilities can be defined in such a way that her actions appear self-interested but simply whether or not self-interest is the real motivation.

9 "There remains," Sen (1977: 342) concedes,

> the issue as to whether this view of man amounts to seeing him as an irrational creature. Much depends on the concept of rationality used, and many alternative characterizations exist. In the sense of consistency of choice, there is no reason to think that admitting commitment must imply any departure from rationality. This is, however, a weak sense of rationality. The other concept of rationality prevalent in economics identifies it with the possibility of justifying each act in terms of self-interest: when act x is chosen by person i and act y rejected, this implies that i's personal interests are expected by i to be better served by x than by y.

Stated another way, there are at least two ways of conceiving of rational agents: as rational fools (with simple preference orderings) or as more complex creatures. See also Lewis (2009) for a discussion of how commitment is connected to identity and why commitment behavior cannot be reduced to instrumental rational behavior.

10 This builds on his earlier work. See, especially, Sen (1973, 1974).

11 As Sen (1977: 337) describes,

> to illustrate, consider a set X of alternative action combinations and the following three rankings of this action-set X: ranking A representing my personal welfare ordering (thus, in some sense, representing my personal interests), ranking B reflecting my "isolated" personal interests ignoring sympathy (when such a separation is possible, which is not always so), and ranking C in terms of which actual choices are made by me (when such choices are representable by a ranking, which again is not always So). The "most moral" ranking M can, conceivably, be any of these rankings A, B, or C. Or else it can be some other ranking quite distinct from all three. (This will be the case if the actual choices of actions are not the "most moral" in terms of the moral system in question, and if, furthermore, the moral system requires sacrifice of some self-interest and also of "isolated" self-interest.) But even when some ranking M distinct from A, B, and C is identified as being at the top of the moral table, that still leaves open the question as to how A, B, and C may be ordered vis-a-vis each other. If, to take a particular example, it so happens that the pursuit of self-interest, including pleasure and pain from sympathy, is put morally above the pursuit of "isolated" self-interest (thereby leading to a partial coincidence of self-interest with morality), and the actual choices reflect a morally superior position to the pursuit of self-interest (perhaps due to a compromise in the moral direction), then the morality in question precipitates the meta-ranking M, C, A, B, in descending order. This, of course, goes well beyond specifying that M is "morally best."

12 Contrast, for instance, North (1990) with North (2005) where he assigns some of these roles to culture.

13 Billig (2000) has criticized the opposite trend within anthropology where, he argues, social institutions are treated as an aspect of culture.

14 Interestingly, Weber (2002) makes a similar point when he discusses the relationship between the spirit of modern capitalism and the rules that govern modern capitalism. Again, as Weber (ibid.: 19) explains, "the 'capitalistic' form of an economy and the spirit in which it is run do indeed stand in a generally adequate relationship to each other." He, however, continued to distinguish between the capitalist form and the capitalist spirit.

15 Admittedly, I am tempted to agree with Jones (2006: xi) and will hint at below that "culture, despite [North's] claim that it is 'central' to economic performance, does not emerge from [his] discussion as particularly influential."

16 As Tabellini (2008: 257) has similarly argued, "well-functioning institutions are often observed in countries or regions where individuals share values consistent with generalized morality, and different identifying assumptions suggest a causal effect of values on institutional outcomes." Specifically, Tabellini (ibid.: 288–9) concluded that

> distant political institutions have left a mark in current attitudes and values . . . This is evident from micro data on second generation US citizens. Descendants of immigrants from countries that over a century ago were ruled by more democratic political institutions are more likely to display generalized trust and respect for others. It is also confirmed by aggregate data on European regions.

Additionally, there is a "contemporaneous link between values and institutional or economic outcomes. . . . Aggregate cross country data reveal that countries where generalized morality is more widespread have better governance indications and specialize in sectors that rely on well functioning legal institutions" (ibid.).

17 See, also, Greif and Tabellini's (2010) discussion of cultural and institutional bifurcation. "Indigenous institutions and culture," they (ibid.: 139) explain, "interrelate to constitute a coherent whole. The implied complementarities contribute to institutional persistence and can hinder inter-society institutional transfer."

18 Lavoie and Chamlee-Wright (2000: 73) argue that the management practices that proved so successful in Japan which included activities to foster comraderie failed in the US because they did not fit the cultural context. "Rather than proving the 'culture as window dressing' thesis," they (ibid.) explain,

> this speaks directly to the importance such cultural influences play in the economic sphere. If the elements of Japanese culture used in management were simply window dressing, then there should have been no differences when they were transported abroad. The fact that they were a weak point in overseas management suggests that these practices "fit" in one context, but not in another.

Referencing her own research on female entrepreneurship in Zimbabwe, Chamlee-Wright (2005) argues that the solidarity loan schemes which are a key feature of many successful micro-finance programs failed in Zimbabwe because of poor cultural fit. As she (ibid.: 9) concludes,

> development initiatives that conflict with the cultural context that guides perception and behavior are not likely to be very successful. The interviews conducted for this study lend weight to this line of argument, in that they provide detail as to why Zimbabwean informal entrepreneurs are so often reluctant to participate in microlending programs, particularly those that stress the use of solidarity loans. The interviews suggest that solidarity loans are a poor cultural fit for the Zimbabwean context, and the widespread participation in rotating credit organizations may indicate that entrepreneurs favor informal forms of cooperative strategies over those initiated through the group lending process.

19 Arguably, the now common recognition that it is not the de facto rules but the de jure rules that matter for institutional analysis is almost a recognition that that institutions do not exist in a cultural vacuum. To admit that an individual's actions are guided by the de facto rules that are in force and not the de jure rules that have been formally adopted is to admit that identifying something as a rule says very little about whether and to what extent it is being followed and how it is understood. That culture might help to explain not only why a rule is adopted and followed in one context and rejected in another but also how the rule is interpreted in a given context.

20 Recall, that Geertz (1973: 5) conceives of culture as "webs of significance" that man has himself spun.

21 Snyder (2002) has also argued that culture and institutions she be viewed as separate but linked. Both Billig (2000) and Snyder (2002) adopt the neo-Weberian/Geertzian approach to the study of culture and its relationship to (economic) behavior and institutions adopted here which defines culture as "patterns of meaning" and sees institutions as "points of orientation." As Snyder (2002: 15) explains, "an advantage of the Geertzian definition, which limits culture to meaningful symbols, is that it permits scholars to investigate the relationship between ideas and institutions empirically, rather than defining them as integrally related under the umbrella heading of culture." As Snyder (ibid.) concedes, however,

> Even with this definition, it is not always easy to draw a sharp line between institutions and cultural symbols in concrete social settings. Both institutions and culture are part of the process by which people coordinate their behavior in groups. Symbols (ideas) may serve as focal points to guide the coordination of expectations in cases where purely pragmatic strategic calculations could yield multiple equilibria or no equilibrium. Moreover, institutions tend to be shored up by symbols . . . that convince people to behave in accord with institutionalized practices for moral reasons, and not simply for the practical benefits of coordinating behavior with the expectations of others. Conversely, norms often require institutionalized enforcement. . . . Thus, I am not claiming that the causes and consequences of culture and institutions are not intertwined. Nonetheless, the conceptual distinction in principle remains clear: Culture is a system of symbols; institutions are conventional, repeated behavior. The distinction between cultural symbols and institutions serves the analytic purpose of clarifying the role of culture as an explanatory variable.

22 "The impressive volume of econometric work," Leontief (ibid.: 2) asserts,

> can be in general characterized as an attempt to compensate for the glaring weakness of the data base available to us by the widest possible use of more and more sophisticated statistical techniques. Alongside the mounting pile of elaborate theoretical models we see a fast-growing stock of equally intricate statistical tools.

23 Boettke (2001), for instance, has explicitly argued that econometric methods fail to help us definitively answer one of the most important questions in economics. Although economics has always sought to ascertain why some countries are rich and others remain poor, according to Boettke, economists have not yet arrived at a way to arbitrate between rival theories of the nature and causes of the wealth of nations. This, according to Boettke, is partly because economists have been focusing on the wrong types of data and empirical analysis. Rather than simply relying on aggregate measures of economic well-being and potential causal factors, Beottke argues that meaningful empirical work

requires that we also conduct history and ethnography. "Aggregate macroeconomic data," he (ibid.: 249) explains,

> is not the only data available from which we can learn about the nature and causes of the wealth of nations—we can approach the question in a multidisciplinary manner and incorporate arguments and empirical information developed in other areas of the social sciences, such as the results of case studies and the evidence gleaned from ethnography.

Calling for economists to make an empirical turn, Boettke (ibid.: 253) suggests that

> a plausible argument can be made that the techniques and data we economists have come to rely on are too "thin" for our own good, and that perhaps it is high time we sought the thicker description . . . In making this turn, individual decision-making is not to be overlooked, but the context of decision moves to the center of analysis as opposed to the behavioral assumptions, and economic actions are recognized as embedded, rather than disembodied and abstract.

While econometric models tend to be neat and parsimonious, they do not allow us to understand the lived experiences of individuals and the meanings they attach to their environments. We therefore require "theory impregnated" but "thick" descriptions of the social world which will allow us to access and understand phenomena that take place in environments outside of our own (ibid.: 253).

24 See Silverman (2004) for a discussion of the strengths and weaknesses of qualitative research.

25 See Chapter 3 for why this is problematic.

26 See Geertz (1973) for a discussion of the differences between thin and thick descriptions. See, also, McCloskey (1988).

27 Thymology, for Mises (1962: 47-8), is a "branch of history" and it "deals with the mental activities of men that determine their actions." It is, Mises (1957: 266) explains, "what everybody learns from intercourse with his fellows." Stated another way, it is the branch of history that deals with how culture impacts behavior. See Lavoie and Storr (2011) for a discussion of thymology and its place within the social sciences.

28 Recall, as Weber (1949) noted, there are three relevant categories of phenomena for the economist who aims at understanding economic life: (1) pure "economic" phenomena (e.g. wages, prices, profits, etc.), (2) "economically relevant" phenomena (e.g. religious and cultural systems), and (3) "economically conditioned" phenomena (e.g. politics).

29 Importantly, interview talk is also consistent with archival work and in-depth case studies. Like ethnographies and structured interviews, qualitative archival research and in-depth case studies "allow us to gain access to not only the actions of others, but also the mental templates shaping their action" (Chamlee-Wright 2011: 166).

30 As Chamlee-Wright (2011: 159) argues, "a greater use of qualitative research methods can help to correct economics' excessive reliance upon quantitative analysis in its empirical investigations and reduce the distance between the investigator and the subject under investigation."

Bibliography

Acemoglu, D. and Robinson, J. (2010) "Why is Africa Poor?" *Economic History of Developing Regions*, 25 (1): 21–50.

Acs, Z. (2006) "How is Entrepreneurship Good for Economic Growth," *Innovations*, 1 (1): 97–107.

Akerlof, G. and Shiller, R. (2010) *Animal Spirits: How Human Psychology Drives the Economy, and Why It Matters for Global Capitalism*, Princeton, NJ: Princeton University Press.

Albury, P. (1975) *The Story of the Bahamas*, London: MacMillian Caribbean.

Aldrich, D. P. (2010) "Fixing Recovery: Social Capital in Post-Crisis Resilience," *Journal of Homeland Security*, 6 (June): 1–10.

Aldrich, D. P. (2011a) "The Power of People: Social Capital's Role in Recovery from the 1995 Kobe Earthquake," *Natural Hazards*, 56 (3): 595–611.

Aldrich, D. P. (2011b) "Ties that Bond, Ties that Build: Social Capital and Governments in Post Disaster Recovery," *Studies in Emergent Order*, 4: 58–68.

Aldrich, D. P. (2011c) "The Externalities of Social Capital: Post-Tsunami Recovery in Southeast India," *Journal of Civil Society*, 8 (1): 81–99.

Allen, K. (2004) *Max Weber: A Critical Introduction*, London: Pluto Press.

Allison, J. and Lin, L. (1999) "The Evolution of Chinese Attitudes Toward Property Rights in Invention and Discovery," *University of Pennsylvania Journal of International Economic Law*, 20 (4): 735.

Arrow, K. (1972) "Gifts and Exchanges," *Philosophy & Public Affairs*, 1 (4): 343–62.

Arrow, K. (2000) "Observations on Social Capital," in I. Serageldin and P. Dasgupta (eds.), *Social Capital: A Multifaceted Perspective*, Washington DC: World Bank Publications: 3–6.

Azariadis, C. (1981) "Self-Fulfilling Prophecies," *Journal of Economic Theory*, 25: 380–96.

Baetjer H. (1998) "Software as Capital: An Economic Perspective on Software Engineering," Los Alamos, NM: IFEE Computer Society.

Barber, M. (2004) *The Participating Citizen: A Biography of Alfred Schütz*, Albany, NY: SUNY Press.

Baron, J. and Hannan, M. (1994) "The Impact of Economics on Contemporary Sociology," *Journal of Economic Literature*, 32 (3): 1111–46.

Basov, S., Jacobson, M. and Miron, J. (2001) "Prohibition and the Market for Illegal Drugs," *World Economics*, 2 (4): 133–57.

Baumol, W. (1990) "Entrepreneurship: Productive, Unproductive, and Destructive," *The Journal of Political Economy*, 98 (5) part 1: 893–921.

Baumol, W. and Strom, R. (2007) "Enrepreneurship and Economic Growth," *Strategic Entrepreneurship Journal*, 1 (3–4): 233–7.

Becker, G. (1973) "A Theory of Marriage: Part 1," *The Journal of Political Economy*, 81 (4): 813–46.

Becker, G. and Stigler, G. (1974) "Law Enforcement, Malfeasance, and the Compensation of Enforcers," *Journal of Legal Studies*, 3: 1–19.

Becker, G., Landes, E. and Michael, R. (1977) "An Economic Analysis of Marital Instability," *The Journal of Political Economy*, 85 (6): 1141–87.

Berger, P. (2010) "Max Weber is Alive and Well, and Living in Guatemala: The Protestant Ethic Today," *The Review of Faith and International Affairs*, 8 (4): 3–9.

Beugelsdijk, S. (2006) "A Note on the Theory and Measurement of Trust in Explaining Differences in Economic Growth," *Cambridge Journal of Economics*, 30: 371–87.

Beugelsdijk, S. and Maseland, R. (2011) *Culture in Economics: History, Methodological Reflections, and Contemporary Applications*, Cambridge: Cambridge University Press.

Billig, M. (2000) "Institutions And Culture: Neo-Weberian Economic Anthropology," *Journal of Economic Issues*, 34: 771–88.

Bird-David, N. (1990) "The Giving Environment: Another Perspective on the Economic System of Gatherer-Hunters," *Current Anthropology*, 31 (2): 189–96.

Bird-David, N. (1992a) "Beyond 'The Affluent Society': A Culturalist Reformulation, and Discussion," *Current Anthropology*, 33: 25–34.

Bird-David, N. (1992b) "Beyond 'The Hunting and Gathering Mode of Subsistence': Culture-Sensitive Observations on the Nayaka and Other Modern Hunter-Gatherers," *Man*, 27: 19–44.

Bisin, A. and Verdier, T. (2000) "A Model of Cultural Transmission, Voting and Political Ideology," *European Journal of Political Economy*, 16: 5–29.

Bisin, A. and Verdier, T. (2001) "The Economics of Cultural Transmission and the Dynamics of Preferences," *Journal of Economic Theory*, 2: 298–319.

Bisin, A. and Verdier, T. (2011) "The Economics of Cultural Transmission and Socialization," in J. Benhabib, A. Bisin and M. Jackson (eds.), *Handbook of Social Economics*, North Holland: Elsevier, 340–416.

Bisin, A., Topa, G. and Verdier, T. (2004) "Cooperation as a Transmitted Trait," *Rationality and Society*, 16: 477–507.

Bisin, A., Topa, G. and Verdier, T. (2009) "Cultural Transmission, Socialization, and the Population Dynamics of Multiple-State Traits Distributions," *International Journal of Economic Theory*, 5: 139–54.

Black, D. (1948) "On the Rationale of Group Decision-Making," *Journal of Political Economy*, 56 (1): 23–34.

Boettke, P. (1998) "Rational Choice and Human Agency in Economics and Sociology: Exploring the Weber-Austrian Connection," in H. Giersch (ed.), *Merits and Limits of Markets*, Berlin: Springer: 53–81.

Boettke, P. (2001) *Calculation and Coordination: Essays on Socialism and Transitional Political Economy*, New York: Routledge.

Boettke, P. and Storr, V. H. (2002) "Post Classical Political Economy," *American Journal of Economics and Sociology*, 61 (1): 161–91.

Boettke, P., Leeson, P. and Coyne, C. (2008) "Institutional Stickiness and the New Development Economics," *American Journal of Economics & Sociology*, 67 (2): 331–58.

Boland, L. (1979) "A Critique of Friedman's Critics," *Journal of Economic Literature*, 27: 503–22.

Boudon, R. (1998) "Limitations of Rational Choice Theory," *American Journal of Sociology*, 104 (3): 817–28.

Boudon, R. (2003) "Beyond Rational Choice Theory," *Annual Review of Sociology*, 29: 1–21.

Bourdieu, P. (1977) *Outline of a Theory of Practice*, Cambridge: Cambridge University Press.

Bourdieu, P. (2002) "The Forms of Capital," in N. W. Biggart (ed.), *Readings in Economic Sociology*, Malden, MA: Blackwell Publishers.

Brennan, G. and Buchanan, J. (1980) *The Power to Tax: Analytical Foundations of a Fiscal Constitution*, Indianapolis, IN: The Liberty Fund.

Buchanan, J. and Tullock, G. (1962) *The Calculus of Consent*, Ann Arbor, MI: University of Michigan Press.

Burrows, D. (1990) *Once Upon a Time: Stories from the Bahamas*, Yellow Moon Press (audio cassette recording).

Browne, K. (2004) *Creole Economics: Cunning Under the French Flag*, Austin, TX: University of Texas Press.

Caplan, B. (2001) "Rational Irrationality and the Microfoundations of Political Failure," *Public Choice*, 107 (3/4): 311–31.

Caplan, B. (2007) *The Myth of the Rational Voter: Why Democracies Choose Bad Policies*, Princeton, NJ: Princeton University Press.

Carden, A., Courtemanche, C. and Meiners, J. (2009) "Does Wal-Mart Reduce Social Capital?" *Public Choice*, 138 (1): 109–36.

Casson, M. and Godley, A. (eds.), (2000) *Cultural Factors in Economic Growth*, New York: Springer.

Chamlee-Wright, E. (1997) *The Cultural Foundations of Economic Development: Urban Female Entrepreneurship in Ghana*, New York: Routledge.

Chamlee-Wright, E. (2005) "Entrepreneurial Response to 'Bottom-Up' Development Strategies in Zimbabwe," *Review of Austrian Economics*, 18 (1): 5–28.

Chamlee-Wright, E. (2010a) *The Cultural and Political Economy of Recovery: Social Learning in a Post-Disaster Environment*, New York: Routledge.

Chamlee-Wright, E. (2010b) "Qualitative Methods and the Pursuit of Economic Understanding," *Review of Austrian Economics* 23(4): 321–31.

Chamlee-Wright, E. (2011) "Operationalizing the Interpretive Turn: Deploying Qualitative Methods Toward an Economics of Meaning," *Review of Austrian Economics*, 24(2): 157–70.

Chamlee-Wright, E. and Storr, V. H. (2009) "Club Goods and Post-Disaster Community Return," *Rationality and Society*, 21 (4): 429–58.

Chamlee-Wright, E. and Storr, V. H. (2011a) "Social Capital, Lobbying and Community-Based Interest Groups," *Public Choice*, 149 (1–2): 167–185.

Chamlee-Wright, E. and Storr, V. H. (2011b) "Social Capital as Collective Narratives and Post-Disaster Community Recovery," *Sociological Review*, 59 (2): 266–82.

Chong, A., Guillen, J. and Rios, V. (2010) "Language Nuances, Trust and Economic Growth," *Public Choice*, 143: 191–208.

Chow, R. (2002) *The Protestant Ethic and the Spirit of Capitalism*, New York: Columbia University Press.

Chow, G. (2010) *Interpreting China's Economy*, Hackensack, NJ: World Scientific Publishing.

Cleare, W. T. (1917) "Four Folk-Tales from Fortune Island, Bahamas," *The Journal of American Folklore*, 30(116): 228–9.

Coase, R. (1988) *The Firm, the Market, and the Law*, Chicago, IL: The University of Chicago Press.

Coleman, J. (1988) "Social Capital in the Creation of Human Capital," *American Journal of Sociology*, 94: S95–120.

Coleman, J. (1990) *Foundations of Social Theory*, Cambridge, MA: Harvard University Press.

Coser, L. (2005) "Preface," in A. Mitzam (ed.), *The Iron Cage: An Historical Interpretation of Max Weber*, Piscataway, NJ: Transaction Publishers.

Cowen, T. (2002) *Creative Destruction*, Princeton, NJ: Princeton University Press.

Coyne, C. (2008) *After War: The Political Economy of Exporting Democracy*, Stanford, CA: Stanford University Press.

Craton, M. and Saunders, G. (1992) *Islanders in the Stream: A History of the Bahamian People*, Volume 1, Athens, GA: University of Georgia Press.

Craton, M. and Saunders, G. (1998) *Islanders in the Stream: A History of the Bahamian People*, Volume 2, Athens, GA: University of Georgia Press.

Dasgupta, P. (2003) "Social Capital and Economic Performance: Analytics," in E. Ostrom and T.K. Ahn (eds.), *Critical Studies in Economic Institutions: Foundations of Social Capital*, Cheltenham: Edward Elgar, 309–39.

David, P. (1985) "Clio and the Economics of QWERTY," *The American Economic Review*, 75 (2): 332–7.

Davidsson, P. (1995) "Culture, Structure and Regional Levels of Entrepreneurship," *Entrepreneurship and Regional Development*, 7 (1), 41–62.

Dickson, T. and McLachlan, H. (1989) "In Search of 'The Spirit of Capitalism': Weber's Misinterpretation of Franklin," *Sociology*, 23 (1): 81–9.

DiMaggio, P. (1979) "Review Essay: On Pierre Bourdieu," *American Journal of Sociology*, 84 (6): 1460–74.

Dore, R., Lazonick, W. and O'Sullivan, M. (1999) "Varieties of Capitalism in the Twentieth Century," *Oxford Review of Economic Policy*, 15 (4): 102–20.

Easterly, W. (2001) *The Elusive Quest for Growth: Economists' Adventures and Misadventures in the Tropics*, Cambridge, MA: MIT Press.

Eliaeson, S. (2002) *Max Weber's Methodologies: Interpretation and Critique*, Hoboken, NJ: Wiley.

Ermisch, J. F. (2003) *An Economic Analysis of the Family*, Princeton, NJ: Princeton University Press.

Farmer, R. and Guo, J. (1994) "Real Business Cycles and the Animal Spirits Hypothesis," *Journal of Economic Theory*, 63: 42–72.

Fernandez, R. and Fogli, A. (2009) "Culture: An Empirical Investigation of Beliefs, Work, and Fertility," *American Economic Journal: Macroeconomics*, 1 (1): 146–77.

Finlay, H. H. (1925) "Folklore from Eleuthera, Bahamas," *The Journal of American Folklore*, 38(148): 293–9.

Fleetwood, S. (2007) "Austrian Economics and the Analysis of Labor Markets," *Review of Austrian Economics*, 20 (4): 247–67.

Folbre, N. (2008) *Valuing Children: Rethinking the Economics of the Family*, Cambridge, MA: Harvard University Press.

Freytag, A. and Thurik, A. R. (eds.), (2010) *Entrepreneurship and Culture*, Heidelberg: Springer.

Friedman, M. (1953) *Essays in Positive Economics*, Chicago, IL: Chicago University Press.

Fukuyama, F. (2001) "Culture and Economic Development: Cultural Concerns," in N. J. Smelser and P. Baltes (eds.), *International Encyclopedia of the Social & Behavioral Sciences*, Oxford: Pergamon, 3130–4.

Gadamer, H. (1976) *Philosophical Hermeneutics*, Berkeley, CA: University of Califonia Press.

Gadamer , H. (1994) "What is Truth?" in B. Wachterhauser (ed.), *Hermeneutics and Truth*, Evanston, IL: Northwestern University Press.

Geertz, C. (1963) *Peddlers and Princes: Social Development and Economic Growth in Two Indonesian Towns*, Princeton, NJ: Princeton University Press.

Geertz, C. (1973) *The Interpretation of Cultures: Selected Essays*, New York: Basic Books.

Geertz, C. (1983) *Local Knowledge: Further Essays in Interpretive Anthropology*, New York: Basic Books.

Giddens, A. (2001) "Introduction," in M. Weber (ed.), *The Protestant Ethic and the Spirit of Capitalism*, New York: Routledge.

Glaeser, E., Laibson, D., Scheinkman, J. and Soutter, C. (2000) "Measuring Trust," *Quarterly Journal of Economics*, 115: 811–46.

Glinton-Meicholas, P. (1993) *An Evening in Guanima: A Treasury of Folktales from the Bahamas*, Nassau, NP: Guanima Press.

Glinton-Meicholas, P. (1994) *How to be a True-True Bahamian: A Hilarious Look at Life in the Bahamas*. Nassau, NP: Guanima Press.

Glinton-Meicholas, P. (1998) *The 99¢ Breakfast*, Nassau, NP: Guanima Press.

Glinton-Meicholas, P. (2000) "Talkin' Ol Story: A Brief Survey of the Oral Tradition of the Bahamas," *Encuentros*, 38, 1–16.

Goldthorpe, J. (1998) "Rational Action Theory for Sociology," *The British Journal of Sociology*, 49 (2): 167–92.

Gorski, P. S. (2003) "Review of S. Kalberg's, P. Baehr and G. C. Wells' Translations of Max Weber's The Protestant Ethic and the Spirit of Capitalism," *Social Forces*, 82 (2): 833–9.

Granato, J., Inglehart, R. and Leblang, D. (1996a) "The Effect of Cultural Values on Economic Development: Theory, Hypotheses, and Some Empirical Tests," *American Journal of Political Science*, 40 (3): 607–31.

Granato, J., Inglehart, R. and Leblang, D. (1996b) "Cultural Values, Stable Democracy, and Economic Development: A Reply," *American Journal of Political Science*, 40 (3): 680–96.

Granovetter, M. (1973) "The Strength of Weak Ties," *American Journal of Sociology*, 78 (6): 1360–80.

Granovetter, M. (1995) *Getting a Job: A Study of Contacts and Careers*, Chicago, IL: University of Chicago Press.

Grant, R., Kleiber, K. and McAllister, C. (2005) "Should Australian Aborigines Succomb to Capitalism?" *Journal of Economic Issues*, 39 (2): 391–400.

Green, D. and Shapiro, I. (1994) *Pathologies of Rational Choice Theory: A Critique of Applications in Political Science*, New Haven, CT: Yale University Press.

Greenfeld, L. (2001) *The Spirit of Capitalism: Nationalism and Economic Growth*, Cambridge, MA: Harvard University Press.

Greif, A. (1994) "Cultural Beliefs and the Organization of Society: A Historical and Theoretical Reflection on Collectivist and Individualist Societies," *The Journal of Political Economy*, 102 (5): 912–50.

Greif, A. (1997) "Cultural Beliefs as a Common Resource in an Integrating World: An Example from the Theory and History of Collectivist and Individualist Societies," in P. Dasgupta, K.-G. Mäler and A. Vercelli (eds.), *The Economics of Transnational Commons*, Oxford: Clarendon Press, 238–69.

Greif, A. and Tabellini, G. (2010) "Cultural and Institutional Bifurcation: China and Europe Compared," *American Economic Review*, 100 (May): 135–40.

Grondona, M. (2000) "A Cultural Typology of Economic Development," in L. Harrison and S. Huntington (eds.), *Culture Matters: How Values Shape Human Progress*, New York: Basic Books.

Gudeman, S. (1986) *Economics as Culture: Models and Metaphors of Livelihood*, London: Routledge.

Guiso, L., Sapienza, P. and Zingales, L. (2006) "Does Culture Affect Economic Outcomes?" *Journal of Economic Perspectives*, 20 (2): 23–48.

Guiso, L., Sapienza, P. and Zingales, L. (2009) "Cultural Biases in Economic Exchange?" *Quarterly Journal of Economics*, 124 (3), 1095–131.

Hall, P. and Soskice, D. (2001) *Varieties of Capitalism: The Institutional Foundations of Comparative Advantage*, Oxford: Oxford University Press.

Harper, D. (2003) *Foundations of Entrepreneurship and Economic Development*, New York: Routledge.

Harrison, L. (1992) *Who Prospers: How Cultural Values Shape Economic and Political Success*, New York: Basic Books.

Harrison, L. (2006) *The Central Liberal Truth: How Politics Can Change a Culture and Save It From Itself*, New York: Oxford University Press.

Hamilton, R. (1996) *The Social Misconstruction of Reality: Validity and Verification in the Scholarly Community*, New Haven, CT: Yale University Press.

Hayek, F. A. (1942) "Scientism and the Study of Society," *Economica*, 9 (35): 267–91.

Hayek, F. A. (1943) *The Road to Serfdom*, Chicago, IL: University of Chicago Press.

Hayek, F. A. (1948) *Individualism and Economic Order*, Chicago, IL: University of Chicago Press.

Hayek, F. A. (1952) *The Sensory Order*, Chicago, IL: University of Chicago Press.

Hayek, F. A. (1960) *The Constitution of Liberty*, Chicago, IL: University of Chicago Press.

Hayek, F. A. (1964) "The Theory of Complex Phenomena," in M. A. Bunge (ed.), *The Critical Approach to Science and Philosophy: Essays in Honor of Karl R. Popper*, New York: The Free Press of Glencoe.

Hayek, F. A. (1979) *The Counter-Revolution of Science: Studies on the Abuse of Reason*, Indianapolis, IN: The Liberty Fund.

Hayton, J., George, G. and Zahra, S. (2002) "National Culture and Entrepreneurship: A Review of Behavioral Research," *Entrepreneurship Theory and Practice*, 26 (4): 33–62.

Hechter, M. and Kanazawa, S. (1997) "Sociological Rational Choice Theory," *Annual Review of Sociology*, 23: 191–214.

Hendry, D. (1980) "Econometrics—Alchemy or Science?" *Economica*, 47: 387–406.

Hermalin, A. (2001) "Economics and Corporate Culture," in G. Cooper, S. Cartwright and P. Earley (eds.), *The International Handbook of Organizational Culture and Climate*, Chichester: John Wiley & Sons, 217–62.

Henrich, J. (2002) "Decision-Making, Cultural Transmission and Adaptation in Economic Anthropology," in J. Ensminger (ed.), *Theory in Economic Anthropology*, Walnut Creek, CA: Altamira Press, 251–89.

Hirshleifer, J. (1985) "The Expanding Domain of Economics," *The American Economic Review*, 75 (6): 53–68.

Hofstede, G. (1980) *Culture's Consequence: International Differences in Work Related Values*, Beverly Hills, CA: Sage Publications.

Hofstede, G. (2001) *Culture's Consequences: Comparing Values, Behaviors, Institutions, and Organizations across Nations*, Beverly Hills, CA: Sage Publications.

Holcombe, R. G. (1998) "Entrepreneurship and Economic Growth," *The Quarterly Journal of Austrian Economics*, 1 (2): 45–62.

Horwitz, S. (2005) "The Functions of the Family in the Great Society," *Cambridge Journal of Economics*, 29 (5): 669–84.

Horwitz, S. (2008) "Is the Family a Spontaneous Order?" *Studies in Emergent Order*, 1: 163–85.

Horwitz, S. (2010) "Economic Analysis of the Family," in R. Free (ed.), *21st Century Economics: A Reference Handbook Vol. 2*, New York: Sage Publishing, 577–84.

Howitt, P. and McAfee, R. P. (1992) "Animal Spirits," *The American Economic Review*, 82 (3): 493–507.

Hurston, Z. (1930) "Dance Songs and Tales from the Bahamas," *The Journal of American Folklore*, 43(169): 294–312.

Iannaconne, L. (1990) "Religious Practice: A Human Capital Approach," *Journal for the Scientific Study of Religion*, 29 (3): 297–314.

Jackson, W. (2009) *Economics, Culture and Social Theory*, Northampton: Edward Elgar Publishing.

Jin, D. (1995) "Bounded Governance within Extended Order: The Confucian Advantage of Synergy under Generalized Constitutional Rules," *Constitutional Political Economy*, 6: 263–79.

John, A. (2010) "Culture as a Constitution" (unpublished manuscript, Department of Economics, George Mason University).

Johnson, H. (1996) *The Bahamas from Slavery to Servitude: 1783–1933*, Gainesville, FL: University Press of Florida.

Jones, E. (1995) "Culture and its Relationship to Economic Change," *Journal of Institutional and Theoretical Economics*, 151 (2): 269–85.

Jones, E. (2006) *Cultures Merging: A Historical and Economic Critique of Culture*, Princeton, NJ: Princeton University Press.

Kalberg, S. (1994) "Max Weber's Analysis of the Rise of Monotheism: A Reconstruction," *The British Journal of Sociology*, 45 (4): 563–83.

Kalberg, S. (2005) "Introduction—Max Weber: The Confrontation with Modernity," *Max Weber: Readings and Commentary of Modernity*, Malden, MA: Blackwell Publishing.

Käsler, D. (1988) *Max Weber: An Introduction to His Life and Work*, translated by Philippa Hurd, Polity Press: 174–96.

Kepner, E. (1991) "The Family and the Firm: A Coevolutionary Perspective," *Family Business Review*, 4 (4): 445–61.

Keynes, J. (1973) *The General Theory of Employment, Interest and Money*, London: Macmillan & Co.

Kirzner, I. (1973) *Competition & Entrepreneurship*, Chicago, IL: University of Chicago Press.

Kirzner, I. (1994) "Book Review: Brigitte Berger (editor), *The Culture of Entrepreneurship*," Advances in Austrian Economics, 1: 327–30.

Kiser, E. and Hechter, M. (1998) "The Debate on Historical Sociology: Rational Choice Theory and its Critics," *The American Journal of Sociology*, 104 (3): 785–816.

Knack, S. and Keefer, P. (1997) "Does Social Capital Have an Economic Payoff? A Cross-Country Investigation," *The Quarterly Journal of Economics*, 112 (4): 1251–88.

Knowles, K. (1998) *Straw! A Short Account of the Straw Industry in the Bahamas*, Nassau: Media Publishing.

Knight, F. (1990) *The Caribbean: The Genesis of a Fragmented Nationalism*, New York: Oxford University Press.

Koppl, R. (1991) "Retrospectives: Animal Spirits," *The Journal of Economic Perspectives*, 5 (3): 203–10.

Kreps, D. (1990) "Corporate Culture and Economic Theory," in J. Alt and K. Shepsle (eds.), *Perspectives on Positive Political Economy*, Cambridge: Cambridge University Press, 90–143.

Kroeber, A. L. and Kluckhohn, C. (1952) *Culture: A Critical Review of Concepts and Definitions*, New York: Vintage Books.

Kulii, E. and Kulii, B. T. (2001) "Brer Rabbit," in W. L. Andrews, F. S. Foster and T. Harris (eds.), *The Concise Oxford Companion to African American Literature*, New York: Oxford University Press, 46–49.

Kuper, A. (1999) *Culture: The Anthropologist's Account*, Cambridge, MA: Harvard University Press.

Lachmann, L. (1951) "The Science of Human Action," *Economica*, 18 (72): 412–27.

Lachmann, L. (1971) *The Legacy of Max Weber: Three Essays*, Berkeley, CA: The Glendessary Press.

Lachmann, L. (1978) *Capital and its Structure*, Auburn, AL: Ludwig von Mises Institute.

Lavoie, D. (1991) "The Discovery and Interpretation of Profit Opportunities: Culture and the Kirznerian Entrepreneur," in B. Berger (ed.), *The Culture of Entrepreneurship*, San Francisco, CA: ICS Press, 33–52.

Lavoie, D. (1994) "Cultural Studies and the Conditions for Entrepreneurship," in W. Boxx and G. M. Quinlivan (eds.), *The Cultural Context of Economics and Politics*, Lanham, MD: University Press of America, 51–70.

Lavoie, D. and Chamlee-Wright, E. (2000) *Culture and Enterprise: The Development, Representation, and Morality of Business*, New York: Routledge.

Lavoie, D. and Storr, V. H. (2011) "Distinction or Dichotomy: Rethinking the Line between Thymology and Praxeology," *The Review of Austrian Economics*, 24 (2): 213.

Leamer, E. (1991) "A Bayesian Perspective on Inference from Macroeconomic Data," *The Scandinavian Journal of Economics*, 93 (2): 225–48.

Leontief, W. (1971) "Theoretical Assumptions and Nonobserved Facts," *The American Economic Review*, 61 (1): 1–7.

Leeson, P. (2007) "An-Arrgh-Chy: The Law and Economics of Pirate Organization," *Journal of Political Economy*, 115 (6), 1049–1094.

Leeson, P. (2008) "Social Distance and Self-Enforcing Exchange," *Journal of Legal Studies*, 37: 161–88.

Leeson, P. (2009) *The Invisible Hook: The Hidden Economics of Pirates*, Princeton, NJ: Princeton University Press.

Leeson, P. and Skarbek, D. (2010) "Criminal Constitutions," *Global Crime*, 11 (3): 279–97.

Levin, P. (2008) "Culture and Markets: How Economic Sociology Conceptualizes Culture," *The ANNALS of the American Academy of Political and Social Science*, 619: 114–29.

Levitt, S. and Venkatesh, S. (2000) "An Economic Analysis of a Drug-Selling Gang's Finances," *Quarterly Journal of Economics*, 115 (3): 755–89.

Lewin, S. (1996) "Economics and Psychology: Lessons for Our Own Day from the Early Twentieth Century," *Journal of Economic Literature*, 34 (3): 1293–323.

Lewin, P. (2001) "The Market Process and the Economics of QWERTY: Two Views," *The Review of Austrian Economics*, 14 (1): 65–96.

Lewis, P. (2000) "Realism, Causality and the Problem of Social Structure," *Journal for the Theory of Social Behavior*, 30 (3): 249–68.

Lewis, P. (2009) "Commitment, Identity, and Collective Intentionality: The Basis for Philanthropy," *Conversations on Philanthropy*, 6: 47–64.

Lewis, P. (2010) "'Certainly Not! A Critical Realist Recasting of Ludwig von Mises's Methodology of the Social Sciences," *Journal of Economic Methodology*, 17: 277–99.

Lie, J. (1997) "Sociology of Markets," *Annual Review of Sociology*, 23: 341–60.

Liebowitz, S. J. and Margolis, S. (1990) "The Fable of the Keys," *Journal of Law and Economics*, 33 (1): 1–25.

Liebowitz, S. J. and Margolis, S. (2002) *The Economics of QWERTY: History, Theory, Policy*, New York: New York University Press.

Lomasky, L. (2011) "Contract, Covenant, Constitution," *Social Philosophy and Policy*, 28: 50–71.

MacKinnon, M. (1988a) "Part I: Calvinism and the Infallible Assurance of Grace: The Weber Thesis Reconsidered," *The British Journal of Sociology*, 39 (2): 143–77.

MacKinnon, M. (1988b) "Part II: Weber's Exploration of Calvinism: The Undiscovered Provenance of Capitalism," *The British Journal of Sociology*, 39 (2): 178–210.

Mankiw, N. (1995) "The Growth of Nations," *Brookings Papers on Economic Activity*, 1: 373–431.

Marchionatti, R. (1999) "On Keynes' Animal Spirits," *Kyklos*, 52 (3): 415–39.

Marshall, A. (1890) *Principles of Economics*, London: Macmillan & Co.

Marshall, G. (1982) *In Search of the Spirit of Capitalism: An Essay on Max Weber's Protestant Ethic Thesis*, New York: Columbia University Press.

Marx, K. (1994) *Selected Writings*, Indianapolis, IN: Hackett Publishing.

McCloskey, D. (1988) "Thick and Thin Methodologies in the History of Economic Thought," in *The Popperian Legacy in Economics*, Cambridge: Cambridge University Press, 245–57.

McCloskey, D. (2010) *Bourgeois Dignity: Why Economics Can't Explain the Modern World*, Chicago, IL: University of Chicago Press.

Meadowcroft, J. and Pennington, M. (2008) "Bonding and Bridging: Social Capital and the Communitarian Critique of Liberal Markets," *Review of Austrian Economics*, 21 (2 & 3): 119–33.

Menger, C. (1985) *Investigations into the Method of the Social Sciences with Special Reference to Economics*, New York: New York University Press.

Mill, J. S. (1848) *Principles of Political Economy with some of their Applications to Social Philosophy*, London: Longmans, Green & Co.

Mises, L. (1949) *Human Action: A Treatise on Economics*, Auburn, AL: Ludwig von Mises Institute.

Mises, L. (1957) *Theory and History: An Interpretation of Social and Economic Evolution*. New Haven, CT: Yale University Press.

Mises, L. (1962) *The Ultimate Foundation of Economic Science: An Essay on Method*, Princeton, NJ: Van Nostrand.

Mises, L. (2003) *Epistemological Problems of Economics*, Auburn, AL: Ludwig von Mises Institute.

Mommsen, W. (1989) *The Political and Social Theory of Max Weber*, Chicago, IL: University of Chicago Press.

Nash-Ferguson, A. (2000) *I Come to Get Me: An Inside Look at the Junkanoo Festival*, Nassau: Doongalik Studios.

Nee, V. (1998) "Norms and Networks in Economic and Organizational Performance," *The American Economic Review*, 88 (2): 85–9.

Newman, D. (2002) *Sociology of Families*, London: Pine Forge Press.

North, D. (1977) "Markets and Other Allocation Systems in History: The Challenge of Karl Polanyi," *Journal of European Economic History*, 6: 703–16.

North, D. (1990) *Institutions, Institutional Change and Economic Performance*, New York: Cambridge University Press.

North, D. (1994) "Economic Performance Through Time," *American Economic Review*, 84(3): 359–68.

North, D. (2005) *Understanding the Process of Economic Change*, Princeton, NJ: Princeton University Press.

Olson, M. (1965) *The Logic of Collective Action: Public Goods and the Theory of Groups*, Cambridge, MA: Harvard University Press.

Parsons, T. (1935) "Sociological Elements in Economic Thought," *The Quarterly Journal of Economics*, 49 (3): 414–53.

Parsons, T. (1937) *The Structure of Social Action*, Columbus, OH: McGraw-Hill.

Parsons, T. (1967) *Sociological Theory and Modern Society*, New York: Free Press.

Pieters, R. and Baumgarther, H. (2002) "Who Talks to Whom? Intra- and Interdisciplinary Communication of Economics Journals," *Journal of Economic Literature*, 40 (2): 483–509.

Portes, A. (1998) "Social Capital: Its Origins and Applications in Modern Sociology," *Annual Review of Sociology*, 24: 1–24.

Portes, A. (2000) "The Two Meanings of Social Capital," *Sociological Forum*, 15: 1–12.

Poulsen, A. and Svendsen, G. (2005) "Social Capital and Endogenous Preferences," *Public Choice*, 123 (1): 171–96.

Pye, L. (2000) "'Asian Values': From Dynamos to Dominoes?" in L. Harrison and S. Huntington (eds.), *Culture Matters: How Values Shape Human Progress*, New York: Basic Books, 244–55.

Reed, I. (2002) "Review: Ann Swidler 'Talk of Love: How Culture Matters'," *Theory and Society*, 31 (6): 785–94.

Remmer, K. (1993) "The Political Economy of Elections in Latin America, 1980–1991," *American Political Science Review*, 87: 393–407.

Ricardo, D. (1821) *On the Principles of Political Economy and Taxation*, London: John Murray.

Ringer, F. (1997) *Max Weber's Methodology: The Unification of the Cultural and Social Sciences*, Cambridge, MA: Harvard University Press.

Rigney, D. and Barnes, D. (1980) "Patterns of Interdisciplinary Citation in the Social Sciences," *Social Science Quarterly*, 61 (1): 114–27.

Ringer, F. (1997) *Max Weber's Methodology: The Unification of the Cultural and Social Sciences*, Cambridge, MA: Harvard University Press.

Rizzo, M. (1978) "Praxeology and Econometrics: A Critique of Positivist Economics," in L. Spadaro (ed.), *New Directions in Austrian Economics*, Kansas City, MO: Sheed, Andrews & McMeel, 40–56.

Robbins, L. (1945) *An Essay on the Nature & Significance of Economic Science*, London: MacMillan & Co., Limited (First Edition 1932).

Rodrik, D. and Subramanian, A. (2005) "From 'Hindu Growth' to Productivity Surge: The Mystery of the Indian Growth Transition," *IMF Staff Papers*, 52 (2), 193–228.

Rotter, J. (1966) "Generalized Expectancies of Internal versus External Control of Reinforcements," *Psychological Monographs*, 80: 1–28.

Ryle, G. (2009) "The Thinking of Thoughts: What is 'Le Penseur' Doing?" in *Collected Essays 1929 - 1968: Collected Papers Volume 2,* New York: Routledge.

Say, J. B. (1803) *A Treatise on Political Economy*, Philadelphia, PA: Lippincott, Grambo & Co.

Schütz, A. (1967) *The Phenomenology of the Social World*, Evanston, IL: Northwestern University Press.

Schütz, A. and Luckmann, T. (1973) *The Structures of the Life-World*, Evanston, IL: Northwestern University Press.

Shane, S. (1992) "Why Do Some Societies Invent More than Others?" *Journal of Business Venturing*, 7 (1): 29–46.

Shane, S. (1993) "Cultural Influences on National Rates of Innovation," *Journal of Business Venturing*, 8 (1): 59–73.

Shapiro, I. (1998) "Can the Rational Choice Framework Cope with Culture," *PS: Political Science and Politics*, 31 (1): 40–2.

Silverman (2004) *Doing Qualitative Research: Second Edition*, Beverly Hills, CA: Sage Publications.

Sen, A. (1973) "Behaviour and the Concept of Preference," *Economica*, 40 (159): 241–59.

Sen, A. (1974) "Choice, Orderings and Morality," in S. Körner (ed.), *Practical Reason*, Oxford: Basil Blackwell.

Sen, A. (1977) "Rational Fools: A Critique of the Behavioral Foundations of Economic Theory," *Philosophy & Public Affairs*, 6 (4): 317–44.

Smith, A. (1776) *An Inquiry into the Nature and Causes of the Wealth of Nations*, London: Methuen & Co.

Smith, V. L. (2008) *Rationality in Economics: Constructivist and Ecological Forms*, Cambridge: Cambridge University Press.

Snyder, J. L. (2002) "Anarchy and Culture: Insights from the Anthropology of War," *International Organization*, 56 (1): 7–45.

Sobel, J. (2002) "Can We Trust Social Capital?" *Journal of Economic Literature*, 45: 139–54.

Sønderskov, K. M. (2009) "Different Goods, Different Effects: Exploring the Effects of Generalized Social Trust in Large-N Collective Action," *Public Choice*, 140: 145–60.

Stark, R. and Finke, R. (2000) *Acts of Faith: Explaining the Human Side of Religion*, Berkeley, CA: University of California Press.

Stigler, G. (1967) "Imperfections in the Capital Market," *The Journal of Political Economy*, 75 (3): 287–92.

Stigler, G. (1984) "Economics: The Imperial Science?" *The Scandinavian Journal of Economics*, 86 (3): 301–13.

Stigler, G. and Becker, G. (1977) "De Gustibus Non Est Disputandum," *The American Economic Review*, 67 (2): 76–90.

Storr, V. H. (2002) "All We've Learnt: Colonial Teachings and Caribbean Under-development," *Le Journal des Economistes et des Etudes Humaines*, 12 (4), 589–615.

Storr, V. H. (2004) *Enterprising Slaves and Master Pirates: Understanding Economic Life in the Bahamas*, New York: Peter Lang.

Storr, V. H. (2008) "The Market as a Social Space: On the Meaningful Extra-Economic Conversations that Can Occur in Markets," *Review of Austrian Economics*, 21 (2 & 3): 135–50.

Storr, V. H. (2009) "Why the Market? Markets as Social and Moral Spaces," *Journal of Markets and Morality*, 12 (2): 277–96.

Storr, V. H. (2010) "The Social Construction of the Market," *Society*, 47 (3): 200–6.

Storr, V. H. and Butkevich, B. (2007) "Subalternity and Entrepreneurship: Tales of Marginalized but Enterprising Characters, Oppressive Settings and Haunting Plots," *International Journal of Entrepreneurship and Innovation*, 8 (4): 251–60.

Storr, V. H. and John, A. (2011) "The Determinants of Entrepreneurial Alertness and the Characteristics of Successful Entrepreneurs," in E. Chamlee-Wright (ed.), *Annual Proceedings of the Wealth and Well-Being of Nations*, Beloit, WI: Beloit College Press, 87–107.

Swedberg, R. (1990) *Economics and Sociology: On Redefining Their Boundaries. Conversations with Economists and Sociologists*, Princeton, NJ: Princeton University Press.

Swedberg, R. (1994) "Markets as Social Structures," in N. Smelser and R. Swedberg (eds.), *The Handbook of Economic Sociology*, Princeton, NJ: Princeton University Press, 255–282.

Swedberg, R. (1998) *Max Weber and the Idea of Economic Sociology*, Princeton, NJ: Princeton University Press.

Swedberg, R. (1999) "Max Weber as an Economist and as a Sociologist," *American Journal of Economics and Sociology*, 58: 561–82.

Swedberg, R. (2003) *Principles of Economic Sociology*, Princeton, NJ: Princeton University Press.

Swidler, A. (1986) "Culture in Action: Symbols and Strategies," *American Sociological Review*, 51 (2): 273–86.

Tabellini, G. (2008) "Presidential Address: Institutions and Culture," *Journal of the European Economic Association*, 6 (2–3): 255–94.

Tabellini, G. (2010) "Culture and Institutions: Economic Development in the Regions of Europe," *Journal of the European Economic Association*, 8 (4): 677–716.

Throsby, C. D. (2001) *Economics and Culture*, Cambridge: Cambridge University Press.

Tomich, D. (1991) "World Slavery and Caribbean Capitalism," *Theory and Society*, 20 (3): 297–319.

Torsvik, G. (2000) "Social Capital and Economic Development: A Plea for the Mechanisms," *Rationality and Society*, 12 (4): 451–76.

Turner, T. (1988) *Once Below a Time: Bahamian Stories*, London: MacMillan & Co.

Weber, M. (1949) *The Methodology of the Social Sciences*, New York: The Free Press.

Weber, M. (1951) *The Religion of China: Confucianism and Taoism*, New York: The Free Press.

Weber, M. (1958) *The Religion of India: The Sociology of Hinduism and Buddhism*, New York: The Free Press.

Weber, M. (1978) *Economy and Society: An Outline of Interpretive Sociology, Two Volumes*, Berkeley, CA: University of California Press.

Weber, M. (2002) *The Protestant Ethic and the "Spirit" of Capitalism and Other Writings*, translated by P. Baehr and G. Wells, London: Penguin Books.

Weber, M. (2011) *The Protestant Ethic and the Spirit of Capitalism: The Revised 1920 Edition*, translated by S. Kalberg, New York: Oxford University Press.

Weigert, A. (1975) "Alfred Schütz on a Theory of Motivation," *The Pacific Sociological Review*, 18 (1): 83–102.

Weingast, B. R. (1995) "The Economic Role of Political Institutions: Market-Preserving Federalism and Economic Development," *Journal of Law, Economics and Organization*, 11 (1), 1–31.

Wennekers, S. and Thurik, R. (1999) "Linking Entrepreneurship and Economic Growth," *Small Business Economics*, 13 (1): 27–55.

Whitefield, S. and Evans, G. (1999) "Political Culture Versus Rational Choice: Explaining Responses to Transition in the Czech Republic and Slovakia," *British Journal of Political Science*, 29: 129–54.

Whitley, R. (1999) *Divergent Capitalisms: The Social Structuring and Change of Business Systems*, Oxford: Oxford University Press.

Wilk, R. (1996) *Economies and Cultures: Foundations of Economic Anthropology*, Boulder, CO: Westview Press.

Wilk, R. and Cliggett, L. (2007) *Economies and Cultures*, Boulder, CO: Westview Press.

Williamson, C. and Mathers, R. (2011) "Cultural Context: Explaining the Productivity of Capitalism," *Kyklos*, 64 (2): 231–52.

Wood, V. (1995) "Rushin' Hard and Runnin' Hot: Experiencing the Music of the Junkanoo Parade in Nassau, Bahamas," *Unpublished Dissertation*.

Woolcock, M. (1998) "Social Capital and Economic Development: Toward a Theoretical Synthesis and Policy Framework," *Theory and Society*, 27 (2): 151–208.

Zak, P. and Knack, S. (2001) "Trust and Growth," *The Economic Journal*, 111 (470): 295–321.

Zaret, D. (1992) "Calvin, Covenant Theology, and the Weber Thesis," *The British Journal of Sociology*, 43 (3): 369–91.

Zelizer, V. A. (1978) "Human Values and the Market: The Case of Life Insurance and Death in 19th-Century America," *The American Journal of Sociology*, 84 (3): 591–610.

Zelizer, V. A. (1988) "From Baby Farms to Baby M," *Society*, 25 (3): 23–8.

Zelizer, V. A. (2010) *Economic Lives: How Culture Shapes the Economy*, Princeton, NJ: Princeton University Press.

Zukin, S. and DiMaggio, P. (1990) *Structures of Capital: The Social Organization of the Economy*, Cambridge: Cambridge University Press.

Index